Black Bart

WITHDRAWN

Wooden diorama of Black Bart by Elwin Millerick. *(Courtesy Sonoma County Museum)*

Black Bart

The
True
Story
of
The West's
Most
Famous
Stagecoach
Robber

by
William Collins & Bruce Levene

Pacific Transcriptions
Mendocino, California

Printed in the United States of America

First Edition

Library of Congress Cataloging-in-Publication Data

Collins, William, 1937-
    Black Bart: the true story of the West's most famous stagecoach robber / by William Collins and Bruce Levene. — 1st ed.
Includes maps, bibliographical references and index.
    1. Black Bart, b. 1829. 2. Brigands and robbers—The West—California—Biography. 3. Outlaws—The West—California—Biography. 4. Frontier and pioneer life—The West—California. [1. Black Bart, b. 1829. 2. Robbers and outlaws.] I. Levene, Bruce, 1936-   . II. Title.
F866.B59C65 1992   364.1'552'092—dc20   [B]   91-67893
ISBN 0-933391-10-2

Front Cover: Illustration by Fred Ludekens
From *Ghost Town* by G. Ezra Dane
Back Cover: Courtesy Wells Fargo Bank

Contents

93-04088

Preface

Black Bart is the best known and most prolific stagecoach robber in American history and he has become a legend in California and the West. In this first book devoted exclusively to the famous outlaw, the authors have tried to extract his true story from the many colorful distortions written during the last hundred years. But because Charles Boles was so secretive, and the activities which made him famous were the result of subterfuge, speculations about his life have been unavoidable. He was not a public person and only his crimes made him more than a marking on a genealogical record.

He also lived at a time when recordkeeping had yet to attain the importance that keeps modern bureaucrats employed, nor was his background the trove of information beloved of biographers. It is not surprising that we know little of his life before he left home, and his frequent moves afterwards did not leave much of a 'paper trail.' He would have made a good spy.

Because he came from a large family, correlations could be made by examining letters and documents of other family members, and some information was gleaned from secondary sources. But many things we either don't know, or couldn't find, because the factual records, if they ever existed, are no longer extant. In addition, with only a few exceptions, everything written about him is suspect.

A few genealogical questions were not answered or even investigated; an exhaustive inquiry into parish baptismal records in Norfolk County, England was beyond the study's range. The name of the ship that brought the Bowles Family to North America was not discovered. We would have liked more information about Mary Johnson Boles' ancestry, but this was not found.

≈

Journalistic practice was quite different in the 19th Century; newspapers sometimes printed a story in one long paragraph. For greater readability, typograhical changes and paragraph breaks have been made in some quotations, but the textual material is unaltered.

Geographic names and locales, particularly stage roads, are sometimes confusing, and many changes, even county boundaries, have occurred during the last century. Maps have been provided showing most of the locations mentioned, but some readers may want to research more detailed sources.

Eureka Express Stage at Lake City Hotel in Lake City, Nevada County.
(Courtesy Nevada County Historical Society)

Introduction
California 1875

If you had met him in San Francisco between 1875 and 1883, Charles Boles — that is not the name he used — would have claimed he was a mining man. But he might have teased himself with, "I rob stages." On the day the bandit soon to be known as Black Bart held up his first stagecoach, California was five-and-a-half weeks away from celebrating its first quarter-century of statehood. The not-so-lucky miner had been there on Admission Day, September 9, 1850. During those twenty-five years, the state had seen an economic boom unlike anything before in the nation's history.

Of course, gold is what did it, what caused the boom and brought Charles Boles to California. The Spanish listened first to the legends of gold: of Cibola, Quivira, El Dorado — and California. They sailed up the Pacific Coast in 1542, to survey Baja and Alta California and to look for the yellow metal. None was found until 1775, by Mexicans at the Colorado River. In 1826 Jedediah Smith probably discovered gold near Mono Lake. A small amount was found in the hills north of Los Angeles in the 1830s; then a little more in 1842. But once the Spaniards and Mexicans began to settle and spread their rancheros out through the rich soil of the central and southern coastal valleys, the legends of gold became less important, and they ignored the area to the north.

By the beginning of the nineteenth century the sparse settlements begun at San Diego in 1769, and the chain of missions extending northwards past San Francisco Bay, had attracted a trickle of non-Spanish immigrants: whalers, merchants, traders. But except for a few mountain men looking for beaver to skin, no Europeans bothered exploring the formidable mountain range, the Sierra Nevada, beginning a hundred miles east of the coastline. A great historic irony is that the Spanish, who found so much gold elsewhere, and were obsessed with the need to possess it, missed discovering one of Earth's largest deposits.

In 1825 Mexico gained independence from Spain. In 1848 the Mexican-American War brought the marginally independent territory of Alta California into United States possession. But for a singular occurrence

California might have remained for years just another faraway territory lackadaisically administered from Washington.

The agent of fate, James Marshall, had contracted to build a sawmill for the Swiss adventurer, John Sutter, on the American River at Coloma. On January 18, 1848 (eight days before Mexico signed the Treaty of Guadalupe Hidalgo, giving California to the United States), Marshall's men were cutting and widening the tail-race for the mill, to increase water flow to turn the wheel. Marshall remarked later:

> My eye was caught by something shining in the bottom of the ditch... I reached my hand down and picked it up; it made my heart thump, for I was certain it was gold. The piece was about half the size and shape of a pea. Then I saw another ...

The word spread more rapidly than seems possible in a society without telephones, telegraph, or nationwide roads. By the middle of 1849 tens of thousands of fortune-seekers, responding to the most outlandish claims about how easily one could pick gold from streams or knock it out of mountainsides, had left families, farms, jobs — everything — to flock to the goldfields. They went overland, braving Indian attacks and scarcity of food and water in the arid plateaus of the Utah and Nevada Territories. Some sailed by ship around storm-beaten Cape Horn; others crossed a disease-ridden Panamanian jungle; once in San Francisco, everyone, including entire crews who deserted their ships in port, rushed toward the Sierras.

Unwilling to lose control over such wealth, the U. S. government admitted California to the Union, the first state not bordering an existing state.

Such was the power of gold.

It must be remembered that we are here in a land of stage-drivers and highwaymen; a land, in that sense, like England a hundred years ago. The highway robber— road-agent, he is quaintly called— is still busy in these parts... I am reminded of another highwayman. He had been unwell, so ran his humorous defence, and the doctor told him to take something, so he took the express box.

The cultus of the stage-coachman always flourishes highest where there are thieves on the road, and where the guard travels armed, and the stage is not only a link between country and city, and the vehicle of news, but has a faint warfaring aroma, like a man who should be a brother to a soldier... Along the unfenced, abominable mountain roads, he launches his team with small regard to human life or the doctrine of probabilities. Flinching travellers, who behold themselves coasting eternity at every corner, look with natural admiration at their driver's huge, impassive, fleshy countenance.

— Robert Louis Stevenson, ***The Silverado Squatters***

Joe Johnson, driving a W. F. Fisher stagecoach in Lake County in 1881.
(Courtesy Healdsburg Museum)

The eleven counties in Northern California and Southern Oregon
where Black Bart robbed 29 stagecoaches
between 1875 and 1883.

Stagecoach routes in Northern California and Southern Oregon
in 1880.

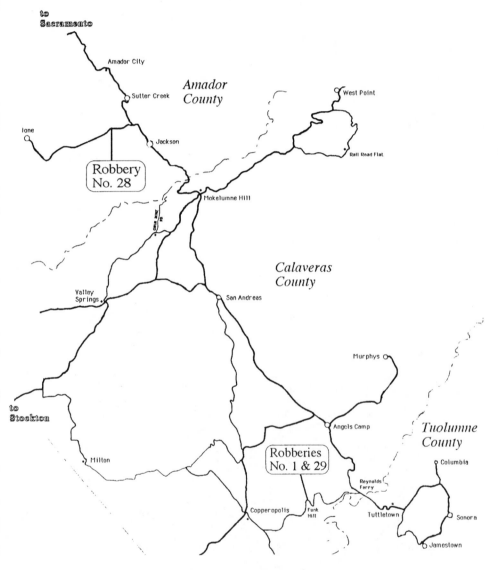

Portions of Amador, Calaveras and Tuolumne Counties showing Robberies No. 1, 28, 29

14

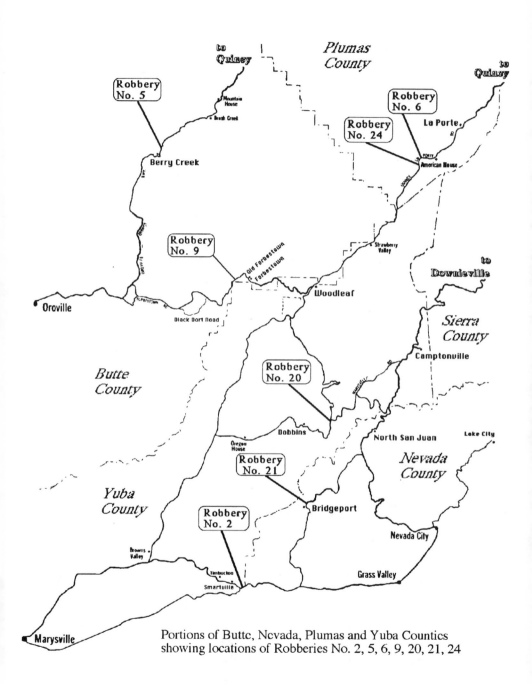

Portions of Butte, Nevada, Plumas and Yuba Counties
showing locations of Robberies No. 2, 5, 6, 9, 20, 21, 24

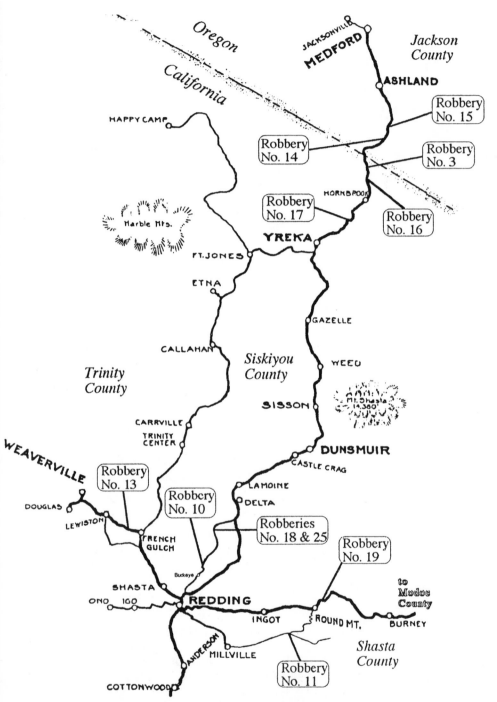

Locations in northern California and southern Oregon of
Robberies No. 3, 10, 11, 13, 14, 15, 16, 17, 18, 19, & 25.

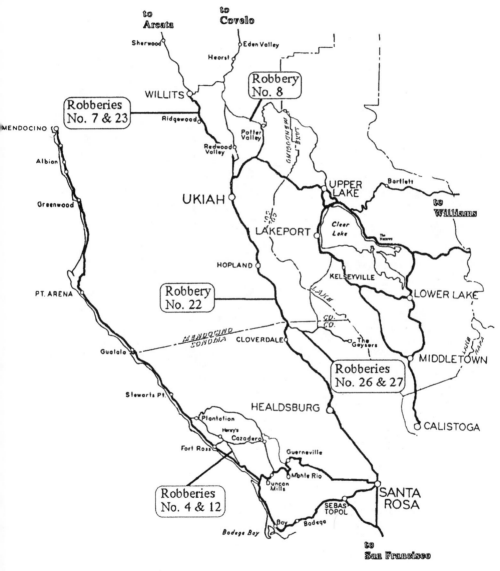

Portions of Lake, Napa, Mendocino and Sonoma Counties
showing locations of Robberies No. 4, 7, 8, 12, 22, 23, 26, 27

From the cover sheet for an address given by William Pinkerton in 1907,
on the subject 'Train Robbers & The Holdup Men.' *(Courtesy Wells Fargo Bank)*

Chapter 1
Calaveras County — *Monday, July 26, 1875*
Robbery No. 1

At 3 a.m. John Shine drove his stage out of Sonora and headed for Milton. He made stops at Tuttletown and Jamestown, then headed for Copperopolis, named for the copper mined nearby.

John Shine would become famous in the Sierras. Born in Wisconsin, he had served in an Illinois regiment during the Civil War. He came to California in 1868, mined in Amador County, then moved to Sonora and began stage driving in 1870. In 1872 he purchased the largest livery stables in the mountains, with a capacity of 75 horses plus his own stock. His company, J. H. Shine & Co., furnished stages to Yosemite and turn-outs for campers, commercial travelers, surveying parties and tourists. In 1876 he received a gold watch from Wells, Fargo for bravery. Shine was fired upon by three bandits but he got his stage and passengers to safety. He was stage line superintendent and stockholder of the Nevada Stage Co., a mine owner, city council member and treasurer of Sonora, California State Senator, and a U. S. Marshall.

On this day the coach held its usual cargo: the green Wells, Fargo strong box, resting beneath the driver's feet in the front boot, a U.S. Mail pouch nearby, and an iron safe bolted to the floor under the back seat. The stage was filled with eight women and children and two men (including John Olive, principal owner of the stage line). Passengers and freight would transfer at Milton, the terminus for a branch of the Stockton & Copperopolis Railroad (which in fact didn't go to Copperopolis) for Stockton.

Shine made good time through the draw at Table Mountain. He had just ferried across the Stanislaus River at Reynolds Ferry (now 300 feet below New Melones Reservoir) and come around Barth Mountain. As the sun

19

emerged from the Sierra peaks behind the coach, the four horses labored up the steep narrow grade of Funk Hill, four miles east of Copperopolis.

Suddenly, a man wearing a short linen coat and light-colored woolen pants stepped into the road directly in front of the lead horse. Dumbfounded, Shine slammed his right foot on the brake lever and frantically brought the stage to a halt. Then the driver saw the double-barrelled shotgun pointing up at him. The man holding the weapon also had a Henry rifle hung over his shoulder. His face was covered by a brown flour sack with eyeholes cut into it, topped by a white hat.

The method the outlaw used to stop the stage — that he would repeat many times — had a two-fold purpose: the horses would be frightened by a man wearing strange apparel and pull up because of him; and the lead animal, which shielded the robber, was too valuable for the driver or shotgun messenger to risk shooting.

With a politeness seldom found in road agents, the masked man called to Shine, "Please throw down the box." When the driver hesitated the robber called over his shoulder, "If he dares to shoot, give him a solid volley, boys." Looking at the manzanita-covered hillside Shine saw a half-dozen rifle barrels pointing at him. The driver had no option, having been caught in the time-tested manner of the professional stagecoach robber, on an uphill grade — any attempt to run down the armed man would be futile and possibly fatal. The policy of stage lines and Wells, Fargo was to shield passengers, its drivers and shotgun riders from danger, so Shine complied. At the brigand's next request he added the U.S. Mail pouch to the booty.

When a woman passenger threw out her purse, the outlaw handed it back, insisting he was only interested in Wells, Fargo's money. The treasure box and mail pouch safely at his feet, he called out "That will be about all, boys, drive on." As he drove away, Shine saw the bandit bending over the express box, holding an axe he'd hidden in the brush.

But then there was an interruption. A second stage, handled by a driver named McClean, had been following Shine's coach from Sonora. Caught on the upgrade also, McClean halted his stage. The bandit demanded the coach's express box. McClean replied that his stage was a private coach, and carried none.

Accustomed as we are to the viciousness of contemporary crime, it is difficult to imagine that a code of honor existed between highwaymen and stage drivers. A bandit would usually accept a stage driver's respectfully given word-of-honor that his coach contained no gold or valuables. In return, the driver understood that he and his passengers would not be harmed by the man (or men) who held the gun. A driver's personal wallet was out-of-bounds to a highwayman, as were, most of the time, the possessions of female passengers. Male passengers might be relieved of

Milton Stage at Angels Camp, Calaveras County. *(Courtesy Calaveras Historical Society)*

their wallets, but wouldn't be harmed unless they tried to resist. Drivers who lied in this balance of trust wouldn't be believed the next time. A bandit who committed gratuitous violence might be hunted down by a posse containing his fellow road agents, anxious to remove the bad apple from their midst. So it was not surprising that the masked outlaw accepted McClean's word, merely ordering him to pass on.

Meanwhile, Shine had stopped his own stage shortly after he drove out of the bandit's sight. Telling the passengers to remain with the coach, the driver cut overland to retrieve the broken strongbox. Seeing the armada of rifle barrels confronting him again, he froze. But when nothing moved for several seconds, Shine (displaying the resourcefulness that would one day launch him into politics) slowly approached the manzanita. The rifles remained stationary — they were, in fact, sticks! He quickly drove on to Copperopolis for help, but when the posse returned, no trace of the robber could be found.

The masked man had doffed his disguise, 'broke' the shotgun so it could be hidden in a bedroll, and swiftly hiked overland. He crossed the San

John Shine

Joaquin River near Graysonville, walked over Pacheco Pass and headed for San Jose. He stopped at a farm, probably to ask for directions and perhaps food, where the farmer's wife offered him $10 for his Henry rifle. The outlaw intended to leave the rifle behind; but the second stage scared him and he carried the weapon away. He suggested to the woman that she take the rifle as a gift, but her strong Protestant ethic resisted, and she handed him a $20 gold piece. Probably with a wry smile, the brigand made change with $10 in paper money, recently carried by the Sonora-Milton stage.

He had stolen $174 in gold notes: cash consignments of $100 to Holt Brothers, $60 to German Savings & Loan Society, and $14 to Glasgow Iron & Metal Co., all in San Francisco. The iron safe inside the stage, that contained $655 in gold and gold coin, was untouched. None of the letters were ever recovered.

The robbery was the debut of America's most famous stagecoach robber and a notice circulated in California with a reward for his capture. Though the flour-sack, grey duster, and double-barrelled shotgun became familiar sights to stage drivers all over northern California, a long time would pass before any reward money was claimed.

~

A long time also passed before this fame began. Although a flurry of newspaper articles appeared when Black Bart was captured, the most notorious 19th Century California bandits were Joaquin Murrieta (much earlier), Tiburcio Vasquez, and Chris Evans and John Sontag; these men, who committed various, and violent, kinds of crimes, received much more notoriety in contemporary newspapers. In contrast, Black Bart, a 'pure' stagecoach robber, was non-violent, quaint and elusive—less newsworthy. Only in the 1920s did his name begin to appear in magazines and books, and it was journalist and historian Joseph Henry Jackson, writing first in the *San Francisco Chronicle* in the 1930s, who really publicized Black Bart's story.

Few later writers, however, followed Jackson's historical perspective and the mythmaking began. For example, in 1946 a writer for the *New York World Telegraph* concocted a tale about Black Bart's first robbery:

Professor Charles Bowles, a mild-mannered schoolteacher in Sierra County locked up his schoolhouse for the day and noticed an approaching stagecoach. As a joke he tied a handkerchief over his face, picked up a stick which looked like a rifle, and called to the driver to halt his stage and throw down the box. The box burst open when it hit the ground and the penurious teacher found himself staring at more money than he'd ever seen. Robbery being so easy, he quit teaching and went on the road as a highwayman.

As will be seen, for a Black Bart invention it wasn't even very clever.

REWARD

WELLS, FARGO & CO.'S EXPRESS BOX

on **SONORA AND MILTON STAGE ROUTE, was ROBBED** this morning, near Reynolds' Ferry, by one man, masked and armed with sixteen shooter and double-barreled shot gun. **We will pay**

$250

for ARREST and CONVICTION of the Robber.

JNO. J. VALENTINE, Gen. Supt

San Francisco. July 26. 1875.

(Courtesy Wells Fargo Bank)

Chapter 2
Stagecoaches, Road Agents & Treasure Boxes

During his eight years as a road agent Black Bart's field of operations ranged over 350 miles in ten counties, nine in northern California and one in southern Oregon. To travel from San Francisco to the locations of the holdups involved patience almost beyond our comprehension. No bridges spanned San Francisco Bay or the Golden Gate. He would have crossed on ferries: from Second Street Wharf to Oakland on the paddle wheeled *Thoroughfare*; to Donahue Landing up Petaluma Creek on the *Amelia*; to Point San Quentin on the *Saucelito*; to Vallejo through Mare Island Strait on the *James M. Donahue*. He might have even journeyed to Stockton or Sacramento on river boats.

No matter how he got to the opposite shores, his difficulties were only beginning. To rob a stage in Mendocino County Bart would have boarded the San Francisco & North Pacific Railroad at Sausalito. The railroad would eventually reach Eureka, but its rails ended at Cloverdale when Bart rode the line. After Cloverdale he would have taken a stage to go further north.

The time necessary to reach remote locales by stage is unimaginable today. While the Central Pacific was laying tracks to Portland, its California terminus was Redding, in Shasta County. Bart committed eleven robberies north of Redding and travelled as far north as Jacksonville, Oregon. To reach Jacksonville from Redding — a distance of 177 miles — he had to ride a cramped, dusty California and Oregon Coast Overland Stage for 34 hours with a change of horses at 17 stage stops! That was during the summer. Winter weather might have added five more cold and uncomfortable hours to the trip. The ordeal would have cost him $29.00.

~

Because the mines were located far from existing towns, the story of the Forty-Niners bears directly on the tale unfolding here. The gold country stretched 180 miles north to south, covering all or part of ten counties and about 20,000 square miles. Mining required tools and timber; miners needed food, clothing, occasional mail, news from the outside world, and, for the lucky ones, goods to buy with their newly-acquired wealth.

The few trails into the Sierras could only be used by horses and mules; then roads were cut into the hills, wide enough for drayers' wagons pulled

A restored Concord stage, used on the Mendocino-Ukiah line.
(Courtesy Mendocino Historical Research)

by teams of bullocks or mules; the miners built some; private enterprise built others and charged toll for their use. Freight costs were high, mail charges exorbitant. Soon the stagecoaches came and transportation in the mountains took on a new dimension.

The best, and most expensive, stagecoaches were the 'Concords,' produced by Abbot-Downing of Concord, New Hampshire, which began as J. S. Abbot and Sons in 1813. The stages were built individually by hand: "The workmanship of the Concord Coach was a joy to behold. Its sturdy frame was built of well-seasoned New England ash and so cleverly put together by Yankee craftsmen that the joints were hardly discernible."[1]

Wheels were made of seasoned elm, with oak spokes and a hard hickory rim. For better maneuverability and greater speed, the body was set lower than in older coaches, and upper parts were constructed of curving hand-laminated bass wood panels, to avoid topheaviness. The exterior was varnished over multiple coats of hand-rubbed pomegranate red paint, the running gear painted yellow and black, the interior damask-lined. Leather or canvas curtains rolled down to protect passengers against the elements. Unloaded, a coach weighed 2200 pounds. None of this came cheap; a Concord cost about $1100.

The whole body rested on thick, sturdy, four inch wide six or eight-ply bullhide 'thoroughbraces:' laced and riveted straps on each side extending between the front and rear axles. The thoroughbrace was a prime example of American ingenuity — shock absorbers for the rough, rutted roads of the time. English coaches, mounted on steel springs, gave passengers a numbing up-and-down jouncing; thoroughbraces provided a rolling motion (which sometimes caused passengers a feeling of seasickness), allowing stages to travel at high speed, easing the ride for people and the strain on horses, by taking severe jolts in rugged terrain.

The space inside a Concord held nine passengers. Three people abreast faced each other in the front and back rows (as seen in countless Western films), and three sat facing forward on a folding drop-seat. One person sat next to the driver and up to a dozen in 'dickey' seats (depending on the bulk of luggage and freight boxes) on the coach's top (the largest number of passengers known to have ridden on a single coach is 34).

The carriage had two boots in the front and rear: leather-covered storage compartments that held passengers' luggage and leather mail sacks. Under the driver's seat the express box, or 'treasure box' held shipments of gold, gold dust, cash, and small valuables — this is what held the interest of Black Bart and his fellow road agents.

Abbot-Downing wasn't the only coach firm — Eaton, Gilbert and Co. made their 'Troys' in Troy, New York, and 'Celerity Wagons' were manufactured in Albany, New York — but Concords were preferred by the newly founded stage companies, particularly for long hauls.

Other stages, generically called 'mud wagons,' were lighter and more efficient in mud and snow on the short valley to mountain runs. They were less expensive and made by many companies, including local carriage makers. Abbot-Downing's mud wagon sold for $500. Studebaker also built a type of mud wagon. The Henderson Carriage Co. of Stockton made the best in California. Most of the stages photographed in California are mud wagons.

Another type of stage was reported in the November 29, 1879 *Mendocino Beacon*: "Len Barnard made his appearance on the street last Wednesday driving his brand new Patent Elliptic Spring Buckboard Wagon, made by Black of San Francisco, expressly for the mail route to Ukiah; the springs are directly under each seat, and the stage rides as easily as a buggy. Len had put on new and good stock and proposes to offer his passengers a comfortable ride to and from Ukiah by day light."

The Yreka-Happy Camp stage, built by Swan & Lemay, 1887. *(Courtesy Siskiyou County Museum)*

Stages were usually pulled by six horses yoked in pairs, though for less arduous routes, without hills, four horses were used. Teams were changed every ten miles or so on regular routes. A stage ran at night, equipped with kerosene lamps fastened on both sides of the coach body just behind the driver. Night travel was slow and perilous, as the lamps barely gave off enough light for the driver to see if his team was still on the road.

Stage drivers, if not an institution, were certainly the local heroes of their day:

The average stage driver ... was lord in his way, the captain of his craft, the fear of timid passengers, the admiration of the stable-boys, and the trusty agent of his employer.[2]

Off the box they were loquacious enough, but when mounted with four or six in hand, they either think it unprofessional to talk, or else were absorbed too much in their business. They each had fifty or sixty miles to make, up one day and back the next, and to the people along the route they were important personages. As bearers of the United States mail they felt themselves kings of the road and were seldom loath to show it. "Clar the road! Git out of the way thar with your bull teams!" was a frequent salutation.[3]

27

W. F. Fisher's stage in either Lake or Napa County. *(Courtesy Healdsburg Museum)*

The 'knights of the lash' were respected, because handling horses on narrow, steep, rough roads — dusty in summer and muddy in winter — was difficult and dangerous:

> The driver was constantly on the alert and the horses almost uncanny in their knowledge of what was expected of them, especially on the mountain grades. At this time, six or seven miles an hour on the mountain roads was considered making good progress. The two rear animals, known as the wheelers, were larger than the two front ones, known as the leaders, and on sharp curves the driver gave rein and the horses did the rest. At the beginning of the curve, the leaders picked up speed and, moving along, swung out near the outer edge of the grade to start the turn. The wheelers, sensing the situation, instinctively held back just enough to stabilize the movement of the leaders to prevent the stage from going out of control.
>
> Time and time again on the curves, this method was employed by the horses. It was frightening to say the least, especially when the leaders swung out so near to the edge of the grade, but the horses evidently knew what they were doing and no mishap occurred. A case of co-ordination and teamwork.[4]

No other personage in a mountain town has the prestige of the stage driver. Every one greets him with liking and respect, and his trifling foibles are passed over with admirable indulgence. If he takes a glass too much when off duty, or spins a yarn to the utmost credibility, by tacit consent the matter is not emphasized by his patrons... In fact, one cannot journey far with a professional driver, before becoming convinced that he merits all the grateful recognition so unostentatiously bestowed upon him. For years he has been equal to a telephone between the remote settlements on his line. To him is due the latest news from the logging camps in the redwoods, and the particulars of the last accident at the mill, all told with graphic homeliness of phrase. From the same source the masters learn how sheep shearing progresses on the high, breezy slopes, the day their fattest beeves may be expected at market, and how the droves of sharp-snouted hogs thrive on the acorn crop... Indeed, the memory of the stage driver has infinite capacity. Seldom a station, camp, or shanty, but has its daily message or package for him to deliver to some one on the route. These commissions are rarely forgotten, though meanwhile the most exacting passenger is not conscious of the least neglect of his personal comfort or entertainment.[5]

Riding a stage as a passenger was also an adventure, with "fifteen inches of seat space with a fat man on one side, a poor widow on the other, a baby in your lap, a bandbox over your head and three or four more persons immediately in front of you leaning against your knees."

In 1877 the *Omaha Herald* printed its *Hints for Plains Travelers*, which probably related to all stagecoah travel:

The best seat inside a stage coach is the one next to the driver. You will have to ride with back to the horses, which with some people, produces an illness not unlike sea-sickness, but in a long journey this will wear off, and you will get more rest, with less than half the bumps and jars than on any other seat. When any old "sly Eph," [a peddler] who traveled thousands of miles on coaches, offers through sympathy to exchange his back or middle seat with you, don't do it. Never ride in cold weather with tight boots or shoes, nor close-fitting gloves. Bathe your feet before starting in cold water, and wear loose overshoes and gloves two or three sizes too large. When the driver asks you to get off and walk, do it without grumbling. He will not request it unless absolutely necessary. If a team runs away, sit still and take your chances; if you jump, nine times out of ten you will be hurt. In very cold weather abstain entirely from liquor while on the road; a man will freeze twice as quick while under its influence. Don't growl at food at stations; stage companies generally provide the best they can get. Don't keep the stage waiting; many a virtuous man has lost his character by so doing. Don't smoke a strong pipe inside especially early in the morning, spit on the leeward side of the coach. If you have anything to take in a bottle, pass it around; a man who drinks by himself in such a case is lost to all human feeling. Provide stimulants before starting; ranch whiskey is not always nectar. Be sure and take two heavy blankets with

A loaded stagecoach at Mendocino. *(Courtesy Mendocino Historical Research)*

you; you will need them. Don't swear, nor lop over on your neighbor when sleeping. Don't ask how far it is to the next station until you get there. Take small change to pay expenses. Never attempt to fire a gun or pistol while on the road; it may frighten the team and the careless handling and cocking of the weapon makes nervous people nervous. Don't discuss politics or religion, nor point out places on the road where horrible murders have been committed, if delicate women are among the passengers. Don't linger too long at the pewter wash basin at the station. Don't grease your hair before starting or dust will stick there in sufficient quantities to make a respectable "tater" patch. Tie a silk handkerchief around your neck to keep out dust and prevent sunburns. A little glycerine is good in case of chapped hands. Don't imagine for a moment you are going on a pic-nic; expect annoyance, discomfort and some hardships. If you are disappointed, thank heaven.

Accidents occurred frequently, as the August 5, 1880 *Redding Independent* reported:

SERIOUS STAGE ACCIDENT. THE CAL. & OR STAGE TIPS OVER ON THE SACRAMENTO RIVER HILL. A LADY PASSENGER SERIOUSLY INJURED. About ten o'clock yesterday morning a messenger arrived from near the Sacramento River Ferry, bearing the intelligence that the stage had run off the bank while going down the Sacramento hill, turning completely over and fatally injuring a lady passenger. The facts are as follows: The stage, with Horace Williams as driver, left Redding at the usual hour Tuesday night having aboard two passengers — Mr. Siffin of Los Angeles and Mrs. Parker of San Rafael, the latter on a visit to Col. Stone and family of Yreka. When just about to descend the Sacramento hill, a very crooked and steep grade a mile long, Horace observed one of the brake blocks out of order, and descended to the ground to repair the same, tying the lines to the brake. The lady was seated on the outside securely buckled to the seat by the leather apron; the male passenger was seated inside. Ahead of the team was a sharp turn, with a high bank on the right, while on the left was a wall twenty feet high, built up even with the road. While Horace was fixing his brake the team started on a run; Horace jumped and seized the lines, making an effort to run the team into the bank and cramp the wheels; but his efforts were unavailing, and after being dragged a short distance the stage ran off the rocky wall, turning on its side and then on the top, the lady passenger striking on her head, and the male passenger bruised up on the inside of the stage.

Horace immediately dispatched Mr. Siffin, who was only slightly injured, to Redding for a doctor. The lady lay in an unconcious state and it was feared that her injuries would prove fatal. The messenger arrived in due time and James Rogers, Stage Agent, in company with Dr. Miller, immediately started for the scene of the disaster. At the present writing they have not returned, but it has been ascertained that the lady will probably recover, but will lose one of her eyes. She was conveyed to the residence of Mr. Smithson, at the ferry, where she received every attention. R.G. Dunn telegraphed to her brother at San Rafael, who will probably arrive by this evening's train. In conversation Mr. Siffin stated that no blame can be attached to the driver; that he did all that anyone could do to stop the team. The road was comparatively level where he stopped to fix the brake, and it was necessary that the brake should be in order before descending the steep grade.

The August 14, 1880 *Yreka Journal* wrote a favorable ending to the story:

WALKER, who drove in town the C & O stage from Redding last Thursday evening, was delayed over an hour, being heavily loaded, and compelled to stop to let a forward wheel spindle cool, besides salting it, to prevent burning up the stage. The axle had probably been sprung enough to cause friction. Dan Cawley started down to Sacramento river station on Wednesday with a light stage, to bring up Mrs. Parker, the lady who was so seriously injured by the late stage accident. She is now able to see out of both eyes, and will no doubt recover from her injuries without any serious detriment to her eyesight, the only danger feared.

A year later a C & O stage tipped over into the Scott River and the driver and horses were killed.

~

A number of express companies vied for routes from the mines in California. The winner might have been Adams Express Company, begun

Express office, Wells Fargo & Co., San Francisco.

in San Francisco in 1849, with whom Wells, Fargo & Company had to compete in 1852 when it opened a San Francisco office. But the 1855 financial panic sent Adams Express crashing into ruin, leaving Wells, Fargo to gobble up its routes, and use its new overwhelming power to become the only significant transporter of goods and services in the American West.

But despite historical memory (and television commercials), Wells, Fargo did not own stage lines in California (although it did operate a few during the 1860s). Wells, Fargo's great overland stage galloped 1900 miles into Sacramento from Omaha — until the trans-continental railroad was completed in 1869 — but the company contracted with local, privately-owned, regularly-scheduled stage companies to carry its express shipments. The image of a 'Wells Fargo Stage,' however, became permanently embedded in the popular mind.

The panic of '55 also consolidated a foundation for trustworthiness that Wells, Fargo had begun to build — guaranteed restitution, to the penny, of valuables lost or stolen while in the company's hands. That was the best deal for miners and the increasing number of merchants who catered to their needs. When Adams Express went under, mobs from Sonora to Portland stormed its offices searching for deposited funds; 196 other businesses in San Francisco alone closed their doors. But Wells, Fargo came through. The better managed company not only survived but was open for business a day after 'Black Friday.'

Early in the gold rush, stage holdups were rare events. Numerous bandits existed near the mines, but they preyed on lone

WELLS, FARGO & CO.
EXCHANGE, BANKING,
AND
EXPRESS COMPANY.

Organized 1852.   *Capital, $5,000,000.*

PRINCIPAL OFFICES:

No. 61 King Wm. Street, - - - London.
No. 33 Rue du Quatre Septembre, - - - Paris.
No. 65 Broadway, - - - - New York
N.W. Cor. California and Montgomery Streets, San Francisco.

EXPRESS LINES

To all parts of California, Nevada, Utah, Colorado, Wyoming, Montana, Nebraska, Oregon, Washington and Idaho Territories, British Columbia, Lower California, and Mexican Ports, New York, Atlantic States, and Europe.

BILLS OF EXCHANGE AND TELEGRAPH TRANSFERS

On New York, Boston, and Montreal, payable in the principal cities of the United States and Canada Also, Bills on London, Dublin and Paris. Letters of credit issued on our New York House, exchangeable for circular letters, payable in all parts of Europe.

COLLECTIONS AND COMMISSIONS

Of all kinds executed, and General Express business attended to promptly in all parts of the United States, Europe, and Canada.

LLOYD TEVIS, President, San Francisco.
Wm. G. Fargo, Vice-President, Buffalo, New York.
James Heron, Secretary, San Francisco.
Theo. F. Wood, Assistant Secretary, New York.
Homer S. King, Treasurer, San Francisco.
John J. Valentine, General Superintendent, San Francisco.

(1875)

miners on foot or on horseback. The first recorded stagecoach robbery in the gold country occurred in April, 1852, when a gang held up the Nevada City coach near Illinoistown and made off with $7,500. Three years later a mule train was held up and $80,000 taken (probably the record robbery of an animal-drawn vehicle in California). On March 12, 1856, a robbery planned by Rattlesnake Dick Barter relieved the Rhodes and Lusk Express of $26,000 on Trinity Mountain.

The era of the California highwayman really began in 1856. During the late 1850s significant amounts of gold were carried on stage coaches. The amounts lost are in the four and five figure range. Black Bart never stopped a stagecoach carrying more than $1,000 in the Wells, Fargo express box (though his take from U.S. Mail sacks may have boosted a few holdups into four figures). Poor Bart — he was too late for the most profitable years of his chosen profession.

Although bandits no longer lurked around every bend in 1875, stages continued to be held up; a stage driver never knew when he would hear 'throw down the box' and his passengers ordered to line up on the ground. Occasionally he could whip up his horses around a highwayman, but not

The holdup of the Raymond-Wawona stage, driven by Walter Farnsworth, on August 15, 1905.
(Courtesy Yosemite National Park Research Library)

often. Road agents who attempted to rob Wells, Fargo gold shipments were usually captured, as they had to contend with a company motto that read "Wells, Fargo Never Forgets," and a policy "never to abandon or relax the pursuit of anyone who commited a criminal offense against it."

Some road agents, of course, were never caught. In two famous cases in Yosemite Valley the brigands got away. One, whose face and hands were covered with charcoal or lampblack, held 39 people at bay, including troopers of the U. S. 6th Cavalry, on June 2, 1900. He failed to open the Wells, Fargo box but obtained $280 by lining up the passengers and passing a hat, to be filled with their money. As the road agent left he handed driver A. H. Foster a crudely written note that boasted 'The Black Kid,' sneering "Here's my card in case we ever meet again!"

34

Five years later a lone robber held up the Raymond-Wawona stage, about six miles above Ahwahnee. The otherwise ordinary crime was unique among stage robberies, as the highwayman permitted a passenger to photograph the event. The photographer, Anton Veith, an Austrian official touring the western United States, testified later how he confronted the road agent:

> He wore a kind of duster over his whole body, with two holes cut out for the eyes. He had a soft hat on his head, and a shotgun hanging on a string in his hands, with one hand on the trigger. The muzzle of the gun was covered with a black cloth about 10-12 inches long... I said, "You have my money, and now I want a favor of you." He said, "What is it?" I said that I wanted to take a snapshot of the whole scene. He said, "All right; nobody would recognize me anyway."[6]

~

There were other links in the stage systems: stage stations, with facilities for horses and passengers, located every ten to fifteen miles; barns to stable and feed the horses; hostlers and grooms to train; mechanics to maintain and repair the stages.

Three components of Wells, Fargo's organization were the company agent, the 'shotgun' messenger, and the 'treasure box.' Augie Heeser (also publisher of the *Mendocino Beacon*) recalled his job in Mendocino:

> I was a Wells, Fargo agent in 1900. The hours devoted to Wells, Fargo's office and the remuneration will be somewhat of a surprise to all but oldtimers. It was a commission office and the company had no rent or other expense, and my remuneration at holiday time would reach a high of $40 for a month. At other times it would descend to a low of $17 a month. The office was kept open from 8 a.m. to 6 p.m., six days a week.
>
> If the stage came when the office was closed the driver had a key to my office. We had a spring lock box built into a side wall large enough to hold the express box and the driver inserted the express box in this.
>
> Other express matter was left in the office. I was on hand the next morning at 7 o'clock to check all waybills and to get the north- and south- bound express off on the morning stages.
>
> The limit of coin shipment was $300. If the amount ran up to several thousand dollars a shotgun messenger was sent along. On his arrival I was called, came to the office, and placed the money in the vault.[7]

Jack Morley was constable of Murphys and a former shotgun messenger:

> The winter of 1889-90 was one of the wettest winters California ever had. And the roads were awful. One night the stage got stuck in the mud going up Funk Hill from Reynold's Ferry to Copper' — that's the hill where stage robbers really took Wells, Fargo & Co. for an awful cleaning. Well, the driver climbed down

and walked back to the Ferry to try and get the ferryman to come on out and take the passengers back to spend the night there. But he wouldn't get up out of bed, and so the passengers, they had to spend the night there in the mired down stage.

The drivers used to carry fifth chains. You know what a fifth chain is? Well, a stage would get mired down on the soft, cut-up roads. There'd be a crust on the surface of the road; either a frozen or a wind-dried crust, depending upon the weather we was having. But underneath the crust the ground was still soft and all cut up, halfway to China.

And the horses would break through this crust and the coaches would go down into the mud to the axles. Then the drivers would unhook the team — on the stages they used horses, never mules — and they'd lead the horses off the soft, cut-up road, out to where they'd have better ground to work on. Then they'd hook up the horses to one end of the fifth chain — and the other end of the fifth chain would be hooked onto the stage. Then they'd pull one way and the other and break the wheels loose and pull the stage out of the mud hole that way.

The Wells, Fargo strong box was bolted to the bottom of the body, on the floor, under one of the center seats. That was the heavy iron box, the strong box you read about. Plates — iron plates — which was bolted to the bottom of the strong box, was bolted to the floor of the coach.

Besides the strong box they always had a wooden chest. This box was carried up in the front boot, up with the driver. It had a heavy iron strap over the lid, fastened with a heavy padlock. It was locked shut but it was loose in the boot — it could be picked up and carried away. That was the box the bandits hollered to the driver to throw down to them when they stopped a stage. I've seen them wooden boxes busted open and laying beside the road and worthless papers, that had no value to them [the bandits], scattered and blowin' all around.

There was something about [stagecoaching, how dangerous it was]. I don't know as I can say it. Having been a shotgun messenger I guess maybe I could see only the danger there was to me, personally, in the job. You just felt something when you climbed up into the seat and loaded your shotgun. There was something about it.

Say, like we were coming into Murphys here. Back there about on Douglas Hill — if I was riding a stage carrying Wells, Fargo treasure and express — I'd likely unload my double-barrel shotgun and get ready to unhook the mail bags from where they hung on nails inside the boot, in front of the driver and me. You see, the mail bags were all leather in those days; anyway, the first class mail bags were. But all of them had handles, or loops, at the top and I had nails driven into the top of the boot, where it curved, you know.

You see, I had it figured out when I first started out as messenger that I'd always do it that way, in case of trouble. The mail bags hanging there would give me some little protection, if I was to drop down in the boot, back of them, and start shooting at a bandit over the top.

So I'd unload my gun and I'd put away the shells so's I wouldn't lose them, and so's nobody else could get ahold of any shells to fit our guns. They was ten-gauge, Colt's double-barrel shotguns, and the barrels were only about sixteen inches long from the breech to the muzzle. And the main reason we were so careful not to lose or misplace a shell was that they was all brass cases, the full length of the shell, and loaded with genuine rifle powder. That was 'specially good powder. Shotgun powder used to be a coarse, black powder that was good enough for 'most any shooting purposes; but rifle powder, that was a much finer powder, finer and stronger.

And Wells, Fargo never wanted anybody to get ahold of one of them shells. They was loaded with seven drams of rifle powder and sixteen big buckshot. Four of the buckshot would fill the circle of the shell. They'd drop four in, then another layer on top of that, until sixteen shot in all was in the shell on top of the powder wad; four layers of buckshot, you see?

We were only allowed to carry each shell for two trips in wet weather because, when it was damp, the shells might lose some of their strength on account of moisture dampening the powder. We had to destroy each shell after every second trip in the wintertime, or shoot them off — that is, if a man wanted to shoot them off. But you didn't want to shoot many of them off — they'd make your shoulder sore. I remember one time, the driver pulled up to rest the team on the way up the hill from Reynold's Ferry to Tuttletown, and I stepped down to shoot off some old shells and it was all of two hundred yards down to the river. But I shot and I could see each spot where the shot struck the water. They landed in a pattern all of ten feet in diameter. And my shoulder was black and blue afterward.

It was a kind of custom in those days of stage coaches for a driver to whip up his horses, comin' into town. They used to like to run 'em down the street on a dead run and pull them up to a fast stop. In summertime folks used to wet down the street in front of their places in town, but there was always a fair sized cloud of dust raised up.

Although you never were allowed to pass a post office, the express office usually come first. Why, I'd get down and put my already unloaded gun back up in the boot. I'd lean it against the seat with the butt up; the muzzle on the floor of the boot. That was the rule. Another rule was to never leave a loaded gun where anybody could get their hands on it.

What if some bandit thought that was a good time to hold me up and make off with the mail bags and the wooden box? I carried a forty-five, a Colt's revolver. That was my belt gun. And I never unloaded that. Anybody that wanted to could get the unloaded shotgun up in the boot. Nobody could get my belt gun.

Then the agent would come out of the express office with the key to the strong box which was bolted to the floor of the stage. He'd unlock the box and take out the treasure, whatever it happened to be. Sometimes it was gold, or money, or jewels or other things. Then he took it on into the office and I stayed right there where I was and watched until he got inside the office door; it was his responsibility from there on. Then he'd put it in the safe and come on back out and take the wooden box and I'd take my shotgun down out of the boot and go on in the office and leave it and my belt gun there with the agent.

But I forgot to tell you — I always had a pocket gun, too. Mine was a thirty-eight caliber Colt's gun.[8]

The portable box road agents wanted to steal (they would have preferred to 'crack' the iron safe, but that was more difficult and time-consuming) — that Wells, Fargo tried to prevent them from taking — was, as a Wells Fargo Bank historian[9] put it, "a modern advertiser's dream."

[It was created by] Joseph Young Ayer, a San Francisco carpenter between 1862 and 1906, and his son Joseph Stetson Ayer.

In a shop on San Francisco's Seventeenth Street, the Ayers used ponderosa pine to fashion their sturdy containers. An oak rim cushioned the knocks of hard use, while iron strapping and hinges strengthened and protected the chest during shipment. To break into one, a robber had to carry along a hatchet or find a good bashing stone.

His package was immediately recognizeable and attracted attention. Our contemporaries, though, might be unimpressed. His boxes were dull green, 20 by 10 inches, and weighed 24 pounds. His iron and wood creations were not the sort of thing a shopper would casually grab off a supermarket shelf. The magic, though, was in the white lettering. It read, "Wells, Fargo & Co." The public did not need Food and Drug Administration regulations to know that these drab containers had golden goodies inside.[10]

Education, liberal; nativity, New York; age about 60 years; occupation, mining; height, 5 feet 8 inches in stockings; complexion, light; heavy mustache, nearly white; heavy imperial, nearly white; size of foot, No. 6; weight, 160 pounds; size of hat 7 1/4; does not use tobacco in any form, nor intoxicating liquors or opium. High forehead, points running well up into hair; large ears, standing well out from head; eyes, light blue and deep set; nose rather prominent and broad at base; high cheek bones; heavy eyebrows; chin square and rather small; head large and long (size 7 1/4); two upper front teeth missing on right side of mouth; two lower teeth missing in center; small mole on left cheek bone; scar on top of forehead, right side; scar inside of left wrist; shield in India ink on right upper arm; two vaccine marks on right upper arm; forearms quite hairy; heavy tuft of hair on breast; gunshot wound opposite navel on right side; well muscled; has been troubled with throat disease and voice at times seems somewhat impaired; is a person of great endurance, a thorough mountaineer, a remarkable walker, and claims he cannot be excelled in making quick transits over mountains and grades; when reading without glasses holds paper off at arm's length; is comparatively well educated, a general reader, and is well informed on current topics; a cool, self-contained talker with waggish tendencies; and since his arrest has, upon several occasions, exhibited genuine wit under most trying circumstances. Has made his headquarters in San Francisco for the past eight years; has made but few close friends and those of first class respectability; is neat and tidy in dress, highly respectable in appearance and extremely proper and polite in behavior, chaste in language, eschews profanity and has never been known to gamble other than buying pools on horse races and speculating in mining stocks.

— from a Wells, Fargo & Company circular, 1888

Chapter 3
Charles Boles

When he was finally captured, Black Bart swore he didn't know much about his origins. In jail awaiting trial for his twenty-ninth and (possibly) last stagecoach robbery, with seemingly little to lose by telling the truth, he told the press he had been born in upper New York state around 1835. In fact, Charles Boles knew very well the circumstances of his birth, because he gave the place and date upon enlisting in the Union Army in 1862.

His family emigrated from England to the United States, departing by ship from London for New York City "on or about the first day of June, 1830." John Bowles, Charles' father, a native of Norfolk County, was born about 1788 in Shelfanger Parish, a few miles northwest of Diss, twenty miles from Norwich. His wife, Maria (Leggett), was born in 1793 thirty miles away in Great Yarmouth, where the couple married on June 27, 1807. Seven children were born in England: Harriet (about 1812), William (about 1815), James (about 1818), John, Jr. (about 1819), Robert (about 1822), Lucy (1824), and Charles (1829). Charles' middle name was possibly Earl, a name the family often used, even today.

The family name, which appears in England as Bowls, Bowels, Bowles, Bolles, and Boles, came from the word Bowler, either a drinking vessel or the occupational term for a maker or seller of bowls. Medieval bowls were made of wood as well as earthenware. It became Bowles permanently after Black Bart's exposure, to obscure the family relationship with a criminal. Why Charles and brother Hiram — but apparently no other family members — changed their name from Bowles to Boles is not known.

No record of the family coming into the United States exists on Atlantic Coast immigration lists, but many ship registers have been lost. John's brother, Leonard Bowles, came on the same ship with them.

The family settled in Jefferson County,[11] New York, north of Watertown near the St. Lawrence River. According to family tradition this land had been 'deeded' (purchased) before they left England. Two more children were born there: Maria in 1832 and Hiram in 1834.

John and Maria Bowles lived with their nine children on a hundred acre farm four miles southeast of Alexandria Bay, four miles west of the village of Plessis, which derived its name from a locale in France. It is familiarly known as 'Flat Rock,' from the prevalent sandstone formation. Present-day Allen Road, Shoulette Road and Center Road met at Godfrey's Corner,

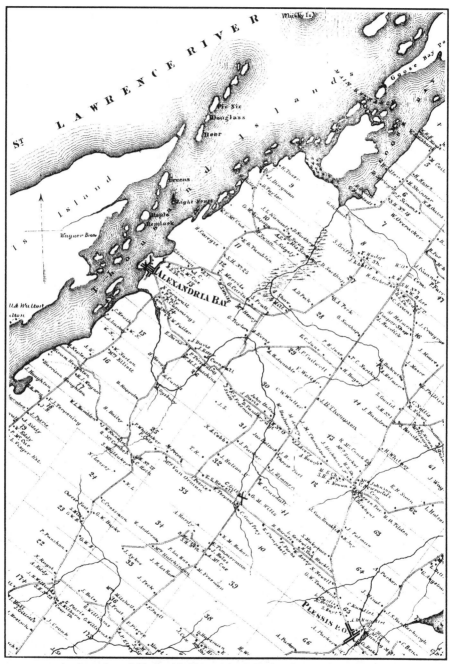

A portion of Alexandria Township, Jefferson County, New York.
From the 1864 Jefferson County New York Atlas.
See J. Boles (Section 39), J. Boles, jr. (Section 36) and Mrs. Johnson (Section 13).
(Courtesy Hazel McMane)

where a schoolhouse was located. Just to the south was the farm of J. Boles (this is the spelling used on the 1864 Jefferson County map), adjacent to the farm of Abraham McCue (possibly a relation of the Bowles family, certainly a long-time friend. He married Harriet Bowles, John and Maria's eldest daughter, in 1836).

Little is known of Charles Boles' early life in Jefferson County.[12] Most likely he had a very ordinary upbringing in an ordinary farming community. He would have attended the nearby school and his surviving letters show he must have received good marks in spelling and writing; his copper-plate penmanship was excellent. This writing ability was almost a family trait.[13]

In 1884, following Charles' trial and sentencing, a letter of unknown origin (probably written by a friend or acquaintance of the family) was printed in the *San Francisco Chronicle*:

> Charley, as we usually called him, received a common school education, and when grown up became better known than any other young man in this section on account of excelling in athletic sports, and was probably for his weight the best collar-and-elbow [Graeco-Roman, rather than today's more common freestyle] wrestler in Jefferson County. He was a young man of excellent habits and greatly esteemed and respected by all who knew him.

Another writer said he was also known as an amateur ventriloquist.

When news of the discovery of gold near Sutter's Mill reached the east coast in 1849, Charles Boles was one of many who contracted 'gold fever.' Typical of young men who search for adventure, he and his cousin David travelled overland and wintered in Van Buren County, Iowa, where Charles' older brother William had settled about 1841. Charles suffered a bout of ague (malaria, one of the common maladies of the age) there and didn't arrive in California until the late summer of 1850, possibly in July or August (they are not listed in the 1850 California Federal Census). The two boys probably mined first, 'with moderate success,' in the region east of Chico, near the most popular, least torturous mountain pass through the Sierras (parallelling the present highway from Reno, Nevada to Quincy). Then they worked with James McCue and his nephew on the north fork of the American River, near Union Bar. In the fall of 1851 the Boles and McCues broke camp and returned East by ship, arriving in New York in January, 1852.

Three months later Charley, his younger brother Robert, David, along with several boyhood companions, set out again for the Golden State. How they travelled is not known; but David Bowles was buried in Yerba Buena Cemetery in San Francisco on July 9th, so most likely they came by ship (their names, however, have not been found on any ship register).[14] Robert also may have fallen ill on board ship, as he died shortly thereafter, but in

PAN, CRADLE, LONG-TOM, AND SLUICE WASHING.

Old mining print from the 1885 book "Gold Mining in California."

the mining region. The group could have made the long 18,000 mile voyage around Cape Horn, or shipped to Panama, enduring a 50-mile mosquito-infested trek across the Isthmus, then caught another San Francisco-bound ship on the Pacific. However, the high incidence of malaria and other then-fatal tropical diseases suggests the Panamanian route; but even had they gone 'round the Horn' the cousins might have contracted diseases from men who boarded the ship at Panama City. Or the deaths could have been due to other causes.

Charles spent two more years in a fruitless quest for the big strike: Butte, El Dorado, Tuolomne, Shasta and Trinity Counties (and possibly mines in the hills surrounding San Jose) felt the blows of his pickaxe and put water in his sluice boxes — but like so many others he found little or no gold. His knowledge of northern California geography, however, would later be put to good use.

He returned overland in 1854 and married Mary Elizabeth Johnson, who, according to census information, was born in 1838. Nothing is known of her ancestry, nor of the couple's courtship, but the Johnson family might have lived near Plessis (the 1864 Jefferson County map shows the name 'Mrs. Johnson' at Browns Corners, a few miles northeast of John Boles farm). The place and date of the marriage has not been discoved either, although it was probably in New York state in 1856.

On April 18, 1857 Charles' youngest brother, Hiram Boles, purchased two parcels of land at $1.25 an acre near New Oregon, Howard County, in northeastern Iowa, not far from the Minnesota border, just south of present-day Cresco. Hiram either moved west then or had lived with their oldest brother, William, in southern Iowa. In 1857 Charles and Mary Boles were in New Oregon,[15] where their eldest daughter, Ida Martha, was born April 26th.

A strange story began then, with peculiar ramifications a decade later. It seems likely Charles either jointly purchased the two parcels in the Turkey River Land District with Hiram, or at least put up some of the money, although the deed was in Hiram's name. In June, 1858 a judgement (circumstances unknown) was passed against Hiram G. Boles in the District Court of Howard County, and Hiram's real estate was put up for public auction. One Almeson Sadler was the highest bidder at $99.13. On May 23, 1859 Almeson Sadler assigned his certificate of ownership of the property over to Charles E. Boles 'of the town of Plessis, Jefferson County, New York.'

Charles may not have physically been in New York state in

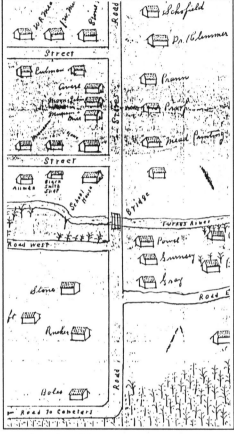

A portion of New Oregon, Iowa in 1868 showing the Boles farm.
(Courtesy Helen & Don Perkins)

1859, but Mary was, because on May 17th she gave birth there to the couple's second child, Eva Ardella.

On May 11, 1860, one month before the 1860 New York Federal Census, Charles E. Boles 'of Howard County, Iowa,' sold his land to Mary E. Boles 'of Jefferson County, New York' for the sum of $400. Certainly a curious transaction! Why did Charles sell the land to his wife for a considerably larger amount than the original purchase price? Why would he sell it to her at all? And where did Mary get the $400?

The 1860 Howard County, Iowa Federal Census does not reveal Charles E. Boles' presence, but this is a difficult census to read in parts and he might have been missed. The 1860 New York Federal Census, however, shows Mary E. Boles, Ida and Eva residing with John and Maria Bowles in Jefferson County, New York.

In 1861 Charles, Mary and the two children were living in Macon County, Illinois, near Decatur, where another daughter, Frances Lillian, was born on June 6th. They were briefly near Forsyth before moving to Hickory Point township, just south of Warrensburg, and lived in a house on a knoll bordering the Bearsdale and Boiling Springs Road to Decatur.[16] At that time Mary still owned the property in Iowa.

During these years in Iowa and Illinois, the frequent moves aside, Charles lived a seemingly honest, ordered life. How he supported his growing family is not known; most likely he was a farmer or maybe, as has been suggested, a schoolteacher. Perhaps Charles Boles would have been content to farm or teach for the rest of his days — but the mortars that fired on Fort Sumter, beginning the Civil War, disrupted millions of lives, his among them.

Boles enlisted as a private in Company B of the 116th Illinois Volunteer Infantry of the Union Army. He is portrayed in the Company Descriptive Book as: "Age, 33; height 5 feet 8 inches; complexion fair; eyes gray; hair brown; born Norfolk, Co., England; occupation farmer. Enlisted 13 August 1862, Decatur, Illinois by A. McClurg; term 3 years."

His unit, 78 privates, eight corporals, four sergeants, a First Sergeant, Second Lieutenant, First Lieutenant and Captain, along with a wagoner and two musicians (a bugler and a drummer), mustered on September 6th.[17] The regiment, almost all men from Macon County, left Decatur on November 8th to join General Sherman's Fifteenth Army Corps at Memphis, Tennessee. From Memphis the regiment started down the Mississippi River and reached the Yazoo River on December 26th. The men ascended the river for fifteen miles, where the regiment received its baptism of fire for three days at the Battle of Chikasaw Bayou.

Two weeks later the 116th returned to the Mississippi and on January 11, 1863 engaged in heavy fighting at Arkansas Post on the Arkansas River. Lieutenant John S. Taylor and two privates were killed, and Company B suffered heavy casualties, with only 25 unwounded men at the battle's end. Charles Boles was injured three times during the war and probably received a flesh wound at Arkansas Post.

Worse was to come. On January 22nd the regiment landed at Young's Point, Louisiana, to help dig a canal during the siege of Vicksburg. Over 100 members of the 116th died from fever, including eight members from Company B. Charles Boles was spared this sickness (if his second trip to the California goldfields was via Panama, perhaps he was immune to tropical fevers).

In March the regiment left the deadly swamps together with the Eighth Missouri to save Admiral Porter's fleet of gunboats from a heavy Confed-

Scene of Sherman's assault against the Bluffs at Chickasaw Bayou. From *Battles and Leaders of the Civil War.*

erate attack; the tide turned in the Union's favor when General Sherman himself arrived, at the head of his Thirteenth Regulars.

In May the 116th was back in action, suffering heavy losses (although not Company B) at Champion Hills and Black River Bridge. The regiment returned to the siege of Vicksburg and witnessed the city's surrender on July 4, 1863. A memorial to Illinois regiments stands at Vicksburg, with Charles Boles' name engraved on the monument.

Just before the blockade's end, on July 1st, Boles was promoted to Commissary Sergeant. On July 5th the regiment moved out to chase General Joseph E. Johnston's Confederate cavalry into Mississippi before giving up. Then the men of the 116th rested at Camp Sherman near Black River for three months.

In October General Grant ordered Sherman and his veteran troops to move to Chattanooga. During the night of November 23rd, the 116th and the Sixth Missouri, commanded by General Giles Smith, floated down the Tennessee River in pontoon boats to the mouth of Chickamauga Creek, where they captured the Confederate pickets. General Smith was severely wounded the following day during a skirmish near Missionary Ridge, his place taken by Col. Nathanael Tupper. On November 24th Sherman massed his forces for the coming battles of Missionary Ridge, Tunnel Hill and Lookout Mountain. The next day, one of the bloodiest of a bloody war, alongside other regiments of the brigade, the 116th formed the Union Army's extreme left flank; at a crucial moment these troops turned the enemy's right flank, which contributed directly to the Union victory.

But celebration was shortlived. General Burnside's army was confronted by a superior Confederate force. So Sherman, without allowing his men to recross the Tennessee River to retrieve their blankets or overcoats, marched his troops through bitterly cold weather toward Knoxville. This would be remembered as one of the hardest campaigns of the war: "The men suffered greatly while camping at night. They would build big fires and hug them close, but the other side would be chilled to the marrow of the bones; rations, also were very short ..."

After successfully relieving Burnside in January, 1864, the Army of the Tennessee moved into winter quarters at Larkinsville, Alabama. On

HARPER'S HISTORY OF THE GREAT REBELLION.   [MAY, 1865.

GRAND REVIEW AT WASHINGTON.—SHERMAN'S VETERANS MARCHING THROUGH PENNSYLVANIA AVENUE.

January 28th Charles Boles received a battlefield commission to 1st Lieutenant.

Fighting began again in the spring. On May 26th, at Acworth on Resaca Creek near Dallas, Georgia, Charles Boles received his most serious wound, a bullet in the abdomen near the right hip (Having been wounded, once seriously, Boles should have been eligible to collect a pension; one wonders why he never applied for one). He was hospitalized in a Georgia field hospital until September 5th, then rejoined his unit during the fall of Atlanta. Sherman's army then scorched its way across Georgia to the sea. The troops reached Fort McAllister, near Savannah, on December 12th and captured the fort after fighting for only five minutes. Then on to the Carolinas where in March the regiment fought its last battle, near Bentonville, North Carolina, against its old adversary, Joe Johnston.

The Civil War ended with Robert E. Lee's surrender at Appomatox Court House in April, 1865. In May Charles Boles wa in the ranks of the 116th Regiment as it marched down Constitution Avenue in Washington, D.C. in the Grand Reunion, a two-day long parade celebrating the Union victory. On the reviewing stand with President Andrew Johnson were Generals Grant and Sherman. The regiment was mustered out following the festivities, on June 7, 1865.

Charles Boles had joined the army as a private, fought in seventeen battles, and demonstrated those qualities that distinguish a soldier. At war's end he was First Sergeant, his unit's third-highest ranking member, and one of only two privates of the eighty who had left Decatur in 1862 to receive, albeit briefly, an officer's commission. Had he stayed in the army, the commission to First Lieutenant (noted without comment in the NAME OF OFFICIAL DOCUMENT) would have been offered to him.

(Courtesy National Archives)

Unfortunately we have no reminiscences by his wife or surviving letters from the front, but there is one brief description of Boles as a soldier. In 1883, after his capture and real identity became known, a reporter called on Christian Reibsame in Decatur. Like Charles Boles, Reibsame had enlisted as a private in the 116th Illinois and had left service as its captain. The December 15th *National Police Gazette* printed Reibsame's recollection:

> [Boles] was one of the bravest men in the regiment, and was often commended for gallantry, and on that account received his promotion. He was always at the front in every fight, and was wounded several times. He was a reticent fellow, but was well liked. He was inclined to sport, and played a good game of poker... He was a perfect specimen of a good soldier and a man of iron nerve.

Whatever he failed to accomplish early in life, whatever shady ends he devoted himself to later, at least Charles Boles could be proud of his military career.

Mary and the children remained in Decatur at least until January, 1865, then moved back to New Oregon, Iowa, where Charles joined them after returning from the war. A short time later the family went to Minnesota, where a fourth child, a boy named Arian, was born. A relative of Mary's, perhaps a sister, was living in southern Minnesota, only a few miles from Howard County. Possibly Mary wanted to be with her sister for the birth.

Arian Boles' birth date has not been discovered, but if he was actually born in 1865 — as stated on the Census report — it must be assumed that Charles Boles had been in Decatur on leave, perhaps recuperating from an injury, in 1864 (he didn't get back from the war until June, 1865). Evidence exists, written in a Bible that Mary gave to him, that he could have been with her on New Years Day, 1865. Mary stated later that she sent the Bible to Charles; in that case Arian must have been born in 1866.

But soon the family of six was back in Iowa, and on March 25, 1867 Mary sold her property to John and Patrick Mooney.[18] Part of the money from the sale probably went to Charles, who was again on the move. He and his family are listed on the 1870 Howard County Federal Census (with real estate valued at $200 and a personal estate of $100):

Boles, Chas. E.	age 40 m	Miner	b. England
Boles, Mary E.	age 32 f	Keep House	b. New York
Boles, Ida	age 13 f	at home	b. Iowa
Boles, Eva	age 11 f		b. New York
Boles, Lillian	age 9 f		b. Illinois
Boles, Arian	age 5 m		b. Minnesota

But Charles was not actually in Iowa when the census taker came around; his wanderlust and gold fever had returned; after he left this time, on May 1, 1867, his family would never see him again. He ventured to Deer Lodge County in Montana Territory, for Montana's 'shallow diggin's' mining boom, and worked a claim with a Missourian, Henry Roberts. The 1870 Montana Census locates him near Deer Creek, close to Silver Bow, a mining camp seven miles from present-day Butte.

The Butte Daily Miner described Silver Bow's origin: "The village is built upon the bend of the stream, which forms a perfect figure of a gracefully curved Indian bow, and from the mountain peaks which surround the beautiful valley, the glistening waters of the 'silver bow' form a striking feature of the landscape." This beauty did Charles little good, as the viciously cold 1868-69 winter froze water necessary for placer or 'free gold' mining; 1870 followed the driest year in the memories of the territory's white settlers, so no water was available for sluice ditches. Silver Bow quickly faded, totally disappearing by 1874.

Mary Boles later said Charles wrote to her as often as four times a week during those years. A few letters survive (in the private collection of a descendent); most contain ponderous sentiments of love and affection, but usually little information about his life or plans. He wrote an unusually informative letter (slightly edited) from Helena City,[19] Montana Territory, on April 4, 1869:

My own dear Mary & Little ones,
   I am indeed thankful for the very kind & loving letters just received from you my dear wife. This is another beautiful Sabbath morning & I am happy to tell you I am well. Oh my dear I was so happy to hear that you [and the children] were also well... I write every week as regular as God sends them & you I know have got plenty [of letters] before this but the late snow blockade prevented them going sooner... Now I will tell you what I have just done. As I told you in my last letter I would tell you today what I would do this summer. Well I have just bought a claim. Paid $260 for it in dust. Now it all depends on how it pays, about my coming home this fall. So I remain in the same place in the same claim & in the same cabin & with the same partner I pay as it comes out. I pay him half I get out of the ground until the claim is paid for. So I will have half I take out to pay expenses & to send home if needed. But it may not pay me, can't tell until we dig. But my dear I don't want to work for any man if I can help it. I will have a wood cabin, stove & everything handy, mining tools too, sluice boxes & can be where I am handy for <u>mail</u>. Quite an item with me I assure you. So if it pays reasonably well we will both come home in the fall... I hope you will not blame me if I fail & be sure not to put it down <u>too</u> strong that I am coming in the fall, but my darling I will [come] if I can and for you only to know how very much I do want to see you all. My dear, at all events I will try & furnish you with what money you will need & use all you need to make you comfortable & happy & you can depend upon regular mail here often. I think the U. P. R. R. [Union Pacific Railroad] is about completed to our

nearest point, which is 480 miles from Helena City. Wells Fargo & Co. will go through to the station in 60 hours soon. So you see our mail will not be too long on the road from here after.

Will my dear kiss all the little ones for me & tell them Papa is aching to get hold of them once more. Now my dear, after once more telling how dearly I love you I will close. So may God bless you all & keep you safe til I return to you again. Good bye, as ever your loving husband.

C. E. Boles

A subsequent letter (August, 1871) contained news that he had made his stake, could take care of his family, and was about to return to his wife and children.

Suddenly the letters stopped — and Mary would not hear of her loving husband again for twelve years! Apparently a rumor reached her that Charles and a party of fellow travellers were set upon and killed by Indians. Certainly the silence, after such a regular correspondence, would seem to indicate a catastrophe. But of what kind? We don't know. Added to this fear and worry was her distress and sorrow over the sudden death of young Arian.

On September 25, 1872 John Bowles died in Plessis. His Last Will and Testament (dated August 24, 1872, when Charles was supposedly dead) named Hiram Bowles as his executor. The puzzle of the land purchase alongside the Turkey River in Iowa in 1857 — if there is a connection — now becomes even more confusing. Current Bowles family lore is that during his California mining days Charles sent either money or gold home to his father, to pay for a new farmhouse in Plessis. If true, that is probably an element in this matter. The fourth item in John's will reads, "I give and bequeath to Mary Bowles, wife of my son Charles Bowles, deceased, the sum of four hundred dollars" — the same amount as in the Howard County land business. The inheritance was to have been paid within one year of the death of John's wife, Maria (who died a few weeks after her husband, in October).

Mary and her three daughters moved to Hannibal, Missouri in 1873. She had received only $80 of her legacy and had difficulty in obtaining the balance from Hiram Bowles, because in October, 1873 she engaged a lawyer. A petition to the Court of Jefferson County, New York states, in part:

> That said legacy became due and was payable to her 25 September 1873, by said executor. That there are assets belonging to said estate amply sufficient to pay all the claims against it. That no part of said legacy has been paid to her except the sum of eighty dollars, for which she gave a receipt to said executor. That she has several times demanded the payment of the balance of said legacy of said executor before filing this petition.

Mary Elizabeth Johnson Boles
(Courtesy Marc C. Reed Collection)

Technically, Mary's attorney was premature in the demand (a year after Maria's death, not John's, would have been October, not September). Eventually, after further legal haggling, Hiram was ordered to make payment, and Mary finally received her legacy.[20]

What she must have felt about the Bowles family — her husband had vanished in the West; her selfish brother-in-law was in the East. Mary's marriage to Charles had never been easy, his restlessness and absences difficult to bear, with added hardships from the frequent moves. For the rest of her life Hannibal was her home, where she eked out an existence as a seamstress. Most likely she never expected to hear from her lost or errant husband again — and would have been better off if she had not.

Perhaps information may come to light someday to fill in Black Bart's 'lost years.' Did he really strike it moderately rich in Montana? If so, what happened to his mine? Did it fail? Did he sell the claim or get cheated out it? If he made a good strike, why didn't he return to Iowa, or at least contact his family? According to unconfirmed sources Charles moved to Salt Lake City in Utah Territory after Montana. When he masqueraded from 1875 to 1883 as the gentleman mining engineer Charles Bolton in San Francisco, he was never known to drink or gamble. Were these lifelong habits, or had he perhaps lost his hard-earned money in a drunken poker game in Montana, and swore off the curses that cost him his security? Did an event take place he never mentioned, that has never come to light, that is lost in the mists of history?

It is not likely that he held up any stagecoaches in Montana. During his years there almost all stage robberies were the work of gangs, rather than loners; the few solo road agents were all either captured or at least identified. Possibly he read about a famous Montana stagecoach robbery that took place on September 6, 1869, when two thieves, one soon killed, the other captured, got $89,000. Although alone, they set up three dummies, which convinced the driver and passengers the stage was being attacked by a large gang. Boles could have filed the information for future use. Or he might have remembered 'Quaker' (harmless) guns, used by both sides in the Civil War. These were typically logs, peeled then painted black, mounted on carriages or laid in embrasures to deceive the enemy. Confederate troops placed them behind fortifications on the Mississippi River.

Or did he make a fair sum in Montana and just decide to travel and spend it — by himself? His most famous alias might indicate that he had returned to California and was in either San Francisco or the Sacramento area in 1871 (see Chapter 9. There is also a persistent rumor that he spent the years 1871-74 teaching in California, either in Sierra County or Concord, over the hills from Berkeley, but was dismissed because of a mania for gambling).

Another dubious report (always that devilish passive voice — who saw him? Whom did they tell about it?) placed him at a racetrack in San Antonio in 1874, where he appeared well to do, and spoke of going to California again. Considering the poignant letters to his wife, that seems doubtful; but supposedly word of the Texas sighting came to Mary Boles' attention, as she hired detectives to search for him.

More likely, he decided he couldn't admit failure to his family again and it was best for all concerned that he disappear. He had married after an unsuccessful second attempt as a miner; perhaps a third without a big strike was too much for him to bear. He had formed no alliances we know of while mining and during the eight years he alternated Black Bart with Charles Bolton apparently had no particular social life. He seems to have been a rare soul who could thrive in an existence with no close companions, either friends or lovers (although the rumor of a mistress exists, even of a second marriage following his release from San Quentin). So he became a loner.

In 1875 Boles was definitely back in California, but his whereabouts is unknown until early 1878, except for the locales of his first robberies. A tale that he worked in a Nevada County sawmill before that time contains too many discrepancies to be credible (see Appendix II).

Market Street, looking towards the Palace Hotel, San Francisco, 1878.
(*Frank Leslie's Illustrated Newspaper,* May 18, 1878)

Wherever he was for those three years, in 1878 Charles 'Bolton' moved into Room 40 of the Webb House, a small rooming house at 37 Second Street in San Francisco (the building still exists, close to the present-day Sheraton Palace Hotel). He presented himself as a mining executive, dressed well, conservatively, and though he sported a diamond stickpin his acquaintances saw nothing dandyish about him. He was known as a regular sort, who made no to-do about his virtues, nor seemed to feel superior to those who lacked them. He was softspoken with a deep voice — a voice people remembered. He frequented the stock boards and Pike & Hayes' fashionable New York Bakery at 628 Kearney Street, where the important mining (and law enforcement) men often dined and discussed their business.

Charles Boles had good ears, an affable manner, and a series of aliases that required an excellent memory. Some mining men knew him as Charles Bolton, others as C. E. Benson. To a few local cops he was Charley Barlow from Ohio, a former Captain in the Union Army who told spellbinding war stories. Quite an actor in real life, he was fascinated by professionals; he stood for hours outside the Bush Street Theater, watching performers (among them young David Warfield, who would one day own a nation-wide chain of theaters) pass in and out of Chris Buckley's Saloon.

Soon after establishing a presence in the San Francisco business world, Charles Boles announced a brief trip to visit one of his holdings. It may have been to Butte County that he went, but his holdings lay all across northern California. They were the Wells, Fargo express boxes carried 'under the seat or in the boot' of stages that crisscrossed the state. He never made a deposit, but he would make an historic number of withdrawals.

Chapter 4
Yuba County — *Tuesday, December 28, 1875*
Robbery No. 2

The U.S. Post Office added 'north' to San Juan's name in 1857, to distinguish it from another San Juan in San Benito County, but local usage of the original name continued for many years.

Timbuctoo, just west of Smartsville, was once one of the largest towns in Yuba County. It was supposedly named by the first person to pan gold there, a black man from Timbuktu, Africa. All that remains are the crumbling ruins of a Wells, Fargo building.

During December, 1875 two stagecoaches were robbed on the San Juan-Marysville line. Only the second sounds like Black Bart but both illustrate the dangers of a stage driver's work:

Marysville Appeal, December 17th — STAGE AND EXPRESS ROBBERY: The San Juan and Marysville stage, on route to this city yesterday, and driven by Mike Hogan, was stopped at 10:30 about four miles above Smartsville, on the road between Finney's hill and Atwood's new house, and robbed of Wells, Fargo & Co.'s express box, which is supposed to have contained but a small amount of treasure. Mr. Hogan informs us that he was half an hour ahead of time, and his team had just got into a walk, from a slow trot, when a masked man jumped up from behind a bush on the lower side of the road, and presenting a rifle at his head, said: "Stop and hold up your hands."

Robert Winans, who occupied a seat on the box obeyed the summons, and the robber repeated his command with more emphasis, "hold up your hands or I'll blow your brains out." Hogan then threw down his reins and whip and held up his hands. The robber then said, "hand down that box and be quick about it." Hogan was some time in getting the box out, as there was a valise in the way, and the robber said, "hurry up." Hogan then threw out the box, and asked, "will I drive on?" "Yes," replied the robber. Hogan said the robber spoke in a tremulous voice, and gave orders, with some space of time intervening, as if a little short of courage. As he drove off he kept his eyes upon the robber with a view of recognition. This the robber did not like, and he said "drive on or I'll blow your brains out," keeping his rifle leveled upon him.

56

Marysville-LaPorte stage, Yuba County. Photographed by Louis Stellman.
(Courtesy California State Library)

After proceeding some distance and being out of sight of the robbers, Mr. Winans, who was armed with a revolver, took a route across lots to the scene of the robbery to watch operations. He reports he was observed, and told to stop. At that time there were two robbers in possession of the treasure box. The robbers broke open the box with an ax, and soon departed with all the contents but one paper. The box was soon picked up and taken to Timbuctoo.

The following passengers were aboard the stage: Robert Winans, Henry Winans, James Smith, Miss Wetzler, and a Chinaman. The robber stopping the stage was a heavy man, about 5 feet 9 inches in height, dark complexion, dark hair, square face, blue eyes, and wore a checked shirt and a pair of tongued boots. Wells, Fargo & Co. offer a reward of $250 and one-fourth the treasure for the arrest and conviction of the robber or robbers. Mr. Hogan says he could identify the robber without the least doubt.

Marysville Appeal, December 29th — ANOTHER STAGE ROBBERY. The Marysville and San Juan stage, en route for this city, was stopped yesterday morning a few miles above Smartsville by four highwaymen and robbed of Wells, Fargo &

Co.'s treasure-box. We did not learn its contents. Mike Hogan, who was driving when the same stage was stopped and robbed on the 16th instant, was again the victim. After the robbery yesterday, Hogan drove his passengers and express matter to the Nevada and Marysville stage, put out his team, and returned with a formidable party in search of the desperadoes. Hogan is probably getting mad. Two robberies in as many weeks is more than he can bear, especially as he is an active and experienced police officer. Hogan was but three hours behind the robbers, and as they cannot cross the river only by the regular bridges, there is hope of his overtaking them.

If a passenger actually saw two robbers in this first holdup, Bart wasn't involved, as he always worked alone. If Bart robbed the second stage, three sticks would have been propped up to look like hidden rifles.

On December 16th Mike Hogan alleged "he could identify the robber without the least doubt." If it was the same bandit, the driver certainly would have recognized that tremulous voice on December 28th.

Bart may have committed neither robbery (although Wells, Fargo blamed him for the second). The lack of information and evidence illustrates the uncertainty and confusion that runs throughout this story to the end.

Chapter 5
Siskiyou County — *Friday, June 2, 1876*
Robbery No. 3

A.C. Adams had little reason to worry about robbery. He was driving his California and Oregon Coast Mail Co. stagecoach south from Roseburg, Oregon to Yreka. The route was subject to banditry, but an experienced thief would rob northern-bound stages, not the other way around. California possessed the gold; some went to Oregon in exchange for goods and produce, or to pay millworkers, but little hard cash flowed back. Oregon's brief gold rush had been over for almost a decade.

Adams had completed the hardest part of his trip, through the rugged Siskiyou Mountains south of Jacksonville. He had just crossed into California, the mountains and their tall trees left behind, and was passing through the rolling scrub hills in the Cottonwood Creek area

north of Yreka, seven miles from Cottonwood itself. At 10:30 at night the team was at a walking pace, the shaky lanterns and the horses' night vision the only guarantees of safe passage. Two miles south from the state border, as the team slowed even more to climb the easy grade of Bailey's Hill, a stout 5'9" masked man stepped out from behind a tree on the uphill side of the road and ordered Adams to stop.

The *Yreka Journal* later suggested, with some justification, that the bandit was a 'greenhorn' for robbing the stage on its southern route, rather than the richer northern one — the treasure box contained only $82.25, though the registered mail may have added to the footpad's meager profits (most accounts say that the box contained $74.25, but a later report to Wells, Fargo indicates that $8.00 more came aboard at Ashland).

Driver John B. Mack, on a C & O 'mud-wagon,' in front of the Franco-American Hotel in Yreka, March 24, 1879. *(Courtesy Siskyou County Museum)*

But in one respect the highwayman acted like a thorough professional. He stood next to the tree on the high side of the hilly trail, pointing his gun down towards the front of the stage. His back was to the moon, further obscuring his face (the driver and passengers were not even sure he was masked), preventing any recognizeable glimpse of him.

Told to drop the treasure box, Adams played dumb, asking "What box," but a bit of the robber's profanity, and an ominous wave of his shotgun, ended the byplay. The outlaw made no attempt to rob the passengers, ordering the driver to move on after the Wells, Fargo box had been heaved to the trail.

Adams drove on to Cottonwood, where arrangements were made to begin pursuit in the morning. A Mr. Shattuck of Cottonwood found the empty treasure box, and Deputy Sheriff John Halleck left Yreka on Saturday morning, hoping to return with the bandit. The town's recently built brick jail needed a tenant. Wells, Fargo offered a $250 reward for the bandit's arrest and conviction, to which the State of California added $300.

Clues on the trail suggested the unknown robber had fled east, up Hutton Creek in the direction of Little Pilot Rock. Bootprints indicating well-worn soles with extremely large nails were plainly visible across the trail that led downhill towards the creek. Bart may have begun wearing canvas boot coverings after reading newspaper reports of his crimes; these didn't always obscure his trail, but they prevented incriminating details about his boots from being discovered.

On Monday morning Wells, Fargo dispatched its chief detective, James B. Hume, to the scene. Shortly after Hume arrived in Yreka, the thief seemed to have been caught. A Wells, Fargo employee, Yreka cashier/ agent A. H. Barrows, had gone to Roseburg on business the day before the robbery; on his return he had noticed a suspicious-looking man on the road near Canyonville, heading toward Roseburg. When Barrows reached Cottonwood and heard about the robbery, he telegraphed the sheriff in Roseburg, who apprehended the vagabond. But after examining the prisoner's boots, Hume declared the Roseburg authorities didn't have the guilty man.

The *Yreka Journal*, forgetting this chain of events, needled their northern neighbor in an article called 'The Wrong Man:' "The boots on the man arrested did not correspond with the description telegraphed, and this Oregon officer made unnecessary cost in telegraphing and getting a detective here from below, besides doing great injustice to an innocent man."

The hunt continued but the trail was cold. Detective Hume's frustration with this wily bandit would continue for seven more years.

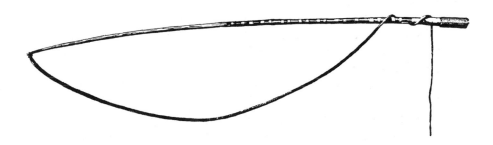

Chapter 6
James B. Hume — Wells, Fargo Detective

An irony of the Black Bart saga is that the man who sought him doggedly for so long looked like the highwayman's slightly more handsome younger brother. James Hume was also born in New York state, at Stamford in 1835, about two hundred miles southeast of Alexandria Bay in the northern foothills of the Catskill Mountains. Like Boles, Jim Hume and his brother John[21] had set out for the goldfields in 1850, but Hume was either made of sterner stuff or had more luck, as he took enough gold out of the Sierras to support himself for ten years.

By 1860 only the large mining concerns could make substantial profits from the seams of gold buried in California hills, so Hume turned to public service. He first became deputy tax collector, then city marshall in Placerville, forty miles northeast of Sacramento. Later, as undersheriff of El Dorado County, he made his name with several newsworthy arrests, and was elected sheriff in 1868. Because of these arrests and convictions he attracted the attention of Wells, Fargo, which had suffered through the gold rush years from stage holdups (and often theft by its own agents, who embezzled almost as much as highwaymen took at gunpoint).

After Hume lost his bid to be re-elected El Dorado County's sheriff in 1871, he accepted the express company's offer to head their detective bureau. But the State of Nevada asked for his services first, after a major jailbreak, to clean up their state penitentiary. Hume battled that state's less honest politicians and restored order in the prison. Then he began his duties at Wells, Fargo, probably relieved to deal with non-elected criminals.

As Chief Special Agent for Wells, Fargo, Hume was a model for lawmen everywhere. He was as ingenious a detective as Black Bart was a criminal. He closed down company embezzlement, and saw the capture and conviction of almost every road agent who robbed his employers. In 1885 Hume wrote a report recording fourteen years of his achievements, from November 5, 1870 to November 5, 1884: 313 stage robberies had taken place against Wells, Fargo; 226 robbers (including Black Bart) had been

James B. Hume
(Courtesy Wells Fargo Bank)

arrested and convicted, and nine killed, either during a holdup or when caught by Hume's deputies or local lawmen.[22] Bandits killed four drivers, two shotgun messengers and four passengers. Black Bart was responsible for 27 (Hume's figure) of those robberies, while Milton Sharp (who specialized on a Nevada stage line between Carson City and Bodie) held up six stages, and Al Hamilton held up seven. Only Black Bart eluded Hume and his men long enough to hit double figures.

Although Hume knew him to be singularly unbloodthirsty, even suspecting at first — and rightly — that Bart's shotgun wasn't loaded, each new report of the deep-voiced man with the floursack mask made him a little more angry, a little more determined to bring the road agent to justice. Detective work also led Hume to deduce that the outlaw was in fact always on foot, never on horseback.

Early on, Hume thought Black Bart was in fact one Frank Fox, a convicted stage robber who had served time in jail and was again free; the detective even sent out a private circular to Wells, Fargo agents describing Fox. But when Hume discovered he had the wrong man, he shrugged his shoulders and settled down to tracking Bart even more intensely.

REPORT

OF

JAS. B. HUME and JNO. N. THACKER,

SPECIAL OFFICERS,

WELLS, FARGO & CO'S EXPRESS,

Covering a Period of Fourteen Years,

GIVING LOSSES BY

Train Robbers, Stage Robbers and Burglaries,

AND A FULL DESCRIPTION AND RECORD OF ALL

NOTED CRIMINALS

CONVICTED OF OFFENSES AGAINST WELLS, FARGO & COMPANY
SINCE NOVEMBER 5TH, 1870.

SAN FRANCISCO:
H. S. CROCKER & Co., STATIONERS AND PRINTERS, 213-219 BUSH STREET.
1885.

NUMBER 519

Chapter 7
Sonoma County — *Friday, August 3, 1877*
Robbery No. 4

Thomas Beacom & Company's stage had left Norton's Hotel in Mendocino City (Mendocino County) the day before at 2 p.m. After an overnight stay at Point Arena, the difficult, 55-mile, 12 1/2-hour trip to Duncan's Mills began at 6 a.m. The seven passengers had paid the $6.00 fare. Stops were made along the coast, then the coach swung inland, to begin a tortuous ascent to the ridgetops of the Coast Range, stopping first at Plantation before moving higher up. Eight miles later, after a well-deserved rest and change of horses at James Henry's Hotel (today's Seaview), the coach ran south, made a quick stop at the stage stop near the crumbling Russian ruins at Fort Ross, then plunged down Myers Grade Road toward Duncan's Mills. Even today this spectacular journey isn't for the faint-hearted, matching in difficulty and beauty any mountain road in California — a stagecoach required 2 1/2 hours to complete the last twelve miles.

NORTH COAST STAGE LINE

Carrying U. S. Mail & W. F. & Co's Express

This line will run as follows:—Leaves DUN-CAN'S MILL every morning (Monday excepted) at 6 o'clock, for TIMBER COVE, FORT ROSS, PLANTATION HOUSE FISK'S MILL, FISH-ERMAN'S BAY, GUALALA, FOURN'S LANDING, POINT ARENA and all points on the Coast. Returning, leaves POINT ARENA every morning (Mondays excepted) at 6 o'clock for Duncan's Mill and Way Stations, connecting with the N. P. C R R. for San Francisco. The Stages of this Company
LEAVE POINT ARENA every morning (Sundays excepted) at 6 o'clock for Manchester, Brukeport, Cuffey's Cove, Navarra Ridge, Salmon Creek, Albion, Little River and Mendocino City, making close connections with stages for all points North of Mendocino City.

CLOVERDALD ROUTE.

Stages of this line will leave Cloverdale every Monday, Wednesday and Friday, for White-Hall, Yorkville, Booneville, Christine, North Fork and Navarra Ridge, connecting with the Company's stages for Mendocino City and all points on the coast.
Returning leaves Navarra Ridge on arrival of Coast Stages From Mendocino City, stopping over night at the North Fork House.
Passengers can leave Cloverdale for Mendocino and return by the Coast route, connecting at Duncan's Mill with the N. P. C. Railroad, making the most delightful trip imaginable.
Tickets for the round trip can be had at the Company's Office at Duncan's Mill, and at their Office in Cloverdale, with the privilege of laying over at any point on the route.
OFFICE, Norton House.
THOS. BEACOM & Co., Proprietors.
jy 27-1y.

Just past a sharp curve at the top of a long, steep climb (Myers Grade), about four miles south of Fort Ross, Bart halted the stage. One account of the robbery states he told the driver[23] to turn his back or be shot down. After gaining his loot the bandit probably hiked overland to the Fort Ross-Old Cazadero Road, then went on into Guerneville.

Only a brief report of the holdup appeared in the *Petaluma Weekly Argus*:

The Point Arena to Duncan's Mill stage was robbed about noon, near Fort Ross, by a masked highwayman. On demand of the robber the driver handed out the Wells, Fargo's treasure box which contained about $60. There were seven passengers in the stage at the time, none of whom were molested.

The *Argus* underestimated the stolen amount, as the express box held more than $300 in coin, and a check in favor of Fisk Brothers (a lumber mill and stage stop north of Fort Ross) for $305.52 on the Granger's Bank of San Francisco (which Black Bart never tried to cash).

Lawmen reached the robbery scene the same day and recovered the broken remains of the treasure box. Nearby, under a rock on a tree stump, they discovered a scribbled message on a Wells, Fargo waybill. During his eight year career Black Bart would hold up twenty-nine stages — twenty more than any other highwayman — but these lines of poetry made him a chapter rather than a footnote in California history:

> I've labored long and hard for bread
> For honor and for riches
> But on my corns too long you've tred
> You fine haired Sons of Bitches
>
> > Black Bart, the Po8
>
> Driver, give my respects to our friend, the other driver;
> but I really had a notion to hang my old disguise hat on
> his weather eye.

Each line was written in a different script. What Bart meant by the postscript has never been established, but by conversing with stage drivers at hotels and saloons when they were off duty, the bandit often learned the contents of express boxes; perhaps he was taunting them for having done so in this case. In any event, the poem is what caught Jim Hume's eye —

66

The North Coast Stage at Plantation. *(Courtesy David & Suzanne Brown)*

and soon the eyes of creative San Francisco and Sacramento news reporters.

> So at last the linen duster man had a name. For years after that everybody [in the mountains] was talking of Black Bart. In all the romance of the frontier there had never been quite such a mysterious and elusive highwayman as he, nor one so original in his methods. Superstitious people began to think there must be something uncanny and supernatural about him.[24]

And from the Russian River came the first of hundreds of stories about this strange hooded character. Black Bart lore can be found everywhere in northern California (and a few places in southern California as well) — most is imaginary, the stuff of myth and legend. The origin of this tale was a line in a Wells, Fargo circular sent to company agents in 1878: "It is believed that he went into the Town of Guernieville about daylight next morning."

These words have caused a misconception, that the stage Bart robbed came on to Guerneville after Duncan's Mills — it didn't. The road from the coast to Guerneville wasn't completed until 1879. Through passengers and freight would have changed stage lines at (old) Duncan's Mills, gone south to Bodega, east through Sebastopol to Santa Rosa, then on to Petaluma for the ferry to San Francisco. The tale became something else:

> On the next morning after this affair, a genial, fairly well-dressed middle-aged man ate breakfast in the little town of Guerneville, a few miles off the course of the looted stage. His brown hair and beard were turning gray; kindly, deepset blue eyes twinkled under heavy brows, and his conversation — in a deep bass voice — was that of an intelligent and fairly well-informed man. He took the next conveyance out of town and was so respectable in appearance that no one ventured upon any prying questions, nor — when they heard of it — did any one think of connecting him with the robbery; that, in fact, least of all.[25]

Chapter 8
"The Case of Summerfield"

One of the first questions officers asked Bart after his arrest in 1883 was the source of his name. He never did tell them his real name; even for his court record and prison admission papers he used his most common alias, Charles Bolton (he used at least ten others — that are known). Where did 'Bart' come in? He told them it had been taken from a newspaper article, "*The Case of Summerfield*," that appeared in the *Sacramento Union* in May and June of 1871 and was reprinted in **Caxton's Book** (A. L. Bancroft, San Francisco) in 1876. However, it was common practice for other newspapers throughout the West to reprint such stories and Boles might have read it some place other than Sacramento. He was definitely in Montana Territory in May and June of 1871. Perhaps he was confused himself and had read the book — which he could have done, as his first poem didn't appear until 1877 — or was intentionally evasive.

The story was a proto-science-fiction thriller, masquerading as a series of news reports, written by a San Francisco lawyer using the pseudonym 'Caxton.' William H. Rhodes was a Harvard and Princeton-educated North Carolinian who gave up a judgeship in Galveston to seek his fortune in California in 1859. Though a competent attorney he was frustrated because his legal work interferred with his creative writing; he circulated his poetry among fellow Bohemian Club members, winning at least local fame, and occasionally wrote reviews and fiction, often using a pseudonym.

In "*The Case of Summerfield*" a seeming miscarriage of justice takes place. A man is on trial for pushing a fellow passenger off a train when it passed over a gorge near Auburn, California. A jury exonerates the man — the death is revealed to have been the wholly justifiable execution of a Dr. Frankenstein-like scientist who has invented a solvent that will set water afire. Summerfield threatens to burn up the oceans and end life on Earth, unless paid a million dollars by San Francisco residents. After half the money is raised, the city fathers suggest the scientist accompany them to New York, where his threats will gain the balance of money from Wall Street's bankers. On California's highest train trestle Summerfield is lured to the observation platform, then pushed to his death so the world might live.

Nothing about Black Bart is in the original "*Case of Summerfield*" (May 13, 1871), but he appears in a sequel (June 10, 1871), a hoax also treated as a news story. Two desperadoes have read the original report and find Summerfield's body at the foot of the gorge. With the dead scientist is a vial of the sinister liquid. One man is 'Bartholomew Graham,' usually called 'Black Bart:'

> Nothing is known of his antecedents. It is said that he was engaged in the late robbery of Wells & Fargo's express at Grizzly Bend [based on an actual robbery near Placerville on June 30, 1864, by supposed southern sympathizers during the Civil War] and that he was an habitual gambler. Only one thing about him is certainly well known: he was a lieutenant in the Confederate army, and served under General Price and the outlaw Quantrill. He was a man of fine education, plausible manners and good family, but strong drink seems early in life to have overmastered him and left him but a wreck of himself. [He] is five feet ten inches and a half in height, thick set, has a mustache sprinkled with gray, grizzled hair, clear blue eyes... He was a Washoe teamster during the Comstock excitement [the silver strike].

> Much of 'Black Bart' Graham's villainous description fits Charles Boles — except he didn't drink (he did gamble) and certainly didn't end up with a vial of liquid that could hold the world at ransom, as did his literary antecedent.

Chapter 9
Butte County — *Thursday, July 25, 1878*
Robbery No. 5

The stage from Quincy to Oroville was stopped on Thursday afternoon, about a mile above Berry Creek, by a masked highwayman, and WF & Co's express box was taken. Three passengers were aboard, but were unharmed. The stage proceeded to Berry Creek [a stage stop], where a gun was procured and two of the passengers returned to the scene of the crime, but could find no trace of the robber or the box. It was thought that there was little coin, if any, in the box. As near as could be seen by the driver and passengers, the robber is a tall, slim man, with iron grey hair and whiskers, probably full beard, vest and shirt, Kentucky jean pants, and long legged boots. He was armed with a shotgun, and had a revolver in his belt. His face was concealed with a white cloth (*Weekly Butte Record*).

For the first time Bart used an old road agent's trick, ordering the driver to unhitch the horses and take them to the rear of the stage while he worked on the express box (probably learned from reading about earlier road agents in the *California Police Gazette*). This gave him more time to escape while the driver rehitched the horses after the express box and mail sacks had been rifled.

Sometime after the stagecoach resumed its journey, the highwayman placed his second and possibly last poem inside the broken express box, for the edification of Wells, Fargo:

> here I lay me down to sleep
> to wait the coming morrow
> perhaps success perhaps defeat
> and everlasting sorrow.
> Let come what will, I'll try it on,
> My condition can't be worse,
> But if there's money in the box,
> It's munny in my purse.
>
> Black Bart the Po8

As in the first poem, each line was in a different handwriting style. Portions of this poem were supposedly copied from *Hutching's California Magazine,* but this had not been verified. Only two of the many poems

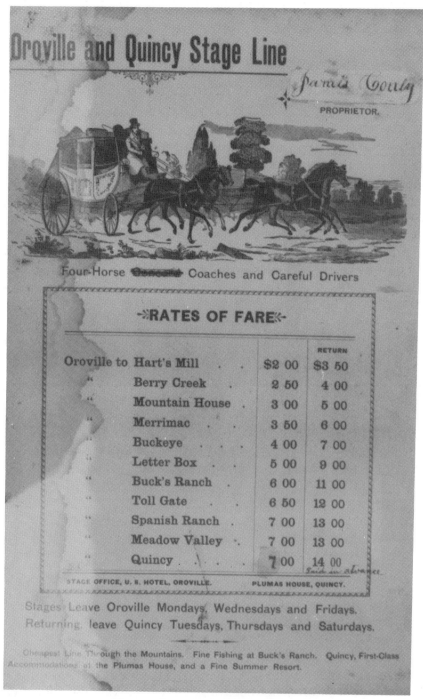

Oroville and Quincy Stage Line

Janiis County

PROPRIETOR.

Four-Horse Concord Coaches and Careful Drivers

→RATES OF FARE←

			RETURN
Oroville to Hart's Mill . .	$2 00	$3 50
" Berry Creek .	2 50	4 00
" Mountain House .	3 00	5 00
" Merrimac . .	3 50	6 00
" Buckeye . . .	4 00	7 00
" Letter Box . .	5 00	9 00
" Buck's Ranch .	6 00	11 00
" Toll Gate . .	6 50	12 00
" Spanish Ranch .	7 00	13 00
" Meadow Valley .	7 00	13 00
" Quincy . . .	7 00	14 00

STAGE OFFICE, U. S. HOTEL, OROVILLE.   PLUMAS HOUSE, QUINCY.

Stages leave Oroville Mondays, Wednesdays and Fridays. Returning, leave Quincy Tuesdays, Thursdays and Saturdays.

Cheapest Line Through the Mountains. Fine Fishing at Buck's Ranch. Quincy, First-Class Accommodations at the Plumas House, and a Fine Summer Resort.

(Courtesy Butte County Pioneer Museum)

attributed to Black Bart are genuine, but he may have written a third poem for his last robbery attempt—which was not delivered—and a fourth while in prison (See Appendix V).

Again the initial newspaper report underestimated Bart's take. The express box held $379 in coin, a silver watch valued at $25 and a $200 diamond ring. Bart liked the ring so much he filed off the name engraved on its inner side and wore it to the day he was arrested.

Writers have been confused about the contents of this second poem, which is usually quoted with Bart's first poem, printed as the second stanza of four lines. The original poems, along with other historical material, probably perished when Wells, Fargo's main office was destroyed by the 1906 San Francisco earthquake and fire. It cannot be determined if Bart repeated the first poem as the second quatrain of the second poem. Or why the Wells, Fargo 'wanted' handbill issued in 1879 reproduces both poems but with the 1877 poem stuck in the middle of the 1878 poem.

What the company expected to gain by printing a facsimile of Bart's handwriting — which was obviously disguised from one line to the next — is inexplicable, unless they hoped someone would notice these differences on a country hotel register (which might have happened, for one example, at the Sperry & Perry Hotel in Murphys in 1880). Whatever the intent, the handbill quickly leaked out from Wells, Fargo agents throughout California, and soon newspapers and word of mouth began to spread the legend of Black Bart.

By mocking lawmen with his verse Bart also connected himself to earlier holdups: Sonoma County, where he'd left his first poem; Plumas County, when he'd worn the same clothing and used the usual method to stop the horses. James Hume realized the same bandit was operating across northern California (apparently the detective didn't extend his research back too far; Bart's earliest holdups were unconnected with the Po8, until after his capture).

LaPorte to Oroville Stage at Woodleaf Hotel in Woodleaf. Louis Stellmon Photograph.
(Courtesy California State Library)

Plumas County — *Tuesday, July 30, 1878*
Robbery No. 6

Laporte, in southeastern Plumas County, at 4,500 feet upon the divide between the Feather and Yuba rivers, served as an outpost for miners combing the Diamond Mountains foothills. In 1851 the town was called Rabbit Creek, because, so a story goes, some miners saw a snowshoe rabbit one evening, unusual at such an altitude. In 1857 the Post Office Department wanted the town to use the name Rabbit Town. The townspeople became indignant and held a meeting to change the name. *Hutching's California Magazine* reported they voted this resolution: "What was Rabbit, then, is La Porte now." The town was renamed to honor a local banker's Indiana birthplace.

Before his next robbery five days later, did Bart hike to Oroville and spend the weekend at the plush Commercial Hotel? Did he play cards on

Saturday night in the smoke-filled poker hall over Sam Mullen's Gem Saloon, and lose some ill-gotten gain or add to his purse? Did he hear a tired stagecoach driver whisper of a large shipment of gold coming from a rich mine near LaPorte? Or was he visiting Mary Vollmer, the illusory sweetheart, 'the belle of Woodleaf,' at the Woodleaf Hotel on the road between Oroville and LaPorte?

Bart's activities that weekend are not known, but the *Butte Record* reported what he did the following Tuesday: "The LaPorte stage was robbed yesterday by a masked highwayman, about six miles from LaPorte. Have not learned the amount taken."

Dan Barry was the driver on the Laporte to Oroville stage line, early on a cool morning (a rarity for July in the Sacramento Valley). He was five to six miles into his journey, at a particularly difficult turn in the road, when a masked figure stepped

LA PORTE STAGE LINE.

SUMMER ARRANGEMENT.

TRAVELERS GOING TO LA Porte, Whisky Diggings, Howland Flat, and Quincy will take the 5 o'clock P. M. train for Oroville, where Sherman's line of stages will connect for all the above places.
feb2tf   CHAS. SHERMAN.

out from behind a tree. Bart greeted Barry with "Hands up! Throw down the express box and the mail bags. You drivers should know the procedure. Quickly, now." A female passenger, anticipating that she would be required to give up her valuables, started to open the door, but the highwayman's words stopped her: "No, lady, don't get out. I never bother the passengers. Keep calm. I'll be through here in a minute and on my way." Which he was. Bart garnered gold specimens worth $50 and a silver watch, marked No. 716,996, made by P. S. Bartlett.

Mendocino County — *Wednesday, October 2, 1878*
Robbery No. 7

In his first venture to the rich timber and farming country of Mendocino County, Bart held up two stages in two days. From conversations in San Francisco, he probably knew that October was sheepshearing season, when large amounts of cash were handled by Wells, Fargo for paying shearers and buying wool. Or else the disguise he had adopted for use in his work — a handyman or ranch hand on the move — brought him the information.

The Cloverdale and Arcata stage had come south after stops at Cahto, Laytonville and Willits, and was about ten miles from its next station, Ukiah, the county seat. Along a series of tricky switchbacks in the stage road, the coach came plodding around a bend north of Forsyth Creek when Bart confronted the driver. This location, afterwards known as Robber's Rock, was perfectly situated for Bart's purpose (and other bandits, who would also use it), as the road sharply curved at that point. Approaching stages could not see the boulder until they were on top of it. But a man hidden behind the rock was able to survey the road for at least a mile in both directions.

From evidence lawmen gathered at the scene, Bart had something of a picnic, munching apples as he waited for the stage. Because of the rock's location Bart abandoned his unique touch of darting in front of the lead horse. Instead he shouted to driver Alec Fowler, who had slowed his team to a crawl coming around the sharp curve, to "Throw down the box".

CHANGE OF TIME!

CLOVERDALE AND ARCATA

STAGE LINE!

Fare Reduced

AND

Speed Increased!

ON and after SEPT. 1ST, 1871, and until further notice—I will run a daily line of Coaches

CARRYING THE

U. S. Mail and Wells, Fargo & Co.'s Express.

Leaving Healdsburg every morning (Sundays excepted) at 5:30 o'clock ... between Cloverdale and Healdsburg with stages for

Santa Rosa, Petaluma, Calistoga, Anderson Valley, Big River and Clear Lake.

Stages for Little Lake, Round Valley, Cahto and Long Valley start from Ukiah on Monday, Wednesday, and Friday after the arrival of the stage from Cloverdale. Returning leave Cahto Tuesday, Thursday and Saturday at 6 o'clock a. m.

W. H. FORSE, Proprietor.

The Cloverdale-Arcata Stage 'Bonanza' at Sherwood.
(Courtesy Bob Lee, Mendocino County Historical Society)

Fowler knew he was caught. The robber had a bead on him. The driver couldn't get the horses up to speed in nearly enough time to avoid being shot at, nor could he shoot through the granite boulder. He dropped his own short-barrelled shotgun, brought the stage to a halt, wound the lines around the brake lever, then lifted the weighty express box out from under his seat. Bart demanded the mail sack, which hit the dirt as well, then yelled at Fowler "Now drive like hell!" Knowing the road agent could follow his progress for a distance down the road, Fowler complied. Sheep season or not, Bart netted only $40 and a gold watch for his troubles.

Ace tracker Sheriff Jim Moore immediately investigated the case, following Bart for 60 miles on horseback, but lost him in the rough country along the Eel River.

There is disagreement about the location of both the robbery and the rock. The October 4, 1878 *Ukiah City Press* said the robbery took place two miles *north* of R. Angle's place. That particular rock (see photo), either blasted away, covered over, or pushed down into a canyon in the late 1940s when the State Highway Department straightened out curves on Highway 101, was about three miles *south* of the present-day State Forestry Station. In 1955 a new section of highway was put through over Ridgewood Summit, passing by an even larger boulder, located about one mile *south* of the Forestry Station; this rock is pictured in local histories and tourist

Black Bart Rock *(Courtesy Bob Lee, Mendocino County Historical Society)*

brochures as Black Bart Rock — that designation is most likely incorrect. One local history expert[26] maintained that the original Robber's Rock was 500 yards *north* of the Forestry Station and was also covered up when the new highway was built. Another rock, Wool Rock — so-called because if wool bales were stacked over the sides, they would get caught on the rock as wagons passed — is *south* of R. Angle's ranch (present-day Ridgewood Ranch) on the old stage road; this rock also has been suggested as Black Bart Rock. There are, therefore, four possible locations for the elusive rock. Take your choice.

Robbery No. 8

Black Bart possessed superior endurance in hiking cross-country over difficult terrain. By the following day he had eluded the posse and was twenty miles due east. The road from Round Valley and Covelo to Ukiah was once a main thoroughfare in Mendocino County, connecting the Indian settlement and cattle town with the county seat. Nat Waltrip had driven his stage through Eden Valley and Hearst, stage stations with accomodations for passengers, then halted overnight at George Coates' Scott's Valley House, at the junction of the Potter Valley and Redwood Valley stage roads. Next morning the coach continued on a now impassable road to Potter Valley, where passengers, mail and freight would be picked up at the two small farming settlements, Centerville and Pomo. A few miles north of Centerville, near the junction with a wagon road that went east to Lake County, Bart struck again — the only time a stage was ever robbed on that route.

Scott's Valley House.

At the Junction Valley and Red Stage of the Potter wood Valley Roads,

G. W. Coates, Proprietor.

THE STAGES RUNNING BETWEEN Ukiah and Covelo stop at this house over night. Here passengers change coaches. There is every accommodation, and the proprietor will spare no pains for the comfort of his guests. THE BEDS are all new and under special care. The Bar-Room in connection with the house is kept by CHARLIE MAUPIN. The health of location and pleasantness of scenery cannot be surpassed. 45

Sheriff Moore returned Tuesday evening. Suspicion attaches strangely to a certain individual, who is no novice in stage robbing, as the one who robbed the stages in this county last week. His position while waiting for the Covelo stage was one that commanded a view of the road for upwards of a mile. While waiting for the stage he amused himself eating peaches, the pits of which were found at the tree from which he stepped behind. On Wednesday Detective Hume went to try his luck. If they are on the track of the right man and catch him, some interesting developments are to be looked for (*Ukiah City Press*).

Hume had come up to Ukiah on the report of the first robbery; the next day he rode the twenty miles on horseback to the scene of the second. Then he tracked Bart east, following his trail over scrub-laden foothills to the Mountain House, twelve miles from Williams in Colusa County, where the trail went cold. Bart had disappeared, after hiking more than 70 miles in

48 hours. He probably boarded the Central Pacific Railroad at Williams and took the train to either Sacramento or the Bay area.

However, at a remote ranch in Lake County, Hume got his first good description of the road agent. Shortly after noon a stranger stopped at the McCreary[27] ranch on Middle Creek, near Bucknell Creek. It was the height of the shearing season. The shearing crew had finished their mid-day meal and returned to the sheep. Young Donna McCreary, 14 years old, was with her mother in the family cabin at 'McCreary Glade.' The stranger, carrying an unjointed shotgun wrapped in a blanket, approached Mrs. McCreary, saying "I'm heading for Lakeport. I'll have to ask you to show me

Jas R Moore Sheriff.

the way. How about some dinner?" (Bart's request was not out of order. A stranger might reasonably expect hospitality in a remote area, though he might be asked — or offer — to do some chores. At the very least he might bring news from 'outside.').

Mrs. McCreary had put away the dishes, but she brought some food from the pantry. As he ate the stranger chatted with Donna, who recalled years later:

> His speech had a certain individuality, a poetic flavor. He made whimsical rhymes. I noticed that his clothing fitted him well. Moreover, when he washed his hands I saw that he had lost one cufflink, and that made me notice the style of the one that remained.
>
> Presently he pulled out a very fine gold watch — I had never seen such a handsome watch [Quite probably stolen from the express box on October 2nd] — and said "Can you tell me the time? My watch has stopped."
>
> I told him the time and he carefully set his watch. Immediately after he had dined he left, saying he was going to Lakeport. We pointed out the road and he departed, walking fast.

Twenty-four hours later Sheriff Jim Moore rode up to the McCreary cabin at the head of a posse. Donna's keen eye gave Moore, and soon Agent Hume, their first accurate description of Black Bart: height about 5 feet 8 inches, weight about 160 pounds, light grey eyes with bushy eyebrows,

A Curtis & Miller Stage at Potter Valley in 1894.
Dr. John Hudson and Grace Hudson are seated next to driver.
(Courtesy Bob Lee, Mendocino County Historical Society)

black hair tinged with grey and thinning at the temples, a heavy moustache, high cheekbones, a mole on his left cheek, hands showing no evidence of heavy labor. Donna also noticed that his coat sleeve was slightly torn and mended with white thread, he had split his shoes with a knife over the ball of the foot (to facilitate cross-country walking) and his watch chain was mended with a leather thong.

After his arrest Bart remembered that day's meal: "I always was afraid of that little girl. She looked at me too closely. I was afraid of her from the first."

The description Hume received was soon sent on a circular to law enforcement officers and Wells, Fargo offices throughout California. Though Bart had concentrated solely on northern California, he would not have been the first road agent to move to another area of the state, or even Nevada. Bart never did, but Hume wasn't taking chances — this shotgun-toting tramp had already committed more stage holdups than anyone else during Hume's tenure as Wells, Fargo's chief agent.

Old Forbestown *(Courtesy California State Library)*

Chapter 10
Butte County — *Saturday, June 21, 1879*
Robbery No. 9

So many stagecoachs were robbed in Butte County between 1875 and 1879 that for a time Wells, Fargo suspended its express services. Stage drivers were usually armed, but they were responsible for the horses, stage and passengers and

STAGES.

STAGES FOR FORBESTOWN AND INTERME-
diate points will leave the Western House at 6 o'clock
A.M. every Tuesday, Thursday and Saturday of each week

Jue15-3m   CHAS. SHERMAN, Prop'r.

couldn't be expected to combat an armed highwayman. To discourage further losses Wells, Fargo hired ace shotgun guards, later known as express messengers. Some, like Mike Tovey (who was shot and killed on the Ione to Jackson stage in 1893), became legends. In Camptonville (Yuba County) a monument was erected in memory of William 'Bull' Meek, a stage driver and Wells, Fargo express agent. One day Black Bart would meet another guard, George Hackett.

Driving alone on this warm Saturday in June, Dave Quadlin was headed to Oroville on his regular run. Three miles below Forbestown Bart confronted him, and the following conversation supposedly took place:

"Sure hope you have a lot of gold in that strongbox, driver, I'm nearly out of funds."

"See for yourself," snapped the driver.

Quadlin threw down the treasure box, but asked Bart to return the waybills and letters, of no value to the robber. The road agent refused and ordered Quadlin to drive on, much to the relief, one thinks, of the lone passenger, an unnamed lady.

The amount of loss is unknown but supposed to be small, as there was no messenger aboard. The Sheriff has already started in pursuit (*Weekly Butte Record*).

Shasta County — *Saturday, October 25, 1879*
Robbery No. 10

Redding has gone through some name changes in its history. It was originally called Latona, in honor of a Greek goddess, but local residents objected to a woman, goddess or not, who, they snickered, "conducted herself in a very improper manner." So they changed the name to Reading, after Pierson B. Reading, a pioneer of Shasta County. In 1880 the town was renamed in honor of B.B. Redding, land agent of the Central Pacific Railroad.

The California and Oregon Stage Road ran north out of Reading up the Sacramento River. It passed through relatively level country, then up a slight grade to Bass Station, the first change station for horses. Between this stop and the ferry crossing at the Pit River was a high ridge known as Bass Hill. By 1879 the town of Reading had begun to challenge Yreka as an important terminus in the northern part of the state. Only a year earlier passengers had to change stage lines in Yreka to go from Roseburg, Oregon to Reading. Now the stage ran straight through, and Black Bart baptised it with a midnight holdup, just ten miles from its destination. Between Bass Station (now at the edge of Lake Shasta) and the town of Buckeye, Jimmy Smithson was urging his horses up Bass Hill. One hundred yards from the top Bart stood in the light of the stagecoach lamps armed with his shotgun and ordered the driver to throw the mail sacks — five in number — out of the front boot. Then he demanded the express box, but Smithson protested that it was chained and locked to the stage. Bart ordered Smithson off the driver's box, telling him to stand at the head of his team. The highwayman then politely requested the passenger, Mrs. Bigelow of Butteville, to get up on the coach's back seat where he could see her.

While Smithson held the reins, Bart attacked the Wells, Fargo box with an axe, trying first to break the box's staple, which kept bending but refused to split. Finally he managed to turn the box over and slashed the other end. All in vain — the box contained no cash. Having already spent so much time with the driver and passenger, Bart abandoned his usual policy and rifled the U. S. Mail sacks while they looked on. The *Yreka Journal* reported correctly that he "may have obtained considerable from registered letters in the mail, from the various offices between Portland and Reading, which Postmasters are not allowed to make known."

The Redding-Weaverville Stage entering Shasta. *(Courtesy California State Library)*

Registered letters likely contained paper money, gold dust, or possibly convertible securities, the reason most road agents 'requested' not only the treasure box but also mail sacks. What Bart and other stage robbers managed to extract from the United States Mail can never be known. Neither local postmasters nor the Postmaster General in Washington released any figures. Occasionally a stage driver would hear in conversation from the postmasters along his route how much money the registered letters contained, and he might include that information in his report after being robbed. Those were the only instances (aside from overly talkative postmasters) which revealed how much Bart, or any other road agent, took from the U. S. Government.

> The next morning special messenger Reynolds and Smithson visited the scene, and down in the gulch discovered the mail lying promiscuously. Johnny then got upon the track of the robber and followed it until within a mile of the Copper City road where he lost it. It has been ascertained that the highwayman made a haul of about $1400, all from the mail, there being scarcely anything in the treasure box... James Smithson has purchased the station on Slate Creek, formerly owned by Mr. Charles. It is too bad that Jimmy's last trip over the road was so unfortunate. The robber should, at least, have waited one day longer before he plied his avocation (*Reading Independent*).

Millville grew up around a grist mill and was a booming settlement with three hotels, two saloons, two doctors and even a newspaper. For awhile, until it was bypassed by the railroad in favor of Redding, the town was a strong contender for the county seat of Shasta County. A newspaper headline about Millville, written some years later when a hotel burned, reflects the humor of the times: "Hotel Burns, One Million Lives Lost (Bed Bugs)."

Perhaps Black Bart passed a tranquil day in a Reading hotel, preparing for his next robbery; maybe he took advantage of Indian Summer and spent the next night under the stars. He could have done either, as his next venture took him only about twenty five miles southeast of the Saturday midnight job. At three in the afternoon the Reading, Big Valley and Alturas stage came rolling in from those lonely Modoc County outposts of Alturas and Adin. About twelve miles northeast of Millville, near where present-day Fern Road becomes Whitmore Road — "about seven miles the other side of Morley's at a place called the Old Canyon House" — driver Ed Payne had his team pulling carefully and slowly at a narrow part of the road. He had twenty-five or so dusty miles to go to Reading when abruptly Bart confronted him, with the usual order to throw down the mail and express. The stage could not be turned with any safety and Payne complied. Bart's booty was thrown down, the stage ordered on, and Payne hurried to Millville, calling for help.

Information has been received by Judge Bush that there were four registered letters from Round Mountain. How many there were from points above it has not yet been ascertained. The express box is thought to have had little in it. John Reynolds, Frank Thompson, a special agent of the government, an Indian and two others are in pursuit. A boy by the name of Parker met a man about a mile from the scene of the robbery, who asked many questions in regard to distances, etc. It is presumed that he was the robber. His pursuers are probably on the trail, as they left word at Eilers, that they would return by noon if they did not strike the trail. They did not return. We understand that the total reward foots [tallies] up $1,300 (*Reading Independent*).

The newspaper report was unusual, for although the mail was robbed repeatedly, U. S. government agents were seldom even mentioned, let alone named.

With only occasional pauses, Bart hiked fifty miles south toward Red Bluff or Anderson, undoubtedly resuming his usual road disguise of an affable, well-educated tramp; a gentleman down on his luck but courteous, who gave good conversation to the kind rural farmers in exchange for the food and shelter they offered to him. Wells, Fargo talked to a farmer who had given breakfast to the road agent. How much loot Bart gained from this holdup is not known, but together with the previous Saturday's take, he had enough to keep him away from the temptation of express boxes for the next nine months.

Research into Black Bart's exploits required extensive reading of local newspapers. Sometimes editors and writers (often the same person) had a flair for the dramatic and a passion for detail; then a single report will explain an incident. Occasionally, however, the story must be pieced together from fragmentary accounts in several newspapers, or sequential narratives over weeks in a given paper — but a researcher still questions his conclusions. Such is the case in Bart's first robbery in 1880. *The Mendocino Beacon* and *Sonoma Democrat* conflict not only in minor details (such as the direction of the stage), but in major ones. The *Beacon* names another robber for the crime, and writes that his confederates are also known and subject to arrest. Unfortunately that newspaper neither follows up nor reports the legal proceedings against the three suspects (nor do other newspapers in Mendocino and Sonoma counties).

This robbery wasn't on Wells, Fargo's preliminary 1883 list of Black Bart's crimes, but does appear on their final 1888 tally. The July 29, 1880 *Sonoma Democrat* (unusual because the writer had a byline, OXGOAD, and a humorous one at that) reported:

Fast Staging to Cloverdale!

ALLMAN'S U. S. MAIL CO., (Carrying U. S. Mail and Wells, Fargo & Co.'s Express,)
ON AND AFTER NOVEMBER 20th, 1879 Stages will leave

Mendocino City

every TUESDAY, THURSDAY and SATURDAY at 4 A. M. for
NAVARRO RIDGE,
NORTH FORK,
CHRISTINE,
BOONEVILLE,
ANDERSON VALLEY,
and WHITE HALL
and will arrive at

Cloverdale,

the same day at 6 P. M: Returning, will leave Cloverdale for the above named places at 6 A. M arriving at Mendocino City at 9 P. M.
THROUGH TICKETS to San Francisco...$10.0.
for sale at POST OFFICE, Mendocino, Navarro Ridge and at the Steamer landing of the S. F. and N. P. R. R. Co., office at foot of Washington St. San Francisco.

COAST LINE.

On and after November 20th, 1879, the Stages of Allman's U. S. Stage Co., will leave Mendocino on TUESDAYS, THURSDAYS and SATURDAYS at 4 A. M., and on WEDNESDAYS, FRIDAYS and SUNDAYS at 7 A. M., for LITTLE RIVER, ALBION, NAVARRO, CUFFEY'S COVE, BRIDGEPORT, MANCHESTER, POINT ARENA, FERGUSON'S COVE, FISH ROCK, GUALALA, BLACK POINT, FISHERMAN'S BAY, FISK'S MILL, HENRY'S STATION and DUNCAN'S MILLS. Returning will leave Duncan's Mills daily, except Mondays, for the above named places at 6 A. M.
Through Tickets for sale at POST OFFICE Mendocino, Navarro Ridge, and at the office of N. P. C. R. R. Co. foot of Clay St., San Francisco
For further information, address
H. M. JARVIS,
Agent at Mendocino.
C. QUEEN, Duncan's Mills.

On Friday of last week the North Coast stage on its way down the coast from Point Arena to Duncan's Mill was stopped about four miles south of Henry's Station. The Wells, Fargo treasure box was demanded. The box being securely fastened to the bottom of the stage the driver [Martin McClennan] was unable to accede to the demand and so informed the masked party at the other end of the shotgun, whereupon he asked the driver to hand out the U. S. Mail. The mail bags were passed out then the stage was allowed to proceed on its way. The bags were found the next day all cut open and the contents gone. There were three robbers. The passengers in the stage at the time — a lady and two gentlemen — were not molested. Shortly after dark on the evening of the same day, Mr. James Curtis , in the employ of John Orr, was stopped at Sheep House Gulch on Markham's ranch near Duncan's Mill, and his money demanded. As the demand was emphasized by a shotgun at very close range pointed at Mr. Curtis that gentleman handed over his entire monetary effects when he was permitted to pass on.

More details came from the July 31, 1880 *Mendocino Beacon*:

This is the fourth robbery that has been committed near the same place, the last having taken place about three years ago. It is supposed that all the robberies have been committed, by persons residing in that county [Sonoma], who are well acquainted with the country round about. At last accounts five of the mail bags have been recovered; one man by the name of Lafayette Nelson had been arrested and identified by the driver. There is a strong suspicion resting upon two others, who, perhaps, will have been apprehended before this paper reaches our readers. Nelson is said to be an old State Prison bird, and lives about ten miles from the coast, in the interior.

On August 7th the *Beacon* printed this notice and wrote:

All persons are hereby cautioned against negotiating for the hereinafter described drafts on San Francisco, which are supposed to have been in the mail bags lately robbed from the stage on the coast line, near Henry's, in Sonoma county:

July 13, 1880, No. 126, L. F. White, by White & Plummer, for Jas. Barnes, $150.

July 13, 1880, No. 114, L. E. White, by White & Plummer, for A. Kankas, $25.

July 16, 1880, No. 125, L. E. White, by White & Plummer, for J. Hanson, $75

July 16, 1880, No. 34, L. E. White, by C. E. White, for W. J. Snow, $400.

July 3, 1880, No. 515, to J. G. Jackson, by S. R. Wade, for George Scott, $90 00.

July 3, 1880, No. 531, to J. G. Jackson. by S. R. Wade, for Charles Halquist, $100 73.

July 13, 1880, No. 3719, to L. Sloss by L. Barnstein, for Frank Kelly, $8 50.

July 3, 1880, No. 100, L. E. White, by White & Plummer, for Burke & Eadie, $20. '

July 7, 1880, No. 134, L. E. White, by White & Plummer, for Burke & Eadie, $25.

FRANK KELLY.

CASPAR, Cal., July 28, 1880

Lane Nellson, the man arrested for robbing the North Coast stage near Henry's, Sonoma County, had an examination before Justice Blackford, and sufficient evidence was found to bind him over in the sum of $1,000 bonds, in default of which he had to go to jail. The driver, McLellan, has identified him, and W. J. Turner and wife, who were passengers of the stage at the time, have corroborated it.

The *Beacon* published its last report of the matter on August 14th:

Another one of the highwaymen, we are informed, that robbed the North Coast stage below Henry's, in Sonoma County, has been captured. It is thought that the third one, will

Guerneville Stagecoaches at Monte Rio Depot.
(Courtesy Monte Rio Area Historical Society [Ed Pedroia Collection])

be caught before many days, as a certain chap in that neighborhood is now being 'shadowed' by an officer.

The holdup took place at the same place, on Myers Grade Road, as the earlier robbery in 1877 (No. 4). If the robber was Bart, certain assumptions must be made. No, he was not working with accomplices. As in his first robbery in Calaveras County (and possibly the second also, in Yuba County), he poked dummy rifles prepared from sticks through the underbrush near the side of the road. The driver quickly called out "Don't shoot. You can have the money box, just be careful of my passengers."

Bart would have told his 'confederates' to cover the driver and passengers while he took charge of the express box and mail sacks; the couple from San Francisco was convinced there was more than one road agent. Afterwards, Bart hiked away alone, his blanket and 'cracked' shotgun hanging over his shoulder.

If Nelson and pals held up the unfortunate James Curtis, the driver and passengers misidentified Nelson when confronted with him — standard police lineups were not yet in use — and the two robberies inadvertently merged. Any other solution would contradict Bart's pattern of only waylaying stagecoaches and never stealing from individuals. Nevertheless, the description of the gunman who robbed Curtis, plus the proximity to the stage holdup, present the possibility that Bart at least once robbed a private citizen.

By 1880 Bart's job was easier (as far as travel was concerned, anyway). Duncan's Mills had moved inland three miles and was a bustling lumber town, with two hotels, a general store, meat market, livery stable, and blacksmith shop. As the terminus of the North Pacific Coast Railroad, with two daily trains and direct rail and ferry service to San Francisco, the town was even then a popular excursion point. Bart would have worn his 'Charles Bolton' gentleman's clothing to and from Duncan's Mills on the train. In between he would have changed clothes off th road, transformed into another vagrant, albeit a polite one, looking for work, hiked to winding Myers Grade Road, halted the coach, then reversed his actions. He could have made the whole trip in two days.

The Weaverville-Redding Stage entering Shasta
(Courtesy Shasta Historical Society)

Shasta County — *Wednesday, September 1, 1880*
Robbery No. 13

Five weeks later Bart was again near the northern mines. The *Trinity Journal* (continuously one of the most readable and eccentric of the era's small-town weeklies) reported the road agent's next foray:

The Weaverville and Shasta stage was stopped by a highwayman last Wednesday afternoon on Trinity Mountain, about two miles this side of Last Chance Station, while going to Shasta. Charley Creamer was driving and had but one passenger, Mrs. P. Eliason [of Steiner's Flat, near Douglas City, on her way to San Francisco to meet her new sister-in-law. She would certainly have a story to tell]. The robber stepped to the roadside and levelling a double-barrelled shotgun at Charley's head ordered him to "Drop that box." This he reluctantly did and was then ordered to throw out the mail; the way bag was tossed out from the front and Charley then had to get off and get the other two lock sacks which were in the hind boot. After securing this much, the highwayman wanted to know if there wasn't another box. The driver told him there was, but that it was stationary. Nevertheless he was ordered to throw that out, too, and this was insisted on several times until the robber was made to understand that it was an iron box securely fastened to the stage. The driver was told to stand at the heads of his leaders [the lead pair of horses] while the robber would try his hand on the stationary box. He dug out an axe which he had conveniently covered by the road-side with leaves and dirt, and with this hacked away at the iron box without succeeding in opening it. Meanwhile the driver kept telling him it was no use as there was nothing in it, and after finding he could not open it, the robber said he would take his word for it and quit the attempt. The stage was then permitted to drive on, nothing being molested except the letter mail and Wells, Fargo & Co's Express box. In the box was only $78 from Weaverville and $35 from Lewiston. The mail contained two registered packages and the usual number of checks and Money Orders, neither of the latter being of any use to the thief or thieves.

It was thought that there were two of the robbers and that the other was probably concealed in the brush near by. The one who did the work was disguised, having his head covered and hands blackened.

Immediately on the receipt of the news here, which was not until the return stage came in Thursday morning, Sheriff Smiley and ex-Sheriff Philbrook started out. We also learn that Under Sheriff Bob Kennedy and an assistant came out from Shasta Wednesday evening and returned on Thursday's stage. They found the box broken open about thirty yards from the road and the mail sacks cut open and rifled of their contents except one package containing one

The 'iron safe,' cut out of a stage by Black Bart, on display at the J. J. (Jake) Jackson Memorial Museum in Weaverville. *(Courtesy Trinity County Historical Society)*

registered letter and five or six other letters which were in the upper end of the sack and had escaped the notice of the thief. They also discovered the track of the robber and followed it to near the old Hoadley mill, finding only one track and tending to destroy the theory of there being two engaged in the robbery. Smiley and Philbrook will follow the track as far as they can and hopes are entertained that they will succeed in capturing their man. This is the first time that the stage has been robbed in Trinity County.

The *Redding Independent* added some rare humor to the serious incident:

The robber was masked by an old flour sack, and disguised by an abundance of superfluous clothing. He was as polite a man as ever cut a throat or scuttled a ship, and his politeness was only exceeded by his facetiousness, for during the robbery he entertained the only passenger, Mrs. Eliason, with his witticisms... He requested the lady to get on top of the stage; but she said that she preferred getting out, as the horses might start. He replied: "Very well; suit yourself." He then got into the boot and proceeded to cut the iron box from

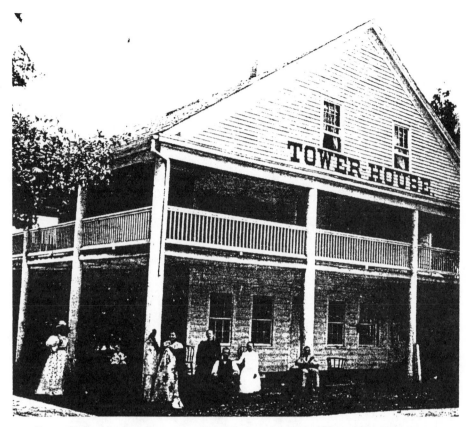

Tower House, the famous stage station at the junction of the Weaverville-Shasta Road and Trinity Mountain Road. *(from My Playhouse was a Concord Coach)*

its fastenings, with an axe. After taking both boxes and going through the mail he departed, requesting the driver to go as fast as he could and hurry the 'hounds' up, as he was quite lonesome in the mountains.

Another newspaper noted that "considerable gold dust is shipped via registered letter from Weaverville." Although the Trinity River gold strike is less known than the slightly earlier Sierra strikes, streams in the Trinity Alps can be panned successfully to this day. The value of the mail stolen in this robbery isn't known, but perhaps Bart was more fortunate than usual.

The actual robbery site was neither in Trinity County nor on Trinity Mountain, but just into Shasta County about 11 miles above Tower House, a famous stage station at the junction with Trinity Mountain Road (one of the old roads to Oregon), and the Shasta Road. Last Chance Station was a mine or vein (near or part of Brown Bear Mine, east of Deadwood), off the

Deadwood-French Gulch Road which intersects with Trinity Mountain Road (all part of the stage road between Weaverville and Shasta). Local lore has it that Black Bart stayed in a cabin near Deadwood. Tower House was 31 miles from Weaverville, to the west; 11 miles from Shasta and 17 miles from Reading, to the east.

The bandit travelled due south and stopped at a ranch house on Eagle Creek (near the village of Ono, not far from Igo. A child in one place had said "I go" and that's what the town was named. In the other, perhaps in response, someone said, "Oh, no!"). The J. T. Adkins family fed Bart breakfast and were impressed "with his gentlemanly manners and soft-spoken intelligence." He then hiked down the Cottonwood Creek trail towards Tehama County, waving goodbye to the homesteaders, carrying a lunch they had packed for him. When questioned later, after giving an accurate description of Bart to detectives, the rancher insisted his friendly visitor could not possibly have been a stage robber.

Siskiyou Toll House
(Courtesy Gary Meir & Southern Oregon Historical Society)

Jackson County, Oregon — *Thursday, September 16, 1880*
Robbery No. 14

Bart seemed to be heading south when the trail went dead September 3rd, but the northern stage lines continued to hold his interest. Almost two weeks later, close to the scene of his third robbery, but over the state line in Oregon, he repeated his 'greenhorn' behavior of three years earlier and stopped the stage southbound from Roseburg to Yreka. This was his first known robbery outside of California.

Last Thursday night, between 11 and 12 o'clock, the Oregon stage, coming southward, was stopped near the summit on the Oregon side [Siskiyou Summit, about six miles north of the border], one masked man presenting a gun at the driver, George Chase, and ordering him to stop. A lady passenger inside the stage says she saw only one robber, but heard others talking near by [Supposedly ventriloquism had been one of Charley Boles' boyhood skills]. The

97

robber stove in the end of the W.F.&Co.'s box, without taking it from the boot where it was fastened by chain and lock, and carried off the contents. He also took the mail sacks with registered letters, and told the driver to travel on. Nearly $1,000 was obtained from the express box, and a larger amount from the mail sacks containing registered letters. John Hendricks was sent out by the express agent, to try and recover the letters and way bills taken from the box, if not the robber. The robbery was committed at the old place for stage robbers, where they can easily escape through the dense chapparal towards the coast on the west, or the Klamath Lake country on the east. The country is full of notorious rascals, and the Oregon stage is seldom robbed on account of not carrying much money from Oregon. South of Yreka, it is a more dangerous experiment to stop the stage (*Yreka Journal*).

Bart realized Wells, Fargo was chaining its express boxes to the boot in the stages; he attacked the box in place at once if the driver couldn't throw it down. The haul from this robbery was one of his best. If he ever read the *Journal's* criticism — that only a 'greenhorn' would rob a southbound stage — the brigand was now laughing all the way away from the bank.

John Reynolds and John Hendricks searched for the robber "without finding any clue to the guilty rascals," and returned with the mail bags, described as "being badly mutilated, showing the robber was greatly excited." Perhaps the large haul (finally) in the express box caused Bart to exuberantly slice open the mail sacks.

Illustration by W. J. Enright. From 'In the Days of Black Bart.'
Wells Fargo Express Company Magazine, 1912. *(Courtesy Wells Fargo Bank)*

There was no time for the messenger to lift the gun from his knees

Summer wagons, foot of Siskiyou Grade on North Side, circa 1886.
First: Dave Curtis; second: Ed Grahams; rear: Henry Giddings.
(Courtesy Siskiyou County Museum)

Jackson County, Oregon — Thursday, September 23, 1880
Robbery No. 15

Undoubtedly pleased with his work, Bart hid out for a week, then struck again in Oregon:

As Nort Eddings was ascending the Siskiyou Mountains Thursday night he was stopped at the last turn near the summit by a road agent and ordered to deliver the mail. The highwayman emphasized his proclamation by the display of a dangerous-looking gun, and Nort saw no other alternative than to obey. Having complied with this, the robber called upon him to throw out the express box, but upon being informed that it was fastened in the boot, commanded Nort to stand at the heads of the leaders while he knocked in the box with an ax he had previously secreted in the brush. Having secured his booty, with all the nonchalance possible, he informed Nort that he might now proceed. There was only one passenger aboard, a lady, and she was not molested. The express box contained gold-dust, etc. to the amount of about $1,000. Eddings was stopped near the same place last year and says he is getting tired of the sport (*Jacksonville* (Oregon) *Democratic Times*).

If Black Bart had waited three days to hold up the C & O stage, he might have achieved an particularly distinct kind of fame (and this story would certainly have taken a different turn). On September 26th President Rutherford Hayes and General William Sherman (under whom Charles Boles had served those many years before) rode through Yreka, sharing an uncomfortable ride to Roseburg, Oregon. The September 11, 1880 *San Francisco Chronicle* reported:

> The reason the President will go to Oregon overland, is that the Constitution of the United States forbids a president going beyond the boundaries of the country during his term of office. To go to Oregon by sea he would get three leagues from shore, and out of the limits of the United States.

Robbing that stage could have added the Secret Service and the U. S. Cavalry to Bart's pursuers!

~

On October 23rd, 1880 James Hume sent a circular to Wells, Fargo offices throughout the west. Curiously, Hume either didn't connect 'H. Barton' with 'Black Bart,' although the writings on this and the 1878 poster (there may have been others, between and after, that haven't survived) show similarities, or else the agent had his own reasons for not placing all the information on the later poster.

Tracing Bart's route is fascinating — on September 2nd (the poster date is incorrect) he was seen heading south toward Tehama County; on September 4th was seen three miles south of Redding. He then went north, robbed two stages in Oregon, then returned to Paskenta in Tehama County, where he stayed the night of September 30th.

What happened next must have outraged Jim Hume. On the evening of October 1st, Bart (or someone resembling his description; Hume would never know and apparently forgot to ask when Bart was finally in his hands) "was arrested by B. F. White and Floyd Vickers, at Elk Creek station, in Colusa County: they released him after detaining him a short time. The robber was then going towards Lake or Sonoma County via Bartlett Springs."

The 'H. Barton' signature was probably found on a hotel register, possibly in Paskenta, or at some other country inn. The outlaw's description had come from Donna McCreary and numerous farmers.

To Agents Wells, Fargo & Co.—Don't Post, but place these Circulars in the hands of Officers and discreet persons only.

$800.00 Reward!

ARREST STAGE ROBBER!

In the forenoon of October 2nd, 1878, the Stage from Cahto to Ukiah, Mendocino County, was stopped by one man, and Wells, Fargo & Co's box and the Mail robbed.

In the forenoon of Thursday, October 3d, 1878, the Stage from Covelo to Ukiah was stopped by same man and Express Box and Mail robbed.

On the night of October 27th, 1879, the California and Oregon Stage was stopped by one man and Wells, Fargo & Co's Box and the Mail robbed.

In the forenoon of October 29th, 1879, the Alturas and Redding Stage was stopped by the same man and Wells, Fargo & Co's Box and the Mail robbed.

In the afternoon of September 1st, 1880, the Weaverville and Redding Stage was stopped by one man and Wells, Fargo & Co's box and the Mail robbed.

It is believed that all of the above robberies were committed by the same man.

On the morning of September 3d, 1880, the robber went to the house of J. T. Adkins, on Eagle Creek, in Shasta County, and procured breakfast and a luncheon to carry with him. On the afternoon of September 4th, 1880, he was seen by McNeill, section boss, on the railroad three miles south of Redding. On the 18th day of September he was in Jacksonville, Oregon. On the night of September 30th, 1880, he stayed all night at Paskenta's, in Tehama County. On the evening of October 1st, he was arrested by B. F. White and Floyd Vickers, at Elk Creek station, in Colusa County: they released him after detaining him a short time. The robber was then going towards Lake or Sonoma County via Bartlett Springs.

The following is an accurate description of the robber:

Name, Harry Barton; American, of Irish descent; aged 47 years; height, 5 feet 9 or 10 inches; eyes light blue; eyebrows heavy and projecting; hair sandy mixed with gray; whiskers about three inches long, sandy, and grayish on side of face; moustache heavy, sandy and gray; forehead broad and high; features long and cheeks a little sunken; two upper front teeth gone, and one lower front tooth pushed in; tonsils of throat affected from salivation, making a peculiarity of voice; reads with paper at arms length; hands long and bony; third finger of right hand crooked at first joint; shoulders and chest quite stout; lower part of body slender; stands up straight and erect, and steps quick and fast when walking.

When last seen, October 1st, 1880, was dressed in steel-mixed coat and vest, checked wool shirt, blue overalls outside and red duck pants underneath; kip boots badly worn and run over on inside; dirty light-colored felt hat; silver watch and heavy link silver chain. While traveling was seen to carry bundle or roll two and a half or three feet long, fastened with blanket straps, supposed to have an unbreeched shot-gun inside. Fac simile of signature:

H. Barton

In addition to the liberal rewards offered by the State and Wells, Fargo & Co. (for particulars see Wells, Fargo & Co's "Standing Reward" posters of July 1st, 1876) the Postal Department offers a reward of TWO HUNDRED DOLLARS upon conviction for robbing Mails.

If arrested telegraph to JOHN J. VALENTINE, General Superintendent Wells, Fargo & Co., San Francisco, or the undersigned at Sacramento.

J. B. HUME,

Sacramento, Oct. 23d, 1880.

Special Officer Wells, Fargo & Co.

(Courtesy Wells Fargo Bank)

Siskiyou County — *Saturday, November 20, 1880*
Robbery No. 16

Unless the man in the poster was someone else, being arrested, detained, and luckily released, didn't deter Bart from his chosen career. Six weeks later, during the last good weather of the year in late November, he was back at work in the northern mountains of Shasta and Siskiyou. This time he took the *Yreka Journal*'s three-year-old advice and held up a stage a mile south of the Oregon border, on its northern journey from Reading to Roseburg. He was pressing his luck.

In the gathering dusk (between 7 and 8 p.m.), driver Joe Mason was nearing the stage stop at Cole's when Bart stopped him. For some reason, rather than his usual shotgun, Bart was aiming a rifle at the driver (or in the dimming light Mason couldn't see properly and misidentified the weapon). Mason suggested to the masked outlaw that what he really wanted was the other stage, from Jacksonville (a mining town near present-day Medford). Bart replied "he guessed not," and ordered the stage driver to throw down the express box and mail sacks. Mason handed him the sack destined for Jacksonville, but complained the box was too difficult for one man to move from under the driver's seat.

> The driver got up on the wheel and commenced trying to pull it out, when Joe seized a hatchet which he held over him, and scared the robber so badly that he desisted from any further efforts to get the box. Possibly he thought Joe's hatchet was a pistol, as he allowed him to start off without any further hindrance, and Joe says he only wished it was a pistol at the time, for he intended business and no fooling (*Yreka Journal*).

Bart leaped down, grabbed the mail sack, and disappeared into the brush.

Driving into Oregon, Mason stopped the Jacksonville stage going south and informed driver Ab Giddings that before chasing the robber away it had been necessary to give up one of the mail pouches. Giddings found the sack on the road, cut open in Bart's distinctive manner, with a few letters strewn about. The postmaster at Yreka confirmed that nothing had been taken from the registered packages. The *Yreka Journal* ended its article with the suspicion that: "The robber evidently became frightened at something [perhaps the sounds of the on-coming stage] when he cut open

THE OREGON STAGE LEAVING COLES.

the sack, and made tracks to escape. He was evidently a green hand, probably some tramp."

Bart's attempt to rob the stage going the 'right' way netted him nothing but a terrible fright, one of two he would experience before finally being caught.

Mike Garvey driving the Yreka-Fort Jones Stage at Yreka, May 1, 1889.
(Courtesy Siskiyou County Museum [Dowling Collection])

Chapter 12
Siskiyou County — *Wednesday, August 31, 1881*
Robbery No. 17

Back in the Siskiyous ten months later Bart halted the south-bound stage from Roseburg via Jacksonville.

The overland stage bound for Redding was robbed about 1:30 A. M. yesterday morning while coming up the Kelly grade from the Anderson ferry across Klamath river, ten miles above Yreka. John Sullaway was driving, and was eating his lunch when he came to a camp fire. Fearing the light would frighten his horses, he drew on his gloves, glancing around to try and discover who the campers were. Suddenly he was startled by the sight of a shot gun close by his head, and a voice commanding him to halt. John immediately complied, telling him to put down his gun and help himself. The robber replied, that he would not hurt him for a thousand dollars, but that he meant business, and told John to get down and go ahead of his team. Sullaway complied with the mild request, got down and grasped his leaders while the highwayman proceeded to break open the strong box, remarking that he did not have very good tools for the business. After getting all the express and mail matter, he told John to drive on, saying he guessed he'd made a 'water haul.' The robber was dressed with a linen coat and light pantaloons, and had a handkerchief over his face, and from the tone of his voice seemed to be an oldish man. Sullaway thinks it was the same one who robbed Smithson on the Bass hill a year ago (*Redding Independent*).

The *Yreka Journal* reported that was the first time a stage had been stopped at that place, with its steep descent from the hilltop to the road, and an even more precipitous dropoff downhill to the Klamath River.

Sheriff Daniel Lash
(History of Siskiyou County, 1880)

Another report said Sullaway complained that the Roseburg-Yreka stage would go broke if the highwayman didn't stop robbing its stages. "They have plenty of money," Bart scoffed. Knowing Bart's reputation for fair play, Sullaway joked that if he hadn't heard Jesse James had been shot down in Missouri, he'd swear Bart was Jesse. Bart replied snappishly "Bosh! I've never shot a man yet doing this work. Now be on your way and no nonsense."

The slashed mail sacks were soon found and lawmen scoured the area. By 5 a.m. Sheriff Daniel Lash was on Bart's trail (or someone's trail; because of Bart's muffled boots and experience in evading trackers, the lawman could have followed an innocent hunter), tracking him to Willow Creek in Shasta Valley, where the trail grew cold.

John Sullaway, son of a pioneer California stage driver, began driving stage as an extra between Redding and Slate Creek in 1876. The next year "he commenced driving steady. They crossed the Sacramento and Pitt rivers on ferry boats. Some times in the spring the water was so high they would have to wait until the water had gone down before they could cross. Men who lived on the river bank operated the boats. The drivers blew their horns to let the boat tenders know they were coming so they could have the boat in position to cross."[28] He was held up three times during his stage driving career.

Stage driver John Sullaway, at right.
(Courtesy Pauline Wheeler Kuechler
& Siskiyou Pioneer)

Shasta County — *Saturday, October 8, 1881*
Robbery No. 18

The *Yreka Journal* had suggested that robbing a stage south of Yreka was more dangerous than halting one in the Oregon border's mountains. Bart pulled off two robberies in that 'dangerous' area in 1879. Now he returned there again, two miles out of Bass Station, sixteen miles north of Redding (as it was now spelled), on the Sacramento Road. Driver Horace Williams, who was robbed twice by Bart (and later by another robber), is one of only three drivers whose experiences with the famous road agent are preserved in their own words. Fifty years later, in the April 1, 1930 *Redding Searchlight*, Williams recalled that first encounter:

In 1881 I was driving the stage for the old California-Oregon Stage Company, which had the contract to carry the mail and Wells-Fargo Express from Redding, Cal., to Roseburg, Or., a distance of 260 miles. The fare on this trip per passenger was $20.

My drive was from Redding to Slate Creek (now known as Lamoine), a distance of 44 miles, with four changes of horses. October 8, 1881 I left Slate Creek at 5 p.m. on my way south. It was one of those beautiful moonlit nights that California can boast of and which makes October such a wonderful month here in northern California.

Coming Up Bass Hill

I had three passengers riding inside and, with fresh horses, was making fine time. We had reached almost the top of Bass Hill, which is 14 miles from Redding, when one of the passengers asked me the time. I told him just 12 p.m.

About three minutes after we had reached the top of the hill I saw what I thought was an animal running down the hill toward me, but when he straightened up and raised his gun, I knew what was up and halted at his command.

"Throw that box out" he said, but when I explained to him that the express box was locked to the stage, he asked me how many passengers I had. I told him three inside and he gave orders for them to get out and walk away down the road. The passengers [Mr. Baxter of the Fishery and a drummer] came tumbling out on his side, but he ordered them back into the stage and out on the other side. As they went down past the team he came toward the stage and when they had gone about three hundred feet away he told me to get down and hold my leaders. I did so and he stood on the front wheel and broke the box open with a small axe he carried under his belt, putting everything into a white sack he carried and also threw out the mail sacks to be opened after I had driven on.

Not Good Haul

I remarked that it was a beautiful night and he answered "It is."

After he had ordered me back on the stage, I said: "How did you make it?" He answered: "Not very well, for the chances I have to take."

He then ordered me to drive on. I did so and picked up my passengers about a quarter of a mile ahead. I don't know what he got, but think it was not very much.

When I made my report to the Wells-Fargo agent at Redding, a posse consisting of Vet Hull, sheriff; Robert Kennedy, undersheriff; William Whiting, deputy sheriff, and others went out, but could find no trace as to which way he had gone.

The *Shasta County Democrat* added more details:

Mr. Curtis coming along half an hour after his up trip, secured the mail and bags and took them on to Pit river ferry. Horace says the fellow was very gentlemanly and allowed him to block his stage and take other precautions to keep the team from running off... From what the express agent Dunn at this place can learn he did not get over $60 from the express box, and Postmaster McCormick has not discovered that he got anything out of the mail bags, as there were no registered letters in them. There were six bags in all, five of them were cut open across the top and slit down the center. Early Sunday morning Under-Sheriff Kennedy went to the scene of the robbery as soon as possible. He found the robber's track and followed it over the divide toward Pit river till nightfall when he was forced to give up the scent till next morning when he put an Indian on the track, with what result we have not learned. The road agent who "went through" Horace Williams was tracked by Robert Reynolds from the scene of the robbery to the old trail that leads to Copper City, and along the trail about half a mile, till he lost his track. A registered envelope was picked up on the way.

A REMINISCENCE OF EARLY DAYS.

from **Picturesque California,** edited by John Muir, 1888

Shasta County — *Tuesday, October 11, 1881*
Robbery No. 19

Ever since he had watched Chicago burn in the great 1871 fire, Lewis Brewster had worn a heavy gold ring on his hand. Some merchants, realizing their shops would be destroyed by the flames, told anyone brave enough to help themselves in the burning buildings. Brewster had gone into a jewelry store, grabbed what he could, then run away from the fire toward safety. Suddenly, something, or someone, hit him and he lost consciousness. When he awoke all that was left was the grasped ring. He soon went west to San Francisco and was shanghaied aboard a sailing vessel; luckily he escaped before the ship weighed anchor.

So Lewis Brewster had seen trouble. And not long after he began driving stage, for the C & O over Trinity Mountain, he had his first experience with stage robbers. Not his stage — his money:

> In June of 1876 a pair of robbers broke into a store in Trinity Center and rifled the safe, getting about $450 in gold coin, $40 of which belonged to Lewis. Hoping to get his money back, Lewis volunteered to help the sheriff hunt for the rascals. Getting someone else to drive his stage, he and the sheriff went by a side trail to the top of Trinity Mountain, where they awaited the robbers. About two o'clock in the morning the two highwaymen came along the road, pistols in hand. When the sheriff and Brewster stood up from their hiding place, demanding surrender, the robbers fired at them. The sheriff had a pistol, Lewis a rifle, and after a desperate exchange one of the robbers was dead and Lewis's head had been grazed by a bullet. The other robber escaped into a gulch in the dark. The dead man was Charles Burch. His companion, Demarest, was captured later and confessed. Whether or not Lewis got his $40 back is not known.[29]

Five years later Brewster was married, a father, and owned a stage station in Burney Valley. He continued driving stage part-time, on one of the longest California stage routes, between Redding and Alturas, which extended to Lakeview, Oregon. During the previous heavy winter he had become a local hero, as the dispatch from Burney Valley in the April 29th *Reading Independent* shows:

> We are indeed 'snow bound' in this upper country. The mail is taken through, but no stages have passed over the mountain for a week, and there will probably be none for as much longer... Mr. Brewster was thirteen hours making ten miles on horseback with the mail one day during the storm... Feed

is almost entirely exhausted throughout these mountain valleys, and stock are starving to death everywhere.

There were no passengers on Brewster's stage when Bart struck again. Because the brake blocks (or possibly a piece of harness) on his stage had loosened, the driver was forced to pull up at Montgomery Creek, two miles from the Round Mountain post office (then known as Buzzard's Roost), about 20 miles from his home. Near 2 p.m. he finished repairing the stage and was ready to climb back up on the box:

> A man dressed in a long linen duster buttoned close up under his chin, a flour sack over his head for a mask and feet wrapped up in sacks, stealthily stepped up behind him from the brush, and presenting his shot-gun said: 'You found me have you?' 'It looks like it,' said Brewster, surveying the man and his villainous shotgun. Of course he was compelled to throw out the express and mail sacks, and after doing this, was ordered to drive on. The last he saw of the robber he was lumbering off into the brush with his plunder. Brewster hurried to the next station, got Palmer to double the road for him, and with Mr. Balch, both armed, started in pursuit of the festive robber. He is undoubtedly the same fellow that robbed Horace Williams last Saturday night. It is not known yet how much the robber got. Detective Hume came up last night and Johnnie Reynolds, as soon as possible started for the scene of the robbery. Up to the time of going to press we had heard nothing further (*Shasta County Democrat*).

In another account, Brewster drove down the road, stopped the stage, grabbed his Winchester rifle and doubled back on foot, before he went for help.

A posse on horseback trailed Bart for 80 miles into Butte County, down the east side of the Sacramento River into the Sacramento Valley, but the trail was lost within three miles of Oroville. Bart stopped at farm houses along the way for food and covered the distance on foot in about three days.

Yuba County — *Thursday, December 15, 1881*
Robbery No. 20

It was rare, even in the great city dailies — *San Francisco Chronicle, Daily Alta California, Sacramento Union* — to find an in-depth interview, much less in a small-town newspaper such as the *Marysville Appeal*. Nevertheless, the *Appeal* printed the most detailed account by a Bart victim. George Sharpe, driver of the Downieville-Marysville coach, related his experience:

THE CAMPTONVILLE STAGE ROBBED. A MASKED HIGHWAYMAN GETS AWAY WITH THE EXPRESS BOX AND THE U.S. MAILS. The down stage from Camptonville was stopped by a robber about four miles above Dobbins' Ranch yesterday morning, and the mails and express box taken. George Sharpe, the driver of the stage, gave this vivid account of the affair to an *Appeal* reporter last evening:

I was driving slowly up a bit of rising ground when suddenly a man jumped out from behind a tree by the side of the road and yelled "Hold on there you — — —." I pulled up the horses pretty quick and set the brake. Then I sat still and looked at the man. I had never been stopped on the road before, and was surprised-like. The man was about my size (pretty stoutly built and about 5 feet 10 inches high). His face was covered with white cotton cloth, but one corner of the cloth was torn so that I could see that his eyes were blue. He had on a long linen duster and a pair of blue overalls. On his head was a little whitish felt hat, with some light colored hair sticking out through the crown. That's about all I remember of his looks.

He spoke in a clear, ringing voice, without any brogue or foreign accent. There was a double-barrelled muzzle-loading shotgun in his hands. I could see the caps on the nipples. I saw all these things in a good deal less time than it takes to tell about them. As soon as I stopped the horses the robber got back behind the tree so as to keep out of range of any guns the passengers might have. He kept his shotgun bearing on me from the word "Hold."

"Throw out that box," was his next order. I supposed he meant the Wells-Fargo box, but I didn't stop to make particular inquiries, and I threw it out on the side of the road towards him. "Now throw out the other box and be quck, — — you," he said. "There isn't any other box, boss," I said. "This line packs only one Wells-Fargo box."

"Well, then, throw out them mail bags, you — — ," was his answer. There was a through mail sack from Camptonville, and some little bags with mail for way stations. I searched around among the bags under my feet, and getting hold of the Oregon House bag, I threw that out. "Throw out the rest of them,

—— — you," he said. "That's all there is," I said, thinking it a matter of principle to lie, under the circumstances.

Then he gave his gun a flourish, squinted along the top of the barrels at me, and yelled out, "None of your — — funny business. Sling out that mail quick, or I'll blow the top of your — — — head off, you — — —, you." It seemed the proper thing to throw out the rest of the mail, and I did so. "Now drive on, you — — —," he said. I drove on. He kept me covered with the shotgun until the corner of the coach shut me out of range, and then he brought the gun to bear on the passengers inside. There were five of them, all Chinamen. I never heard such a pow-wow as those Chinamen made when they saw the gun pointed at them.

There was a white boy on the box seat with me. He was badly scared. After I had driven on a piece, he said to me, "I'm glad that robber didn't get my parcel," showing me a little package wrapped up in a newspaper. "What have you in that ?" I asked him. "I've got my lunch in it," he said. And that was all the poor little cuss did have in it.

A telegram was received from Camptonville at Wells, Fargo & Co.'s agency here last evening, stating that there was no money in the express box taken from the stage. It is not known whether or not there was any money in the mail bags. Probably there was. Deputy Sheriff Aldrich starts out this morning for the scene of the robbery.

The profanity attributed to Bart would have been unusual behavior by the highwayman, maybe brought on by the slim pickings garnered in recent holdups. Perhaps, like many people, driver Sharpe naturally used profane interjection, ascribing to Bart language the driver himself would have used. Or possibly the reporter wanted to make the holdup seem more menacing. Bart was never known to say anything stronger than 'damned' (as in "Throw down the damned box," though of course his most famous poem contains the phrase 'sons of bitches.').

In the pursuit, like so many before him the deputy sheriff was no match for one of the best long-distance hikers since the ancient Greek, Phidip-pides of Marathon.

Nevada County — *Tuesday, December 27, 1881*
Robbery No. 21

Bart continued hitting a general area more than once and twelve days later held up a stage in nearby Nevada County. Again he came up empty, gaining nothing from the Wells, Fargo box. The brief report in the *Grass Valley Union* didn't even name the driver:

The stage running between San Juan and Smartsville was stopped yesterday near Bridgeport [where a covered wooden bridge built in the 1850s to cross the South Fork of the Yuba River still stands] by a single highwayman, but he did not succeed in obtaining anything of value. It is believed that the would-be robber is the same man who last week stopped the Camptonville stage and a few days previously the stage near Smartsville [a robbery Bart did not commit] and in each instance failed to be compensated for his trouble. The Express Company is fighting shy of highwaymen now, and when there is any treasure aboard it is so well guarded that no one or two robbers would have any chance to get it.

The highwayman might have taken some money from U. S. Mail pouches, as San Juan was still a well-off town, but the government failed to announce possible losses.

Bart was lucky that Steve Venard, Nevada County's ace tracker, had retired. The 1880 **History of Nevada County** graphically describes Venard's most famous exploit, which took place on May 15, 1866:

As the stage was on the brow of the hill south of the South Yuba river, and above Black's crossing, at half-past four on the morning, it was stopped by three masked man, the passengers ordered out and the driver commanded to unhitch his horses. Two attempts were then made to blow open Wells, Fargo & Co.'s treasure box, the last of which was successful. After appropriating the contents, $7,900, the box was returned to the stage, the horses again attached and the vehicle allowed to proceed. All haste was made to Nevada City to give the alarm, and a posse ... started in pursuit.

[Steve] Venard and [James] Lee soon found the trail and followed for a mile and a half over extremely rough ground, until it became necessary for Lee to take a more circuitous route with the horses, and Venard, armed with a Henry

Stagecoaches in front of National Hotel in Nevada City, the hub of seven different routes.
(Courtesy Nevada County Historical Society)

repeating rifle, followed the trail alone. He soon came to Meyers' ravine, where it opens into the Yuba, up which the robbers had evidently gone to a crossing that lay above. He was alone in that rugged gorge, with precipitous mountains frowning down on either side, while shrubs, trees and rocks on every hand offered ample concealment for an ambushed enemy. Where the waters of the ravine came rushing and roaring over their bed of rocks, rose a rock, towering to the hight of twenty feet, surrounded by smaller ones, all forming an island, upon the lower end of which several trees raised their knotted limbs, the foliage screening the jagged rock above. Below, the waters pitched down a precipice fifteen feet in hight. Here he decided to make the passage of the torrent. He crossed upon a log to a rock in the center of the stream, above which rose the huge mass of granite, the approach to which lay between two smaller rocks in front.

Glancing up this alley, Venard saw George Shanks, *alias* Jack Williams, the leader of the bandits, sitting upon the ground and in the act of taking aim at him with his revolver. Quick as thought, Venard aimed his rifle, and at the same

115

instant discovered that another robber was aiming at him from over the top of a rock. There was not time for hesitation, he fired, and the leader fell dead with a bullet in his heart. The other, Bob Flynn, *alias* Caton, endeavored to shield himself behind the rock, but as soon as his head appeared above in the effort to aim his pistol, a bullet from the unerring rifle sped swiftly through his brain. Venard sprang forward, determined that the last of the three should not shoot him down from an ambush. An instant, and he was among the rocks. Here lay the treasure and the bodies of the two robbers, but the third had escaped. He covered the treasure with earth and leaves, took the pistols from the lifeless bodies, and dashed across the stream. The fleeing outlaw was seen hastening up the side of a hill some sixty yards in advance. The fatal rifle was again leveled, and a bullet brought the fugitive to the ground, another shot and George W. Moore rolled lifeless down the hill.

Venard soon found his companions and related to them the incidents of the fight, regretting that he had wasted a shot on the last man when one ought to have been enough. They repaired to the scene, uncovered the spoil, and by two o'clock in the afternoon it was returned to Wells, Fargo & Co., at Nevada City. After the departure of the posse the express company had offered a reward of three thousand dollars, which Venard promptly received. They also presented to him a gold mounted and tastefully inscribed Henry rifle.

Bart usually took 'vacations' during the rainy California winter and early spring, when overland travel by foot on muddy trails and roads was extremely difficult. He had held up three stages in December, but his usual 'season' began in late June or early July, lasting through November. Perhaps his run of bad luck late in 1881 forced him into the next robbery, which was back in Mendocino County after a four year hiatus. These takings, however, were enough to keep him off the highways until his usual early summer debut:

Last Thursday considerable excitement was created in town [Cloverdale] by the report that the Ukiah down stage had been robbed by a masked robber, armed with a rifle, just a half mile about the toll house, six miles from this place. Harry Forse, the driver of the stage, gives the following account. When the stage, which had no passengers in it, was within half a mile of the toll house, he saw a man in the middle of the road, and noticing that his coat was turned inside out and a white cloth drawn over his head, with only two

The Cloverdale-Arcata Stage in front of the U. S. Hotel in Cloverdale, 1885.
(Courtesy California State Library [Thurston's Photographic Studio])

holes in it for his eyes, he at once suspected the situation, and when he drew nearer the robber demanded him to stop, and at the same time bringing his rifle up to his shoulder and further, to get down and throw out the treasure boxes and mail sacks, which the driver instantly complied with, while the robber held the horses. He ordered the driver to "git," and he "got."

Harry Forse whipped up his horses and in a few minutes gave the alarm at the toll house, where the keeper, J. A. Lance, accompanied by others instantly, armed with guns, went in pursuit. Harry Forse, upon arriving here in town instantly informed Mr. I. E. Shaw, the Postmaster and agent of the Wells, Fargo's Express, and Mr. Shaw telegraphed to Ukiah, and from whence Sheriff Donahue and party left immediately in search of the robber. Mr. Shaw also telegraphed to Hopland, from whence also a party of men left in search. At 4 o'clock [in the afternoon], about one hour after the affair took place, six men armed left Cloverdale, and inside of an hour were on the spot. After examination of the ground, the searchers found his tracks for about a mile and a half, and as yet heard from they had not been able to trace it further.

It seems after the stage left the robber took the treasure boxes — those of Hopland and Ukiah — together with the registered letters, and climbed up the bank from the road, and skirting the hills for a mile and a half he again came down to the road and broke open the boxes, took the coin and made off into the hills. The regular mail sacks of letters have been recovered and were brought in last Thursday by Lee Smith. The amount of money in the treasure is not exactly known; Shaw, Bowman & Co. had $240.00 in it. The reward for the arrest of the robber is $800.00 and probably $1,000 (*Cloverdale Reveille*).

The *Sonoma Democrat* had a slightly different, somewhat playful, report, writing that the stage was running *north* at 4:00 and held up "by one man and a double-barrelled shotgun, who asked the driver to jettison a part of his cargo in the shape of two express boxes and a mail sack. This was done with the festive stage driver's usual grace, and he thence proceeded on, leaving the highwayman in possession of the field and $300 obtained from a Wells Fargo box."

A posse followed Bart's tracks as far as Kelseyville, on Clear Lake, where the trail petered out. Bart could have crossed the lake by steamer at the Narrows or hiked 55 miles south to Calistoga, resumed his 'city' identity, and taken the California Pacific Railroad to the San Francisco ferry at Vallejo.

"UNCLE JIM" MILLER.

Mendocino County — *Thursday, June 14, 1882*
Robbery No. 23

On an unseasonably cold June morning Bart returned to Mendocino County for his last adventure there. This time another son of William Forse, the owner of the Cloverdale and Arcata Stage Line, would be Bart's victim. The stage left Willitsville[30] at 2:30 a.m., heading for Ukiah. Near 3:00, about five and a half miles south on the stage road, "coming up on an old mill that served as a landmark" (near Robbers Rock), driver Tom Forse was halted by the familiar hooded figure. The only passenger aboard the stage was Hiram Willits, postmaster of Willitsville and former Mendocino County Supervisor. Willits and Forse reported their inability to identify the highwayman. A posse led by Sheriff Jeremiah Donohue and Forse recovered the broken express box and slit mail sacks, but couldn't find the robber's escape route. Bart made $300 from his efforts.

～

On a warm day that summer, a few miles away in Sonoma County, one of the stranger incidents occurred in stage coach history. If Bart had attacked that stage, he might have ceased his career as a road agent immediately. Wash Gilham was one of the last of the old drivers. Coming into Bloomfield one day he had a heart attack but remained erect in the box, clutching the reins in his gloves. Just after the incident these graceful lines were penned by his friend Tom Gregory:

> The old stage driver came quietly into town just as he had done off and on for some fourteen years. But this time he came slower than usual. He had a new team but the horses tramped solemnly along as if they knew that pace suited the occasion or knew that something was amiss with the solemn man behind them. The old driver had a strange look on his face that we had never seen before — the look of one who is moving deeply in a mystic spell. He always was rather quiet, but now his silence was almost appalling. When the team stopped, his old friends gathered around him, but he did not seem to know them, for he spoke not a word. One grasped his hand, but no pressure was returned (1889 *History of Sonoma County*).

Plumas County — *Monday, July 13, 1882*
Robbery No. 24

A month later Bart was back on the Laporte to Oroville road, at nearly the same place he had success in 1878. But the bandit's twenty-fourth attempt to rob a stagecoach was almost his last.

The *Marysville Appeal* 's interview with driver George 'Hank' Helm graphically tells what happened:

> I was driving three horses, with George M. Hackett, Wells-Fargo's messenger, on the box beside me. [Hackett was well-known for his bravery and coolness. Three years earlier he had not only thwarted an attempted robbery by two masked men near Marysville, but had also chased them to their hideout, captured one, and recovered almost $900 from their previous stage robberies]. There were no passengers. We had $18,000 in bullion aboard. The stage was stopped about seven o'clock [a.m.], about five miles this side of Laporte and a mile and a half beyond Diamond Springs. The road at that point is level and the horses were trotting along quietly. Nobody would expect to find a robber in such a place. Hackett was sitting sideways in the seat, talking to me, when a man ran out from the left side of the road and tried to catch hold of the leading horse. He was a tall man, in size and build resembling Frank Manning of Marysville. He wore a linen duster and his face was covered with a big white mask.
>
> As soon as I saw him I whooped up the horses, with a view to get past him. But the lead horse was frightened and swung off to the right side of the road and against the side of the hill, stopping the team. The man carried a double barrelled shotgun. He didn't say a word, and didn't raise his gun, but carried it in one hand hanging by his side. As soon as Hackett could get his gun ready, he fired. The gun was loaded with buckshot. The robber then made a motion as if to shoot, but didn't seem able to get his gun to his shoulder. He then ran around to the other side of the leader and I yelled to Hackett to "sock it to him."
>
> Hackett then fired over the heads of the horses the contents of his second barrel. The robber then took to his heels. He ran down the hill, straight away from the road. Hackett jumped down and ran after him for a short distance. Hackett had a buttoned glove on his left hand and had his cartridges in his left pocket, so that he couldn't reload his gun in time to get another shot at the robber. When he saw that pursuit was hopeless, he came back to the stage. We picked up the robber's hat on the road. It was a soft hat, of black felt, very old and weatherbeaten and full of ragged rents. It had four fresh buckshot holes in it, with hair sticking to some of them. The man's hair was light in color,

George Hackett, one of the most famous Wells, Fargo & Company express messengers.
(Courtesy California State Library)

streaked with grey. As he ran down the hill he tore off his mask, and I noticed that he had a bald spot on the top of his head.

Hackett had no pistol with him. If he had had a pistol, he could have dropped the robber easily. He can drop a rabbit at a hundred yards with the big pistol he generally carries. The robber was no doubt green at the business. He never opened his mouth, and instead of covering us with his gun and singing out 'throw up your hands' as an old hand would have done, he just made a target of himself. Neither Hackett nor the robber said a word. The whole thing happened in half a minute.

It wasn't Hackett's business to follow the robber; he had to come back and take care of the treasure. Put up jobs have been made before now for one robber to get the messenger out of the way while another one would come up and go through the stage. From the place where the stage was stopped Hackett went in with me to Forbestown, and from that place he went on another stage with the treasure to Oroville.

Bart travelled more slowly than usual despite the scare. At one point the sheriff walked past a hollow fir log in which the brigand lay quivering, almost stifled by polecat stench. The sheriff's tracking dog was interested in the log; but the sheriff thought the dog had gotten off Bart's scent, favoring the polecat. He called the animal away and went on, allowing the frightened, slightly wounded thief to escape. Wells, Fargo reported that

Bart was heading south and was seen the following day near Camptonville, in Yuba County.

James Hume later commented that "Black Bart got in front of the lead horses, his usual style of proceeding, and ordered a halt, but George opened on him at great disadvantage, because he didn't want to kill a good horse, and the brave B. B. dusted like a whirlwind for the brush on the side of the road ... with two scalp wounds from Hackett's buckshot" (*San Francisco Examiner*, 4/3/87).

This was by far the richest stagecoach Black Bart ever attacked. If he'd gotten the drop on Hackett before the guard could bring up his gun, if he'd stolen the $18,000 (one report states $23,000) in bullion, would Bart have ever robbed another stage? He might have retired comfortably, fading into an even greater legend, uncaught and unidentified, the mysterious 'last of the great road agents.' This conjecture , however, might be flawed, as that much gold was probably inside an iron safe (not the small wooden box) anchored to the stage; Bart would have had trouble getting the safe open.

While Bart licked his wounds (not only chagrin at failure, but pain as well), George Hackett kept working until the $18,000 in gold was delivered to Oroville. After Helm's coach arrived at Forbestown, the shipment was loaded onto the Forbestown-Oroville stage. With Hackett on the box with driver Frank Morse, the coach left Forbestown at 1:00 p.m. Near Boston Ranch, about seven miles south of Forbestown, a masked highwayman attempted to board the stagecoach from the rear, unseen. Hackett saw him, drew up his gun and the two men fired simultaneously. Although creased in the face, the messenger got a bead on the fleeing outlaw, but his gun misfired, which allowed the unknown bandit to escape.

Hackett's wounds have been dressed and are not dangerous. He says that this last man was not at all like the one that attacked them [earlier]. The man who made the last attack was of medium size, and had on a linen duster. The other was tall, with a dirty duster. The news of the attempted robbery caused some little excitement about the express office here last evening. Helm was obliged to tell the story a good many times, and to such an extent that his throat became seriously affected. Hackett was in Oroville last evening. It will be remembered that he accidentally shot himself in the foot last winter and as a result is partially crippled. It is not at all surprising that he was unable to overtake the robber (*Marysville Appeal*).

No shotgun messenger had ever repulsed two holdups on the same day, and in recognition of this feat Wells, Fargo rewarded George Hackett with a gold watch. Hackett, who worked for Well's Fargo for 20 years, would eventually be regarded as the best of the company's 108 express messengers, fending off and tracking criminals almost until the day he died. His *San Francisco Chronicle* obituary in 1895 reads in part: "He left many

friends, and if he left any enemies they are such as he helped to send to San Quentin or who bear scars from the sawed-off gun that made him a terror to road agents."

~

In 1935 the Butte County Road Department placed a monument to Black Bart on the Forbestown-Oroville road. Unfortunately, they muddled things up. This is the location of the second attempted holdup on July 13, 1882—but the holdup man was not Black Bart. Frank Morse (his middle initial is N on the marker and E in his obituary), who died in Oroville at age 81 in 1938, was either confused (saying also that he drove the last stage Bart ever attempted to hold up) or disingenuous when he gave information for the engraving. When a new section of the Forbestown highway was put in, the old stage road, where the monument stands, was renamed Black Bart Road.

John Sullaway, driving a California & Oregon Coast Overland Mail Company Stage, at Sisson Tavern, Mount Shasta, August, 1883. *(Courtesy Sisson Museum, Mount Shasta)*

Shasta County — *Saturday, September 17, 1882*
Robbery No. 25

Two months later Bart made his last strike against a California and Oregon Coast Overland Mail Co. stagecoach. Again it would be driven by Horace Williams, climbing the Bass Hill grade, at just about the spot where the outlaw had stopped him almost a year earlier. Williams was recalling that experience when he found himself facing the familiar masked man again, this time (so he reported later) armed with a revolver. An article in the *San Francisco Chronicle* (but no other newspaper) said Bart yelled, "Well, I have called on you again. Make haste and throw out the box and mail bags." Bart ordered Williams to stand by his leaders and the two passengers to walk down the road, while he rifled the mail sacks and broke open the express box.

Then he told the driver to move on. "They'll catch you one of these days," growled Williams. "Perhaps," responded Bart, "but in the meantime, give my regards to J. B. Hume, will you?" One hopes the jibe was worth Bart's time, as he realized only thirty-five cents from this robbery, the express charge on a package. In an article titled BLACK BART AGAIN, the *Chico Enterprise* reported that "All the treasure is sent by the other route... J. B. Hume went up to interview the robber if he can get a hold of him."

Bart closed his 1882 activities with a strike in Sonoma County, just south of the Mendocino County line. The 30-mile stage route between Lakeport, in Lake County, and Cloverdale, in Sonoma County, was over the tortuous Squaw Creek Toll Road (also know as the Matt Lea, Donohue or England Springs toll road). The private road opened in 1875, to give Lake County passengers, freight and mail better access to the railroad, which reached Cloverdale in 1872. It crossed Adobe Creek seven times without a bridge south of Lakeport, continued down a crooked trail to England Springs, went up over the Mayacamas Mountains at Sam Hand Opening, next along Lone Pine Ridge, and down to Tyler Valley into Sonoma County. Then the road twisted slowly up another moun-

Shortest and Cheapest.

THE S. V. & C. L STAGES
WILL LEAVE
LAKEPORT
For CLOVERDALE daily, at 6.00 a. M.

Connecting with the trains, so that passengers by this line can go or come through from San Francisco to Lakeport in one day, without stopping over at Cloverdale.

STAGES LEAVES
CLOVERDALE
For LAKEPORT daily, at 12.30 P. M.

Through tickets from Lakeport to San Francisco over the Sonoma Valley & Clear Lake line can be purchased at Greene's Hotel for $6.50

The line is equipped with first-class coaches, and none but skillful drivers are employed. Stages will leave Lakep rt for UPPER LAKE and BARTLETT SPRINGS, daily at 6 A. M.
W. C. VAN ARNAM,
P. oprietor.

tain grade and down Squaw Creek, ending at the junction with Geyser Road (a public road) at Sulphur Creek, about eight miles from Cloverdale.

One point in the toll road, named 'Cape Horn' by stage drivers and freighters, "was of solid rock for about a mile and the roadway through it was very narrow. It had been built so narrow that it was nearly impossible for one vehicle to pass another. Mail, stages and freight teams knew the schedules and always travelled so that everyone at that time was going only one way. If someone did not know of this system and met another party in Cape Horn, then one of them had to unhitch and pull his vehicle backward until a spot could be found to allow for passing."[31]

Driver Dick Crawford left Lakeport at 6:00 a.m., his S. V. & C. L. stage on a tight schedule to reach Cloverdale in time for the San Francisco and North Pacific Railroad departure at 2:30 p.m. After Lakeport there were two stops to change horses: at the Matt Lea Place and at the Tyler Road House in Tyler Valley, which had accomodations for passengers. Crawford was on Geyser Road near to ending his run when Bart surprised him.

> Yesterday afternoon the down stage from Lakeport when about five miles of Cloverdale was stopped by a masked man, who had a shot gun. The driver, Dick Crawford, was driving along at an easy jog, and had got just opposite the Bancrof cottage, making a little bend, when before he realized what he saw, the horses stopped, and right ahead about ten feet, stood a medium sized man with a broad slouched hat, a black overcoat, and stripped pants. He wore a white cloth mask across the upper portion of his face. He, as quick as the horses stopped, raised a double barreled shot gun to his shoulder and demanded the express and mail. The driver asked a friend on the seat with him to throw it out, which he did, and the stage drove on. The passengers were not interferred with, although there were several ladies and gentlemen on board. The driver says he only saw one man although he carefully looked for others.
>
> Mr. Sanderson, of the stage company, passed over the same road the night before, and at Livermore Flat he saw two men camped in the brush. The chances are they were the same set, and no doubt there were more men than were seen on the grounds at the time of the robbery. At this late hour as we go to press, we cannot learn anything about the treasure and mail, if it contained any money or not. Chas. Cook started out in pursuit a little after the stage arrived (*Cloverdale Reveille*).

The *Sonoma Democrat* (Santa Rosa) ran a somewhat different story:

> As the down stage was coming along at a stiff jog, at a point called chicken hill, about four miles out of Cloverdale, the driver saw a man standing on a little elevation and leaning on a double-barrelled shotgun, who, as the stage approached, brought the gun up to his shoulder and demanded him to halt. The driver not understanding, did not stop, and was told twice and three times to stop, which he finally did. The man then, still keeping the gun at his shoulder, said, 'express box;' the driver threw it out. He again said, 'mail,' the driver immediately responded by throwing out one sack. He then demanded the rest which were also thrown out. The driver was then ordered to drive on.
>
> The robber is described as a man of five feet, four or five inches in hight, dark complexioned, wore a black hat, short coat and light pants. He wore a mask of white cloth. His gun was a double-barrelled one, and was apparently a new one. Upon the arrival of the stage here, two or three men left in search of the robber, but it is very possible that he is the old offender, known as 'Black Bart.' His manner of operations are very similar to several other little jobs that have transpired hereabouts, and it is thought that it was him again. He, to all appearances, is always alone, and invariably selects some spot on the road, from which he can command a good view of the road from both directions. As we go to press nothing new has been heard from the searchers.

The *Reveille* had a brief item the following week:

A Sonoma Valley & Clear Lake Stage at Highland Springs, Lake County.
(Courtesy Lake County Museum)

Nothing definite has been, as yet, learned of the whereabouts of the stage robber who stopped and robbed the Lakeport stage last week. Detective Aull, of Wells' Fargo & Co's express, and Detective Culver, of the United States Service, have both been out in search, but as we have been able to learn nothing definite is known. He is, the robber, an old timer, and thoroughly familiar with these mountains, which gives him a great advantage. The amount lost by the express is about $250.

The actual amount Bart stole was $475.50,[32] but aside from that discrepancy there are some interesting aspects to this robbery. The *Reveille*'s report is only the second Black Bart holdup where a U.S. government agent is named. Also, there seemed to be some question at the time (and at present) if the stage was even robbed by Bart, although he was blamed. Wells, Fargo had a suspicion that Buck English, a moderately famous Northern California outlaw, had committed the holdup.

On November 26, 1882 Wells, Fargo Detective Charles Aull sent the following to his division superintendent, S. D. Brastow:

One man. The robber is without any doubt 'Black Bart.' The mail sacks are cut the same as all of the robberies he has committed (T). I start out this morning with the constable ... I think that he goes out through that County [Colusa] and by notifying the Ranchers right & left we might cut off his retreat.[33]

The T, Bart's unique method of cutting open mail sacks, was one of the first things Hume saw to tie Bart's robberies together. The next day Aull wrote to Brastow again, from Calistoga:

Dear Sir, I wrote you on yesterday from Cloverdale, came through to this place last night via the Geysers. The stage robber was tracked along top of Ridge 15 near the Geysers, he came to scene of robbery and went the same route. I found on arrival here that "Buck" English was discharged last month from San Quentin. "Buck" has served two terms from Lake Co., once for robbery, last term 8 years. During the last term he was the inseparable companion of Jack Bowen (Black Jack), Big Frank Clark, Billy Miner, et. al. He fills the modern rendition of the Jeffersonian test, "He is capable, he is 'on it.'" He lives at Middletown, Lake Co., 18 miles north of this place, and on direct line of route the stage robber went and came from scene of robbery. While all the ear marks are those of Black Bart, still "Buck" is bright enough to ape his style if he knew it. I go to Middletown and Lower Lake on stage today.[34]

Perhaps English was guilty, but no evidence was found to charge him.

~

Black Bart said his favorite author was Edward Bulwer-Lytton (author of ***The Last Days of Pompeii***, one of the most popular books of the 19th Century); others said he read Shakespeare. These are indications of an intellectual bent, but it is doubtful that Charles Boles was an historian of his crimes. Unless he kept a written record (none was discovered after his arrest), he could not have remembered the details, even the number, of so many robberies, and through the years subtleties would have merged, then become blurred in his memory. So it is plausible that certain holdups blamed on Bart were committed by other bandits, or that he was responsible for more than the 29 crimes recounted in this book.

Although he supposedly only robbed from Wells, Fargo, (which wasn't true — he liked the U. S. mail also), some stages carried packages the express company had not forwarded. Wells, Fargo cared only that their own green strongbox was neither stolen nor damaged; if goods they had not insured were taken, the company had only a mild interest — and the robbery, even if Black Bart was suspected, would not have appeared on the firm's list.

Numerous unsolved stagecoach robberies occurred in northern California between 1875 and 1883; Black Bart might have been responsible for some of them and he might have been blamed for some he didn't commit. Or after his capture Bart might have accepted blame for a robbery he wasn't responsible for — if it was to his benefit.

Chapter 14
Sonoma County — *Thursday, April 12, 1883*
Robbery No. 27

To begin his eighth year as a road agent, Bart again returned to the Lakeport to Cloverdale line, at almost the same milepost. The *Sonoma Democrat* (with its wonderful motto 'The World Is Governed Too Much') reported:

> The stage was robbed by an unknown individual. He took Wells, Fargo & Co.'s treasure box and the mail bag, the former containing about twenty-seven dollars and the latter nothing of value except several checks, which though drawn for large amounts, are of no use to the robber. He ransacked the mail thoroughly, however, in his search for something valuable, tearing everything open and scattering the contents about everywhere.
>
> Though we have spoken of him as unknown, he is supposed to be an old hand at the business, who has committed several other robberies in the same locality. He is described as being a man about thirty-five years old, five feet, eight inches in height, of sandy complexion and having two front teeth missing. He travels about like an ordinary tramp, carrying a roll of blankets within which, however, is rolled up a shotgun, the stock and barrels being separate. When he wishes to stop anyone it is but the matter of a moment to arrange his weapon and have it ready for use. After the robbery is accomplished and the victim is gone, he replaces the gun in the blankets and trudges on, the same harmless looking "vag" as before.

After stopping the stage Bart used the old outlaw trick and ordered driver Connibeck to unhitch the horses and lead them to the rear of the stage. Sheriff Tennessee C. Bishop of Cloverdale, aided by two of Hume's Wells, Fargo agents, tracked Bart east to the Geysers area of Sonoma County, but lost the trail.

Cloverdale Wells, Fargo agent Isaac E. Shaw wrote to Superintendent S. D. Brastow: "No doubt but it is 'Black Bart' as he opened the T Box and Mail sacks in his old style — and answers to his description." The official amount stolen from Wells, Fargo was $32.60.[35]

Amador County — *Saturday, June 23, 1883*
Robbery No. 28

Mail and express packages from several towns were taken to Jackson, then staged twelve miles on a toll road to the Amador Branch Railroad terminus at Ione. The town, previously called Bedbug and Freezeout, was named after the heroine of ***The Last Days of Pompeii***. Describing Black Bart's only stagecoach robbery in Amador County, the *Amador Sentinel* captured the details and flavor of the outlaw's last profitable day before his luck ran out:

Saturday morning the Ione stage was stopped at the head of the Morrow grade [Four miles from Jackson, its point of origin] by one masked man, who used the persuasive eloquence of a double-barrelled shotgun to enforce obedience to his command. There was but one passenger aboard. The driver [Clint Radcliffe] handed out the two express boxes and four United States mail sacks, and drove on to Ione. After the stage had gone a little distance the highwayman fired off one barrel of his gun, it is presumed accidentally.

The express boxes and mail sacks were taken a few feet from the road, the boxes broken open and the sacks cut open by splitting them across the top and down the center in the form of a T, all being cut alike. Only sixteen dollars was in the Jackson express box, but the amount in the Sutter and Amador box swelled the haul on W. F. & Co. to $574. The registered mail packages, eight in number, were taken, one package from Sutter Creek contained $87, one from Mokelumne Hill contained $60. Three dollars was in a registered package from Railroad Flat, and $15 in one from West Point, which swells the cash booty of the robberman to $750. A five hundred dollar check was also secured, but this cannot be made available.

The robber left an old hat, an old pair of pants, his mask, a piece of a woman's dress, and an old ax by the demoralized boxes and bags. The ax is said to have been stolen from the Morrows. A man was seen the night before near Ione, at the Dog ranch, who wore the hat and pants found, and his description given to the officers. Sheriff Murray and assistants at once started out to obtain a clue if possible. Detectives Hume and Thacker arrived in town Monday night. They are confident they know the man, but as he is supposed to be the hero of twenty-two successful stage robberies, this knowledge is not of much use.

It is said he has never been seen in a town, always does his work in the identical manner that this last robbery was performed, is not supposed to be of a drinking or gambling character. Eight hundred dollars is the reward on him,

The Ione-Jackson Stage at the National Hotel in Jackson.
(Courtesy California State Library)

and he goes by the name of "Black Bart the Po8." No trace of the highwayman has been obtained as yet.

This is the only robbery when Bart supposedly used a loaded weapon. Perhaps being shot at and unable to return fire caused him to rethink his methods. Perhaps the accidental discharge of the shotgun in this case made him change his mind again and keep his gun unloaded. Or maybe, as he couldn't see Bart, driver Clint Radcliffe was mistaken about the source of the sound.

As a successful bandit this was Black Bart's last hurrah — at least he got a decent haul.

WELLS, FARGO & CO'S EXPRESS,

SPECIAL INSTRUCTIONS IN REGARD TO STAGE ROBBERIES.

To Agent Wells, Fargo & Co.

DEAR SIR:

Since the publication of the accompanying Circular, Dec. 18th, 1882, the fellow, Black Bart, has robbed the stage from Lakeport to Cloverdale, April 12, 1883, and the stage from Jackson to Ione City, June 23, 1883.

Hereafter, should the stage to your place be robbed by one man, (your office being nearest place of robbery), I desire you to IMMEDIATELY send two competent persons to scene of robbery, instructed to gather up box, mail bags, (if taken,) and everything that they may find in way of disguises, tools, etc., and one to hasten back and report, the other to stay on the ground taking measurements of all tracks and noticing and noting everything that may tend to bear in any way upon the robbery, or aid in pursuit by those who follow. You will also please take from the driver, upon his arrival, a full statement of the features of the robbery, and immediately telegraph me in about the following form:

" Stage from .... to .... driven by .... robbed at .... o'clock......M to-day..... miles from .... by one man armed with .... masked with .... wearing......... came out .... (in front of team or on driver's side as case may be,) ordered driver to throw out box and mail (as case may be), then ordered driver to move on, keeping gun on him until he passed (as case may be); .... about .... high, etc."

As soon as your messenger returns from scene of robbery, telegraph again in about following form:

" Box found, broken open in end with axe, (as case may be), mail bags cut .... (if taken, describe how cut or opened), way bills and way pocket (found or not, as case may be); robber on foot or horseback (as case may be); wears about No.....boot; tracks indicate he went S., E., W., N., (as case may be); disguise and axe found, (as case may be), etc.

Have a full understanding with your drivers, requesting them *when there is any time to be saved* to forward a messenger (at our cost), to nearest telegraph office to notify our Agent nearest the scene of robbery, and also citizens along his route. Each driver should be supplied with this and the circular accompanying.

I would advise, also, that you at once have an understanding with some proper persons in your community, who will at all time be prepared with arms, etc., for quick work, when required.

Familiarize yourself with accompanying circular, and if, in your judgment, from reports made, mode of opening box, cutting mail bags, etc., you are reasonably satisfied it was Black Bart, telegraph to the " Associated Press, San Francisco," giving particulars and stating that the robber is probably Black Bart.

Take the names, residence and statements of passengers, and fill out a blank (" Stage Robbery Report ") and send by first Express. If waybills are found, telegraph loss; if not found, telegraph your Division Superintendent as soon as loss is ascertained

I would suggest that you immediately call the attention of active men to the standing rewards offered, for arrest and conviction:

Wells, Fargo & Co...$300
State of California.. 300
United States, if mail is robbed.. 200

See Instruction Book, Page 47.

And, further, that, from formation of country and knowledge of direction taken by robber, information of same should at once be sent ahead of him, as well as trying to overtake him by following his tracks.

The foregoing instructions will apply and should be followed in nearly all cases of robbery.

J. B. HUME,

Special Officer W. F. & Co.

SAN FRANCISCO, September 5th, 1883.

To get to Funk Hill from Copperopolis, you continue out Main Street, past the Corner, past the old Armory Hall and past Goey Hendsch's tall, two-storied house on the left. It is the last house in the town and stands like an outpost before advancing fields and rolling hills. And, after a mile, there is a break in the fence on the left side of the road where a cattle guard is set into a small, little-used dirt road. Here the old Funk Hill road you seek bears to the left ... you pull over to the side of the narrow road and stop. You sit and look at a narrow, rubble-rock strip ... worn and depressed by the heavy travel of long-ago years into the grass-covered surface of the country. And your eyes trace the depression to its crossing of Black Creek at a very shallow and wide ford. And you see, to left and right of the shallow ford, where the creek bed narrows and becomes a gulch, sharp ledges and reefs of rocks, irregular and jagged and gaily colored in blues and greens by copper and other minerals. You stand at the ford and look up the steep hillside across Black Creek and you trace a narrow, rains-washed , brown-earth strip which is the abandoned Funk Hill road, long valiantly struggling against an inexorable, strangling pressure of thick brush and scrub trees to keep alive the memory of its former existence as a main thoroughfare.

In a silence that ushered into the present a fantasy-something out of the nothingness of time and space and out of the nowhere, and which materialized upon that struggling strip of former roadway ... surely a dusty stage loomed into focus and took material form and motion. Surely out of the dimness of the dead past, from somewhere along the way to the yesterdays, that stagecoach rocketed over the top of the hill, across Black Creek, and came plunging down a roadway, miraculously widened now and secure from the reaching arms of the brush-monster. And we heard the wheel hubs cluckin' on the exes and an errant breeze brought the urgent voice of Reason McConnell to us out of the silence of the yesterdays and he was shouting to his team and, using his whip on horses already plunging down the precipitous down-grade into the shallow ford of Black Creek, leaving Black Bart behind, after that last robbery on his record, whose memory will outlast them all: 'the gentleman robber!'

"Get th' hell down the hill, nags! Go on you goats! There's a chance of gettin' this hooded bandit this time; if I can only get the word to Copper' in time! He's up there somewheres right now... He's still up there this minute; somewheres! Giddup, you slow-pokin' sons ... ! Go on! Hi, yup! Go on!"

— *Owen Treleaven,* **Old Men in the Sun**

Black Bart Rock on Funk Hill, 1959.
(Courtesy Wells Fargo Bank)

Chapter 15
Calaveras County
Saturday, November 3 — Tuesday, November 6, 1883
Robbery No. 29 & Pursuit

Black Bart seemed to live by the old saying "The criminal always returns to the scene of the crime." Give or take a few miles, the outlaw had gone back to previous holdup sites nine times. But he had never returned to the scene of his first holdup, the Funk Hill area near Copperopolis on the Sonora to Milton road. After eight years of challenging Wells, Fargo's best efforts to catch him, after holding up twenty-eight stagecoaches, with only two close calls, Bart finally went back to Calaveras County. There he pressed his luck — too hard.

Sometime before October 25th Boles left the Webb House in San Francisco and took either the train or riverboat to Stockton, at the head of the San Joaquin delta. From Stockton, with his essentials in a satchel and still dressed as a gentleman, he could have taken the train to Milton, then a stagecoach to Tuttletown. In Tuttletown he determined when the Patterson Mine would ship their next packet of gold to Milton. From Tuttletown he walked the stage route on the way to Sonora, resuming the hobo-like disguise while reconnoitering the territory.

At Angels Camp, on October 25th, he bought some supplies (a dollar's worth of Knic Knack crackers and a quarter's worth of granulated sugar) at Jeannine Gardiner Crawford's grocery store. He stayed one night, October 27th or 28th, at Reynolds Ferry, at the small hotel and stage station on the Calaveras side of the Stanislaus River run by 'Grandma' Rolleri; her son Jimmy operated the ferry which transported the Milton-Sonora stages, owned by John H. Shine, across the river. Bart told his hostess he was a miner from Bostwick's Bar, a few miles down the river; as there were many 'goldwashers' along the Stanislaus, he was taken at face value. Accustomed to camping in the wilds, this concession to comfort had unpleasant results.

Olivia Rolleri, in whose lodgings Bart slept, was a local legend. Born in Genoa, she had sailed around Cape Horn with her mother and sister, reaching Tuolomne County in 1860. There she married Gerome (later anglicized to James) Rolleri, who was a hydraulic miner. When such environmentally-destructive mining was outlawed, the family moved to Cherokee Hill, then to Big Oak Flat, and opened a general store. There is a spurious story that the famous bandit Tiburcio Vasquez once plundered the store and held Olivia Rolleri at gun point, but the date of Vasquez' death does not coincide with the legend. James Rolleri was elected Tuolomne County Public Administrator, but the family soon moved to Reynolds Ferry in Calaveras County, to operate the inn and ferry.

A half-century later one of Grandma Rolleri's daughters, Louise Rolleri Barden recalled the evening of Black Bart's visit:

The house was very old fashioned. It was painted ... sort of yellowish brown... There was a porch that ran all along the front and along the side — that was the side by the river. Coming in from the front, you went into a very large room. At one time it had been a barroom. That was before my day. And once it was a store and the old bar was a counter then. Well, the bar ran all along one side of the big room. And at the end of the bar there were three steps ... going up to the dining room. To the right, as you stepped into the dining room, were steps leading upstairs. There were three bedrooms up there ... where the boys [Louise had eight brothers, six living] slept.

Downstairs, a door led from the dining room into the kitchen. Then there was one step into a hall... On the right of the hall was the spare bedroom and then Mama's bedroom. Across the hall were three bedrooms; that's where us girls [Louise had four sisters] slept. At the end of the little hall was a great big back parlor. And then, beyond that, was a bedroom. And that's where Black Bart spent that night. We didn't exactly run a hotel. But sometimes travellers would want to stay overnight, as well as eat a meal or two; so we used the back bedroom for them.

[Black Bart] came before supper and asked for a room to stay all night. He was on foot. And I remember distinctly that when Mama showed him the spare bedroom he was to sleep in, he asked her for a key to the door. It semed so funny to us girls. Nobody had ever asked for a key before. That seemed to us like a very peculiar thing to do. I remember I couldn't understand that; nobody ever locked their door in those days.

He ate supper with us that night in the big dining room. We had a great big long table. And I remember another thing we talked about afterward; a thing that seemed so peculiar to us girls especially. He didn't seem to want to sit around after supper and talk with the family. That's the way everybody else did who ever stayed there in those days; they'd sit around after supper and we'd get acquainted. But he went right to his room and stayed there.[36]

At first light Bart was gone. Only Jimmy Rolleri was awake, to ferry Bart across the river. The outlaw sought out familiar territory, pitching camp near the best site for his intended holdup, the Funk Hill grade, where he'd made his first unofficial withdrawal from Wells, Fargo & Co.

To describe Funk Hill is to describe thousands of similar places in the Sierra foothills. The gentle slope up from Reynolds Ferry (or from where it used to be, before the construction of the New Melones Dam) is mirrored

Reynolds Ferry, over the Stanislaus River, between Calaveras and Tuolumne Counties.
(Courtesy Calaveras County Historical Society)

by an equal descent westward toward Copperopolis. The land is dotted with scrub oak and manzanita brush surrounding stands of large oak and pine, with more trees at the robbery site now than existed in Bart's time. At the crest a lava-capped ridge flanks the road, where Black Bart watched for the oncoming stage from the east.

He cut tall grass for bedding to spread under his blankets. Mixing sugar with ground corn brought from San Francisco, he fed himself a simple Mexican trailside meal, pinole, and brought up water from the Stanislaus River, two miles away. On the night of November 2nd he camped within a few yards of the stage road, waiting for the Sonora to Milton stage, which would come about 6:30 the next morning.

Near 4:00 a.m. on November 3rd Reason McConnell eased his Nevada Stage Company coach out of Sonora and headed for Milton. The first stop was Tuttletown, where McConnell picked up a Wells, Fargo express box containing 228 ounces of amalgam from the Patterson Mine quartz mill (valued at $4100), $550 in gold coin, and 3-1/4 ounces of gold dust valued at $65. Nearing 6:00 a.m. McConnell changed his horses and had breakfast at Reynolds Ferry and was on his way to Copperopolis. Louise Rolleri Barden continues the story:

> Mr. McConnell ... had told [my brother] Jimmy that he often saw deer near the road up on Funk Hill... He saw them almost every morning after he left the Ferry, he said. And he told Jimmy he ought to ride up with him one morning and get us some deer meat. But Jimmy told Mr. McConnell that he didn't have any shells for his rifle and so he couldn't go with him. And Mr. McConnell, he said that he would get some for Jimmy and bring them along with him on his next trip.
>
> So, that morning, soon after the family got up ... [McConnell arrived and] said he had got Jimmy's shells... And Jimmy went and got his rifle and money to pay for the shells and he got up on the driver's seat with Mr. McConnell and they started off.
>
> Well, as luck would have it, they didn't see a single deer that morning [another omen for Black Bart; if Jimmy had shot at a deer before the stagecoach arrived at the Funk Hill grade, Bart would undoubtedly have cancelled his plans for that day] and, by the time they had nearly reached the top of Funk Hill, Jimmy began to think he had gone about far enough. So he asked Mr. McConnell to stop and let him down; he said it would make a long enough hunt for him if he got off there and hunted all the way down the hill, home. So he got off the stage and Mr. McConnell started up the horses and drove on and Jimmy started working his way down the hill.

Other sources claim Jimmy Rolleri planned to ride the stage through to Copperopolis and come back on the returning coach later that day. In that version McConnell suggests that Jimmy get off the coach and cut around the base of the hill on foot; the boy might scare out a rabbit or squirrel and could rejoin the stage on the downhill side. Jimmy hops off and begins his overland hike. Louise Rolleri Barden's story is equally detailed, though slightly different. In any event, some 200 yards from where John Shine had been stopped in 1875 by a flour-sack-masked outlaw wielding a shotgun, and covered by what looked like the rifles of a desperado gang, Jimmy Rolleri got off the stagecoach with his gun and began walking diagonally down hill.

McConnell was within sight of the top of the grade when Bart, hiding in the brush, stepped out in front of the lead horse. McConnell had driven stage for many years and been held up before (three times in 1876 alone). He recognized Black Bart immediately and halted his stage.

For once Bart didn't say "Throw down the box," with or without adding the usual "please". Instead he demanded "Where's the man that was with you a few minutes ago." McConnell told him it was a boy — perhaps to protect Jimmy from Bart's shotgun. He also lied, saying Jimmy was searching for some stray cattle.

Knowing the express box was bolted to the stage, Bart ordered McConnell down, but the driver protested, telling the masked man the brake was bad.

McConnell had been through it all before. Joseph Henry Jackson (the first researcher to study Black Bart seriously, when people who knew of events first-hand were still alive) suggests that a duel of wits was taking place and Bart was losing: "[Bart] did not really think fast; he merely thought of many things. And this time he thought of something — the wrong thing."

If gripping the brake lever wouldn't stop the stage from rolling backwards, Bart should have told McConnell to back up and turn the stage; then the vehicle would end up across the road, against the hillside, unable to roll at all. What Bart decided to do instead was to block the wheel with a rock, which is what he told McConnell to do. The driver replied, "You do it" (rather cocky for a man facing a shotgun-toting outlaw).

Making sure McConnell was unarmed — the driver was momentarily out of shotgun range — Bart bent over to place a heavy rock behind a front wheel. The highwayman ordered McConnell off the coach and to unhitch the horses. Bart was so nervous he helped with the straps. After the horses were freed, Bart told McConnell to walk them over the hill a short distance. With the driver and horses out of sight Bart took an axe from a hiding place and attacked the gold-laden express box.

McConnell, standing next to his horses, listened to Bart's hammering axe. Suddenly the driver saw Jimmy Rolleri working his way around the slope of the hill. Louise Rolleri Barden related what happened next:

> [Jimmy] had only gone a very short way when he noticed he couldn't hear the stage moving any more; it seemed to him that all at once everything got awful quiet. He wondered if the stage had broken down, or something, and listened but couldn't hear a sound. So he worked his way across the road and through the brush and he got to a clear place where he could see back up the road to the very top of the hill. And he could see the stage horses standing there, and he saw Mr. McConnell standing there by his horses, holding the reins.

"I attracted Jimmy's attention," the driver said later, "and signaled him to walk in a detour around the foot of the hill and come to me out of sight of Black Bart." Seeing McConnell with his horses without the coach, Jimmy understood immediately what was happening. He was only eleven when Bart first robbed the Sonora-Milton stage, but the route had been hit numerous times afterwards by other, less fortunate highwaymen, although not since 1881 (Between May, 1876 and March, 1885, twenty-one men were sentenced to state prison for robberies on the 35 miles of stage road between Sonora and Milton).

Finally Jimmy reached McConnell; then they cautiously made their way up the hill. At the crest they looked down at Black Bart, on the right side of the stage, the side nearest the trees, hammering at the express box, less than 100 yards away with his back to them.

Harry Morse, Jim Hume's assistant detective, later reported that Bart had "a sledgehammer, a big crowbar, a wedge for splitting wood, a couple of picks and an axe." Joseph Henry Jackson commented wryly that if Bart had carried all that across country, along with his shotgun, provisions, and robbery clothes, he would have needed a pack mule at least. The November 10, 1883 *Calaveras Chronicle* might have reported it correctly: "His tools consisted of a crowbar, a sledge hammer and an iron wedge with a ring through the head of it. One or two blows with the hammer upon the fastening sprung it so that the wedge could be inserted conveniently and then driven in, after which introducing the crowbar through the ring in the wedge, the box was easily pried open."

The next sequence of events has been told in several conflicting versions, but Joseph Henry Jackson concluded that Jimmy's own story was the most accurate. McConnell grabbed Jimmy Rolleri's rifle and fired, missing Bart, who ran for cover. McConnell shot and missed again. Jimmy cried "Let me shoot. I'll get him and won't kill him either," took the gun from McConnell and fired a third shot as Bart got to the bushes. The bandit stumbled and dropped a bundle of letters, but held onto the bag with the gold and money, disappearing before Jimmy could shoot again.

As soon as Bart was gone, McConnell hitched the horses back up to the coach and set out into Salt Springs Valley for Copperopolis. He made a fast run to Gilmore's watering station, yelling "I've had a holdup!" He also claimed (then, but not later) that he'd exchanged shots with the road agent. McConnell moved his stage out again and met a local cowboy, Joe Ratto, a half mile down the road. He sent Ratto to San Andreas to inform Calaveras County Sheriff Ben Thorn about the holdup, at first suggesting the cowboy go look for the holdup man. Ratto was carrying a Henry repeating rifle but he didn't like the odds in a shootout with Black Bart.

At Copperopolis, in case Ratto hadn't reached him yet, McConnell sent a telegram to Sheriff Thorn at San Andreas. He also wired Wells, Fargo in San Francisco. Sheriff Thorn later recalled:

> The stage was robbed on the morning of Nov 3rd near Copperopolis. Upon hearing of the robbery I proceeded immediately to Copperopolis reaching there about noon of that day — and with the stage driver R. E. McConnell repaired at once to the scene of the robbery. In the mean time, W. H. Case, Agt. W.F&Co. at Copperopolis, had gone out taking with him Billy Fagan, Milton Curry, and James Rolleri, the latter being the young man who rode up the hill

141

The Dechamps Stage at the Union Hotel, Copperopolis. Driver is believed to be Reason McConnell. William Fagan is inside the coach. *(Courtesy Charles Stone)*

with McConnell, and whose rifle indirectly accomplished such satisfactory results.

These parties soon found the rendezvous behind the rocks, and took possession of all articles which have since figured in the case, including the handkerchief, and they at once discovered the laundry mark, and there and then discussed the probabilities of the mark leading to the capture of the robber.[37]

Charlie Fontana also had memories of that posse:

Billy Fagan and I were good friends ... W. P. Fagan. He afterward ran the Union Hotel. He went out with us that morning after the holdup took place. He never would have missed anything like that any more than I would have. It's been so long ... I can't be sure who the others were. There was Milt Curry and ... I think maybe Bill and Goey Hendsch were along. The chances are, about fifteen or twenty of us altogether — all young fellows — went over there to the top of Funk Hill in a bunch. We went up there as fast as we could, after we got the word. You know how it is. Whenever there's an excitement like that ...

142

Anyway, we ... looked around a lot and walked all over the place, looking. And we came across this great big boulder of a rock and we came across this flour sack. There was a lot of little stuff in it; oh, there was salt and pepper and crackers and cheese, and all such little stuff as that. And I think the salt and pepper was tied up in this handkerchief... That's all there was to it.[38]

The first find was a derby hat, which McConnell said Bart lost as he fled into the brush, but nothing else was discovered for several hours. Near dusk the men stumbled on Bart's camp behind a large rock, finding paper bags from Crawford's grocery in Angels Camp, flour sacks bearing logos of mills in Stockton and Sonora, the leather case for a pair of opera glasses (but not the glasses themselves), three dirty linen cuffs, a razor, a magnifying glass, a belt and a handkerchief full of buckshot.

According to a Calaveras County legend, retold in the *Overland Monthly* some years later, the handkerchief was spotted apart from the rest of Bart's leavings, and dismissed by the members of the posse as probably a remnant of an old Indian burial shroud. It makes a good story, but the detail of the buckshot — or even salt and pepper — wrapped in the handkerchief effectively belies it.

Sheriff Thorn continues:

Mr. Case took entire charge of the articles found and carried them to his office in Copperopolis. McConnell and myself reached Copperopolis after dark that evening not having encountered Mr. Case in our search during the afternoon... Thacker and Mr. Langmaid [Oren Langemate, law officer] of Stockton, arrived at Copperopolis about 2:00 A. M. the morning of the 4th and after daylight Thacker, Langmaid and myself called at the Office of Mr. Case and then and there, together, received the handkerchief cuffs opera glass cases etc. and as a matter of fact had our attention called to the laundry mark by Mr. Case.[39]

Everyone in the Wells, Fargo agent's office crowded around the dirty, torn white silk crepe handkerchief lying on Mr. Case's desk. On the handkerchief's margin a laundry identification mark, in faded India ink, could faintly be seen: Fxo7. If Black Bart had washed his own linen he might never have been caught (or if he hadn't lost his handkerchief on Funk Hill — a loss that soon became the greatest funk of his life).

Historians have credited Sheriff Thorn with discovering the laundry mark, but he refutes this himself — as did others. The following year John Thacker would write to his sidekick, Oren Langmate:

Do you remember who was present when you and I found the mark of the handkerchief B. B. lost... Do you remember the conversation between [the Wells, Fargo agent] and myself, when the handkerchief was handed to me with the buckshot in it [and] the agent said there is no marks on it. And I said never mind I will examine it for myself and I spread it out and found the mark on

Sheriff Benjamin Thorn of Calaveras County
(Courtesy Calaveras County Historical Society)

it and you took a memorandum of it... If you do remember just what was done and said you will oblige me much by writing the full particulars to me.[40]

For a day Sheriff Thorn was confused by a false lead. Coming back from Funk Hill with the remains of Black Bart's camp, W. H. Case stopped to see a rancher named Campbell, who said the tools Bart used to break open the express box had been stolen from his place about two weeks earlier. If Campbell told the truth, so much for Bart's constant claim that he never robbed anyone but Wells, Fargo. The newspapers noted that his mail robberies gave the lie to his statement, but they missed, or chose to ignore, this crass theft of a rancher's tools (the newspaper report for Robbery No. 28 also stated that he stole an axe).

Campbell, however, suggested another candidate for the road agent, an olive-skinned Italian-looking tramp who had come by a few days before looking for work. After giving the 'Italian' breakfast Campbell pointed to a pile of wood to cut; but the tramp, snorting that he wasn't looking for that kind of work, walked off instead toward Funk Hill. Black Bart's general description had been available for several years and Campbell's 30-year old Italian in no way resembled the infamous outlaw, but Thorn circulated the description anyway.

Then the sheriff set out to comb the countryside for other clues. San Joaquin County Sheriff Cunningham and Tuolomne County Sheriff Mc-Quade joined the Calaveras County sheriff in the manhunt. The posse spread out through the formidable Bear Mountain range, using Tom Cunningham's tracking dogs, trying to find someone who had seen the robber. A hunter, T. P. Martin, whose cabin in York Gulch was about 3/4 of a mile from the robbery scene, had met "an elderly man with gray whiskers." The stranger was bound for Jackson, after being in Chinese Camp and Jamestown on business. Martin became suspicious when the man asked if he had to go through Angels Camp to get to Jackson. The hunter thought it extremely odd that someone who lived in the area — had just hiked through it — wouldn't know the right trail. He would recognize the stranger if he saw him again, Martin declared. The hunter's description tallied with Black Bart's accepted portrait, so Thorn sent word to Copperopolis to cancel the alert for Campbell's 'Italian.'

Branching out up Nassau Valley, Thorn next encountered Ineous Peaslee Sylvester, a local character known as 'Doc:'

'Doc' was no physician. He had acquired his nickname from a private fancy which he never hesitated to make public — the notion that pills rolled from dried angleworms would cure anything. Aside from this crotchet, he was as sharp as the next man.[41]

'Doc' had also met up with a man with a gray mustache heading toward Jackson inquiring about the distance to Angels Camp.

Thorn and his men reached Angels Camp the morning of the 5th and spoke with Mrs. Crawford at her grocery store. The stranger had been her customer a week earlier; several townspeople were in the store remembered him also.

The next day in Tuttletown the Patterson Mine manager told the lawmen that on November 2nd a man had passed himself off as a prospective mine investor, perhaps obtaining information about the stage shipment the following day. It seems unlikely that Bart would have left his perch the day before a robbery. He could have made the round trip to Tuttletown from Funk Hill, but would have been tired, good walker that he was. Maybe that is why Bart's usual alertness failed him during the robbery attempt.

Meanwhile, Wells, Fargo's Detective Thacker was hearing amazing news from Jimmy Rolleri — the man Jimmy had shot at rented a room at the Rolleri hotel about a week before the robbery! Like his sisters the boy thought it strange for someone to ask for a room key. While ferrying him across the river the following morning, Jimmy had chatted with the stranger.

Wells, Fargo rewarded Jimmy with a fancy rifle, inlaid in silver with a hand-carved stock, which exploded the first time he tried to fire it. So the company gave him another one. After travel decreased on the Reynolds Ferry road, Grandma Rolleri moved to the more populous Angels Camp and managed the Calaveras Hotel, than a small restaurant and rooming-house. Jimmy's rifle was above the bar until it was destroyed in 1938 when the hotel burned to the ground.

Louise Barden Rolleri ended her interview with these words:

[B]ut we found the metal plate that had been on it with the wording about Jimmy. I'll show it to you... 'James Rolleri, Jr., For Meritorious Conduct, November 3, 1883.'

The express company must have thought Jimmy was brave and a good shot, too, ... because they offered him a job as a messenger on the stages. But Mama wouldn't let him take the job. She said she wasn't going to have her boy be a target for anybody to shoot at.[42]

Reason McConnell received a $105 reward, promotion to messenger, and possibly a rifle from Wells, Fargo. He later left the stage-driving business and became chief agent for U. S. Customs in San Francisco.

Two months later S. C. Richards of Angels Camp sent a package and message to the Wells, Fargo agent at Milton: "I was out hors hunting on funk hill today and found this pouch with a bundle of letters and it being in the vacinity of wher the Stage was robbed, I sent them to you as they may be of Som Value to the Company."[43]

The *Calaveras Chronicle* would later publish a tongue-in-cheek post-script, of sorts:

The Milton stage has been robbed so frequently of late that the reoccurence of this trifling incident has ceased to be the subject of comment. In fact the stopping and robbery of that unfortunate vehicle has to be regarded as a matter of course and the omission of the crime creates more surprise than its commission. We don't credit the story, however, that the driver has become so accustomed to handing out the box at a particular point on the road that he frequently stops and sets it out on the wheel without being asked. That is a gross libel.

(Agents of WELLS, FARGO & CO. will please place this in the hands of local Officers and Business Men and preserve a copy in Office. ☞ DO NOT POST. ☜)

ARREST STAGE ROBBER.
LIBERAL REWARD.

The Stage from Sonora to Milton, Cal., was stopped by one man Saturday morning, the 3d inst., about three miles east of Copperopolis, and Wells, Fargo & Co's Express robbed of $4,700 in treasure, described as follows:

One cake of retorted gold amalgam of a conical shape, $5\frac{1}{2}$ inches in width across the top, $5\frac{1}{2}$ inches in depth; of a rich yellow color; weight 228 ozs.; fineness 874, and assay value $18 per oz.

One parcel gold dust $3\frac{1}{4}$ oz. fineness and value unknown.

Several parcels coin $553, mostly gold.

In addition to the *standing reward* of $300, offered by the State for the arrest and conviction of each such offender, Wells, Fargo & Co. have a like *standing reward* on same terms, and will also give one-fourth of any treasure recovered.

Gold Dust buyers, Bankers and Assayers are especially requested to keep a sharp lookout. Any person giving the undersigned, information that leads to the arrest and conviction of robber or recovery of treasure will be suitably rewarded.

JAMES B. HUME,

Special Officer W. F. & Co.

San Francisco, No. 5, 1883.

(Courtesy Wells Fargo Bank)

Chapter 16
San Francisco — *November 7-13, 1883*
Capture

By coincidence, two other principal players in the Black Bart story (together with Boles himself and James Hume) were also from New York state. Benjamin Kent Thorn was born in Plattsburg, about a hundred miles due east of Alexandria Bay. Like Charles Boles, Thorn crossed the country overland in 1849 to join the gold rush, working his way down from Lassen County to Calaveras County. However, like James Hume, his lack of success as a miner turned him toward law enforcement. Thorn first worked as a deputy sheriff, then was elected sheriff of Calaveras County in 1867. His combined service as a law officer was 47 years.

Thorn and Hume were long time friends, but had a serious falling out in 1893, when William Evans was arrested and convicted for the murder of Wells, Fargo messenger Mike Tovey. In a strange twist of fate Hume came to the defense of Evans — who spent 13 years in prison — and the case destroyed the friendship between the two lawmen.

In 1851, at age fourteen, Harry N. Morse jumped ship (where he was serving as a common seaman) to participate in San Francisco's gold fever. Turning to law enforcement he became sheriff of Alameda County, achieving such success as a manhunter that he was in demand all over central California. Known for his ability in shootouts, he killed a number of wanted criminals in gun battles, including Juan Soto in 1871. In 1874 the governor of California picked him to head a state-funded posse to run down Tiburcio Vasquez, the most famous California outlaw of the time. Morse tracked Vasquez to Los Angeles County, but the outlaw was finally captured by Los Angeles officers. In 1878 Morse established a private investigation bureau in San Francisco, and it was in this special capacity — so that he would be eligible for reward money — that Hume hired him in June, 1883 to conduct an independent inquiry into the Black Bart case.

Morse would later publish two short-lived San Francisco journals (*San Francisco Mercury*, and *Pacific Monthly*, which published a poem by Elizabeth Barrett Browning in August, 1886 called 'The Women's Question,' and reprinted 'The Case of Summerfield'). He acquired mining properties and wealth, dying in his fourteen room house in Oakland in 1912.

Attention now turned to the handkerchief, with its laundry mark, which together with the poetry has become a core element in the Black Bart

(San Francisco Bulletin, December 4, 1905)

drama. As the hunt for the laundry began, a controversy smoldered, fired
by newspapers attempting to boost circulation and the egos of the various
law officers — the glory and rewards that would come from Bart's capture
caused strong personalities to clash. Perhaps James Hume might have
sorted out the truth, but he — not Wells, Fargo & Co. (although Morse's
expenses appear on the company's cash books) — had hired Harry Morse
to find Black Bart and loyally backed his personal employee. Unfortunately, no official Wells, Fargo & Co. report exists with the sequence of events.

Thorn and Thacker brought the evidence from Bart's overnight camp
to Hume's office in San Francisco. While Thorn and Hume tried to find
where the opera glasses and case had been purchased, Harry Morse
focused on the handkerchief, saying: "The first worthwhile clue we've
uncovered yet. It won't be an easy job but maybe we'll be lucky."

The newspapers reported how time consuming it was to find the
laundry and to check for the identifying mark. In a 1905 *San Francisco*

Bulletin interview, Morse declaimed about his task: "I knew that I had a job before me, as there were only ninety-one laundries in this city at that time. After days of search I was rewarded by finding on the books of a laundry on Bush street, conducted by a man named Ware, the identical mark for which I had hunted."

It is possible that Morse might not have told all. As a private investigator, familiar with the city, he would have preferred to buy information and avoid tedious leg work. Wells, Fargo Cash Books show a payment of $20 paid to the bookkeeper of the United States Laundry.[44] It is difficult now to sort through the confusing ownerships of San Francisco laundries during the 1880's, and there may be a simpler explanation. The mark (with which there are also problems) was discovered to be used by the California Laundry at 113 Stevenson Street, owned by Phineas F. Ferguson, John J. and William J. Biggy. But Phineas Ferguson, who was also, or had been, a co-proprietor of the What Cheer Laundry, changed business partners and became co-owner of the United States Laundry. In addition, William J. Biggy later became San Francisco Police Chief (and mysteriously drowned in 1908). Conceivably, Morse could have known Biggy. The detective might have learned how the system worked or found the laundry very quickly — it was only a few blocks from Wells, Fargo. Perhaps Morse got caught up in the media attention, and after preening in the spotlight either couldn't or wouldn't extricate himself from an exaggerated situation. He always maintained that finding the laundry was due to solid footwork, not from any great detective ability.

Sheriff Ben Thorn certainly questioned Morse's role, later thundering:

Don't you think that if it were generally known *just what you* had to do with the finding of that mark, that the figure you would have made in the reports of the capture would have been rather insignificant, and instead of your being the hero of the handkerchief it would be generally known that the Herculean task of visiting 91 laundries existed only in the fertile and imaginative brain of a *Call* reporter, and that the Laundry man who really found it is entitled to the credit, and that you had very little to do with the matter?[45]

By some means the mark was discovered to be assigned to a California Laundry agency, Thomas C. Ware, whose tobacco shop was near Chris Buckley's Saloon and the Bush Street Theater. But different stories were told about what happened next. Harry Morse's words:

I found out on inquiry that the laundry mark belonged to Charles E. Bolton, who was well known at the laundry. The laundryman said that Bolton was a mining man who was frequently called out into the country to see his mines. Sometimes he would be gone one week, sometime two, or even a month, when no laundry would come into the office.

THE BULLETIN: SAN FRANCISCO, DECEMBER   1903.

HOW BLACK BART
WAS · MADE · TO · CONFESS
AS · TOLD · BY · DETECTIVE · HARRY · MORSE · WHO   CAPTURED   HIM

I assumed as a pretext that I wanted to consult him about some ores that were in my possession, and also said that not being certain whether it was Bolton I was hunting for, asked Ware to describe the man and asked him where he lived. He did so willingly, and told me that Bolton lived at the Webb Hotel on Second Street.

An article and letter in the *Examiner* declared something else:

Mr. Ware said to an *Examiner* reporter last evening that he had no marks on his book and would not have known Bolton's marks… All he knew was that a person calling himself Mr. Hamilton called and inquired for Bolton. "The handkerchief was never shown to me," Ware said, "but was taken to the laundry, where the washing was done and there identified by Mr. Ferguson, the proprietor, as the mark* of C. E. Bolton, sent from my office at 316 [Post] Street. Morse then came to me and inquired if I was proprietor of the place and agent for the laundry? I told him I was. He then asked if I would be good enough to let him look at my book for the name of a gentleman who he understood had been getting some washing done here; said he understood the gentleman was a mining man, and being a mining man himself he desired to see him on business. I asked what name he wanted to find? He said Bolton. "Why certainly," said I, "I know Mr. Bolton well. He is in the city now; just arrived from his mine two days ago, and if you will call later you will probably meet him here, for he is an old acquaintance and makes this his headquarters when he is in the City." After asking numerous questions about his mine, etc. he left, saying he would call later.

And what had Bart been doing up until this time? Reason McConnell had missed with the rifle, but Jimmy Rolleri's shot had creased the robber's hand, bloodying a knuckle, which caused him to drop the registered mail that looked so promising. After lugging the 15-pound sack filled with treasure for over a quarter of a mile, Bart buried the amalgam and gold dust under a tree stump, but took the gold coins with him. Nearby he also hid his shotgun, a British-made Loomis IXL No. 15 sawed-off breechloader (the weapon was found by an Indian some time later and purportedly saved when Wells, Fargo's office burned during the 1906 earthquake and fire).

One newspaper later claimed the bandit hiked across the Sierras in two days (over 120 miles) to cash in the amalgam at the Carson Mint in Carson City, Nevada — perhaps he'd done something like that during another Sierra robbery, but not this time. He did walk northwest toward Sacramento, avoiding Angels Camp (the reason he had asked directions from Doc Sylvester and T. P. Martin) and went around Carson Hill. Along the way he threw away everything he carried, except the gold coin. He passed the night of November 4th in a deserted cabin, finding a 'fairly respectable hat' to replace the one lost at Funk Hill. The next morning he began his last cross-county hike, on a trail close to the Gwin Mine, and walked more than a hundred miles in two days!

*Some comments are necessary about the mark, because naturally there is a dispute about what it actually was. Sheriff Thorn said it was F. X. O. 7. in capitals (see Page 218). John Thacker said the mark was F. O. X. 7. Harry Morse, in both 1883 and 1905, said it was F. O. K. 7. One would tend to accept Morse's version, considering he was most familiar with the handkerchief, however Boles himself clearly wrote in a letter (see Page 182) that the mark was Fxo7. But Boles was extremely farsighted, or the ink might have spread, making a K look like an X. Unfortunately, though he mentions the mark, Charlie Ware doesn't state what it was, which would have settled the matter.

By Monday, November 5th, Bart was in Sacramento and picked up a valise he'd left at the International Hotel two months earlier. He luxuriated in a shave, ordered a $45 suit from Thomas Bromley ('merchant tailor, fine assortment of goods, perfect fit guaranteed') at 4th and J Streets, then took a train to Reno. He stayed there for a few days, writing two letters, informing his landlady at the Webb House, and his friend and tobacconist, Charlie Ware, that he'd soon be back in San Francisco. By Thursday, the 8th, he had returned to Sacramento, picked up the suit, ridden the train to Oakland, and taken the ferry to the City.

The linen duster that fit like a Mother Hubbard was packed away in his room at the Webb House, together with clothing farmers thought gave him almost a clerical appearance. Now he wore his new suit and 'dice box' Derby hat, looking every bit the prosperous businessman, or even, as someone jibed, 'a Gilded Age dude.' As well they might — the Funk Hill job earned him by far the largest amount he had ever stolen. Who knows what he thought of doing with it. Certainly the money could have supported his lifestyle for quite some time without the need to venture back onto the highway.

Perhaps he indulged himself that evening. Courtwright & Hawkins Minstrels were performing at the Bush Street Theater. The entertainment consisted of "*Kate Castleton's Return — An Olio of Entirely New Acts, Songs, Specialties, Jokes, Etc.,*" during the first part, and after intermission "A Grand Production of Courtwright's New Musical Melodramatic Operatic Melange, '*Fun on the Petaluma, or A Trip Across the Bay,*'" with the entire company, starring Minnie Tittel. If he was in the mood was for something more elevating, "*The Romany Rye*" was playing at the California Theater, while Bellini's "*Norma*" was being sung at the Tivoli Opera House.

Thus Bart must have felt jaunty the following day, when he spotted Charlie Ware strolling along with an unknown gentleman just a block from the Webb House. T. C. Ware continues his story:

> In about an hour [Morse] returned and said he would like to have a little private talk with me if I could spare a few moments from my business. I consented, and we started down the street together, but before he had time to divulge whatever he wanted to say to me, fortunately for the detective, but unfortunately for poor Bolton, he rubbed right by us and spoke to me before we noticed him. I then hailed him and told him the gentleman wished to see him; then turning to the stranger I said, "I don't know your name, sir." "Hamilton is my name," said he. I then introduced Mr. Bolton, and they walked down the street together and I returned to my business ...

The *Examiner* concluded its article about T. C. Ware:

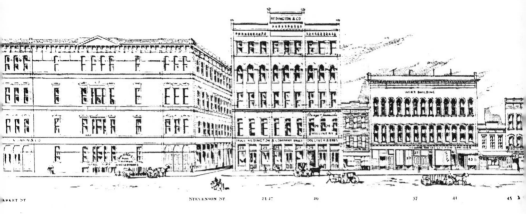

The Webb House, in Webb Building at 37 Second Street. *(Courtesy Sutro Library)*

He did not give 'Hamilton' the number of Bolton's room, and does not think the detectives knew it at that time. He very frankly adds, that, having known Bolton a long time and knowing nothing against him, he would have been much more likely to notify him, if he had any idea that detectives were looking him, than to introduce one of them to him.

Harry Morse's recollections were different:

Then I went away and placed a watch on the [Webb] house but for two days nothing happened. I afterward learned that Bolton, or rather Black Bart, had been out of the city at the time. Soon I went back to the laundry office, and reopened the conversation with Ware. While we were talking Ware looked into the street.

"Why," he said, "here comes the very man now. Come out with me and I'll introduce you."

It was about 5 o'clock in the afternoon. I knew at once from the description of the fellow that this was Black Bart. He was elegantly dressed and came sauntering along swinging his cane. He wore a natty Derby hat, a diamond pin, a large diamond ring and a heavy gold watch and chain. He was about five feet eight inches tall, straight as an arrow, with fine broad shoulders, with deep sunken blue eyes, high cheek bones and a handsome gray mustache and imperial. One would take him for a gentleman who had made money and was enjoying his fortune — anything, in fact, but a stage robber.

Ware introduced him to me and we shook hands, while I asked him if he were not Bolton, the mining man. He assented, and then I asked him to walk a few steps with me and look at some ores that I had in my office.

"He said "Certainly" in the most cordial way.

So we walked, I with my arm in his, to Bush and Montgomery streets, and into Wells, Fargo & Company's office.

Bolton was perfectly calm, but great drops of perspiration stood out on the bridge of his nose as we entered the office.

154

I introduced him to Mr. Hume, the detective for the company, who started to question him about his mines.

Another version of the story, which in part confirms Ware, is that after he got the name from the tobacconist, Morse easily traced 'Bolton' to his residence at the Webb House. With a plainclothes detective watching Bart's hotel, Morse returned to the vicinity of Ware's tobacco shop and laundry agency, and questioned bartender Billy Winthrop at nearby Buckley's Saloon. Winthrop knew Mr. Bolton, of course, and told Morse and his fellow detective (still masquerading as 'mining men') that Mr. Bolton's usual practice was to visit Buckley's in the afternoon. Morse then returned to Ware's tobacco shop.[46]

James Hume began what on the surface was an amiable, rambling conversation, but he was probing. Where did Mr. Bolton have his property? Mr. Bolton replied in generalities. Noticing Bolton's wounded hand, Hume asked about it. Nervously Bart responded that he'd hurt it getting off a train in Truckee. Well then, was Mr. Bolton's mine in Truckee?

"No," Bolton vaguely replied, "In Nevada on the California line."

At this point Bart became truculent: "I am a gentleman, and I don't know who you are. I want to know what this inquiry is all about." Hume assured Bart that he just wanted to ask a few more questions, and slipped out of the room, leaving Morse to placate the suspect. Hume sent for Captain Appleton W. Stone of the San Francisco Police. Then the detective began to close in on the evasive Mr. Bolton, pointing out that a gentleman would certainly know the location of his own mine.

By the time Captain Stone arrived from the City Prison, Bart would answer no more questions. Hume asked about Mr. Bolton's whereabouts in the last few weeks. Bolton was evasive, especially concerning the first days of November. Hume urged:

> If you will tell me where you were on the 1st, 2nd, 3rd, 4th and 5th days of November, I'll keep the telegraph offices open all night in order to verify your statement and if you will not do that I am going to take you down and lock you up. Bolton responded quickly: "Take me down and lock me up."

The four men, led by Hume, took a hack over to the Webb House to search Mr. Bolton's rooms. They found three valises and a large trunk. The trunk contained three suits; one was ragged and snuff-colored, matching Reason McConnell's description of the Funk Hill bandit's clothing. There were cuffs, collars, and a handkerchief, all waiting to go to the laundry, all bearing the Fxo7 mark. Hume was certain the perfume he smelled on this handkerchief matched the faint scent clinging to the one found on Funk Hill. In one valise was an unfinished letter with handwriting resembling a line of Black Bart's verses (Unfortunately, no information about this letter exists). Near the letter was a Bible with a faint, but still readable inscription:

This precious Bible is presented to Charles E. Boles, First Sergeant, Company B, 116th Illinois Volunteer Infantry, by his wife as New Years gift. God gives us hearts to which His [passage smudged] faith to believe. Decatur, Illinois, 1865.

Black Bart maintained his composure, but cracks began to show. Asked about the laundry mark his response was that other people in the city used the Ware agency; even if the incriminating handkerchief was his, well, someone could have stolen it; he could have lost it and someone else found it. What did they take him for, a stage robber? Yes, they did, and Captain Stone arrested him.

The legal situation concerning Bart's apprehension and detainment is somewhat shocking to us today. There were virtually no civil rights, and concepts such as illegal search and seizure and forcible entry apparently didn't apply. Wells, Fargo detectives were private investigators, not sworn officers, and their only legal right was to make a 'citizens arrest.' But as suspects were considered guilty until proven innocent, Hume could detain Bart if he had 'reasonable cause;' but Captain Stone had to be brought in to make the actual arrest.

His valises were repacked in a large trunk and carried down to the front hall of the Webb House.[47] Now pale and sweating, Bart had to borrow a dollar from a detective to pay his rent; his landlady, Mrs. W. Warner Henry (who also co-owned a millinery and dressmaking parlor at 131 Post Street) couldn't make change for one of the bandit's gold pieces. Though obviously distraught he managed to keep up his genteel pretence, telling her that he was suddenly called away on business. Considering what his business had been for eight years, he wasn't really lying.

A *Chronicle* reporter talked to his landlady the following day. "Can you tell me where he is?" she asked, "He went away very mysteriously last night." Hearing his real identity nearly caused her to faint.

Taken to the Central Police Station, his name was placed on the 'small book,' a secret register for prisoners whose cases were under investigation, not ready for public knowledge. However, the *Call's* beat reporter speculated that someone booked as 'Fleming' back at the City Prison might actually be Black Bart. When the desk sergeant asked his name, Bart replied 'T. Z. Spaulding,' adding another alias to his list. Perhaps the *Call* reporter mixed up Fleming with Spaulding, or perhaps Hume provided the 'Fleming' name to further confound the ever-inquisitive press.

Bart had $160 in gold and $10 in silver on his person. The silver he was allowed to keep.

The law officers involved in the capture of Black Bart.
Front: Tom Cunningham, Ben Thorn, Harry Morse; Rear: A. W. Stone, John Thacker
(Courtesy Wells Fargo Bank)

At some point (possibly even the following day) one of the most famous and endearing stories of Black Bart's humor — that waggish tendency — took place. The detectives produced the derby hat found at Funk Hill and asked Bart to try it on. "Why gentlemen," Bart teased, "it fits very well, doesn't it? And it is a very good hat. Perhaps you'd allow me to buy it from you."

Chapter 17
Calaveras County — *November 14-15, 1883*
Confession

Now began a flurry of activity by the various law enforcement agencies concerned with the Funk Hill holdup. Because Bart had been arrested in a different county, and only a sworn officer could legally take him anywhere, Hume asked San Francisco Police Chief Patrick Crowley to permit Captain Stone to accompany the prisoner to Calaveras County. Hume himself had to go off to Bakersfield on another case, but arranged to get Bart/Bolton/Spaulding to Stockton, then to Milton, where witnesses might identify him. On the morning of the 14th Harry Morse, John Thacker, Captain Stone and Bart took the 7 a.m. ferry to Oakland, then went on by train to Stockton.

It would seem unlikely that the method the party traveled should be in dispute but it is. Some writers have stated the journey was by river boat from Alameda to Stockton; others by train from Oakland to Stockton. Harry Morse said it was by boat. It really doesn't matter, of course, except to point out (again) that nothing about Black Bart is ever perfectly clear. The train seems the logical choice, as the trip on the bay and river took 12 hours; if the boat left Alameda at 8 a.m., it would not have arrived in Stockton until 8 p.m., rather late for what took place.

After receiving a telegraphed request from Hume, Sheriff Thorn had a warrant sworn out in San Andreas against 'C. E. Bolton,' then met the train in Stockton at noon. With Thorn was the hunter Martin, who had run across Bart shortly after the robbery. Thorn held Martin back, asking him to pick Bart out from passengers getting off the train. Thorn and Martin wormed their way through several hundred people who had gathered at Court House Square near the train station after hearing the news that Black Bart might have been captured. "That's the man! That's him!" cried Martin, pointing to the descending figure of Charles Boles. Another story is that when Martin came up to him, Bart "smiled pleasantly, offered his hand and greeted the hunter with composure, saying, 'We meet again, I see.'"

Thorn took over official custody of Bart from Captain Stone, and guided his charge, accompanied by Morse and Thacker, to J. Pitcher Spooner's photography studio, where photographs of the suspect were taken. Bart became indignant, saying they had no right to force him to do that, as he was innocent of any wrongdoing. He objected at first to "looking into the machine, but Sheriff Cunningham talked sweetly to him and he melted." Posed before the camera lens he regained his composure and even joked with the photographer, "Will that thing go off? I'd like to go off, myself."

Six photographs of Black Bart are known to exist. Two sets of two each might have been taken by different photographers, or J. Pitcher Spooner could have taken both sets. The real money was made by I. W. Taber's photo gallery at 8 Montgomery Street in San Francisco. Black Bart's photograph "in front of a Montgomery street gallery is daily surrounded by an eager crowd." Photographers sold 'studio cards' to the public, and it was common practice to copy and sell other photographers' work. A November 13th, 1883 letter from Hume to Wells, Fargo Detective Charles Aull says: "They wire me that they have taken first class photographs of him and will send me 2 or 3 dozen ..." The Wells, Fargo & Co. General Cash Books list payouts of $18.00 to Spooner and $45.50 to Taber for photographs.[48]

The third and fourth photographs appear to be the same, except for the bowler, but are actually different. An original of the latter has not been located. The shot without the bowler has been reproduced often, at times heavily retouched by an artist and captioned 'authentic.' The fifth photograph (and a similar sixth one not located), was probably a 'mug' shot taken at City Prison in San Francisco.

The photograph most often reprinted shows a dapper man wearing a low crown derby hat, Cumberland broadcloth overcoat with its silk lapels and satin lining almost concealing his snowflake Harris tweed suit, the diamond stickpin fixing the cravat at his throat, cane in hand, with his left foot confidently planted a bit ahead of the right. Would you have done mining business with this man? Probably.

Bart's good humor continued for a while. When Sheriff Cunningham served him with a summons drawn up by Wells, Fargo to recover what he still had in the way of valuables, Bart asked "This don't cost anything, does it ?" The Sheriff replied that it was free, to which the robber responded pleasantly "Well, I'm taking free things now, so I'll take this."

A *Stockton Daily Independent* reporter gave Bart a complimentary newspaper and spoke with the prisoner . Bart thanked him, commenting that "he was travelling with a party of fine fellows, as they pay all his expenses and keep him supplied with the delicacies of the season." The reporter went on to write:

> He is very talkative and while with the officers he keeps them laughing constantly. Bart is a very intelligent man and being extremely fond of good reading he took pleasure in reading yesterday morning's INDEPENDENT. While holding the paper out a considerable distance, as is his habit in reading, J. C. Williams [the reporter] looked in the wicket and surveyed him. Bart raised his

Charles Boles — Black Bart
(Courtesy Wells Fargo Bank)

eyes from the paper and pleasantly asked Mr. Williams: "Do you think you have ever seen me before?" Mr. Williams answered the genial highwayman that he was a stranger... The prisoner was wounded while in the army in the right hip, and the effects of the wound still affect his walking slightly.

After a night in the Stockton jail Bart was taken by train to Milton, where another crowd had gathered. "Look," he said, "The whole town has turned out to meet me. I guess they'll know me when they see me again." Reason McConnell was brought up to him while Morse engaged Bart in seemingly innocent conversation. McConnell had only seen a bandit wearing a floursack mask, so all he could say was that this man's general build resembled that of the road agent. But hearing Bart speak, McConnell interrupted Morse: "That's enough! I could recognize that voice anywhere."

A horse and buckboard were hired from the McDonald & Mead Livery Stable in Milton and the four men drove to the county seat in San Andreas. The crowd at the courthouse momentarily mistook the adequately-dressed Morse for the highwayman and the nattily-attired Bart for the detective. Bart was locked into the San Andreas jail and the lawmen went out for dinner. At 7 p.m. Morse began an intense interrogation in the jail that he hoped would finally break down the criminal and produce a confession. For over a century the accepted version of what happened that night has been an account the detective first gave to the *San Francisco Call* shortly after Bart's sentencing, and repeated in 1905 for the *Chronicle*. According to Morse, for five hours he bombarded Bart with questions: the laundry mark; the derby hat; Martin's identification at the Stockton wharf; the evidence found at Funk Hill; 'Bolton's' inability to precisely locate the mine he claimed to own; the handwriting on the letter in the valise; the wounded hand; the man's many aliases; his presence at Grandma Rolleri's a few days before the robbery.

With each new question Morse asked his prisoner how important he thought that item would be at the trial — there would be a trial, and soon. Some Bart responded to, dispassionately weighing their possible importance. At other times a question would set him off on Civil War reminiscences or biblical quotations. Morse recalled that "he would branch off on Bible matters, in which he seemed well posted. He thought that Moses had a great deal of pluck to reprove the Lord for his harsh dealing with the children of Israel on different occasions." Finally, near midnight, Bart himself asked a question: "Mind you, I do not admit that I committed this robbery. But what benefit would it be to the man who did acknowledge it?"

This was the crack Morse had been waiting for, but the detective gave no sign that he sensed the highwayman was weakening. The trial itself, he explained, would bring out the fact that the accused had committed

Charles Boles — Black Bart
(Courtesy California State Library)

numerous other crimes, but "if he made restitution and should go into court and plead guilty, it would save the county the great expense of a trial, and it would no doubt be taken into consideration by the court."

Morse knew he had Black Bart, whose 'list' at Wells, Fargo included twenty-two stage holdups. He had seen the bandit's lifestyle, probably concluding (though his account of the case doesn't mention this insight) that the booty from previous holdups was gone — for rent at the Webb House, to good food and stylish clothing, perhaps to a chippy or two — and Wells, Fargo would never get it back. But Bart couldn't have spent almost $5000 from the Funk Hill robbery. Most of that money could be recovered. So Morse, according to his own story, gradually spun out his line.

Bart wanted to know just what 'mitigation of circumstances' might imply. "Would it be possible for [the robber] to get clear altogether?" No, Morse responded, but if all of the criminal's robberies were brought into evidence at a trial, he'd probably get a life sentence.

At this Bart showed his first violent reaction. "I want you to understand that I am not going to San Quentin Prison! I'll die first!"

As Joseph Henry Jackson notes, Morse did not point out that the hypothetical highwayman had now given way to 'I.' Instead Morse hammered at the point just planted in the prisoner's psyche. The hypothetical robber should understand how easy it was to prove his last crime, one he was definitely going to go to jail for. But if the loot was returned, and he pled guilty, the judge might look favorably on him for not forcing an expensive trial — where his other crimes would be brought up. Some of those might be hard to prove, but enough evidence existed to get him a long sentence. Pleading guilty to the Funk Hill robbery meant no trial, no mention of other robberies — and with restitution ...

Bart didn't fold quietly. He complained about witnesses. "These men may all come up and testify just as you say. Men are apt to commit perjury, and courts are apt to be prejudiced, and whether a man is guilty or not he has to suffer the consequences."

It was half past midnight. After five hours of intensive, masterful grilling, Harry Morse broke his man. He hadn't admitted anything yet, but Morse called in Stone and Thorn — Bart would lead them to the loot from the Sonora to Milton holdup. With a feeling of relief, Bart got up and sighed "Well, let's go after it."

Thus far the story of Black Bart's confession is according to Harry Morse. Sheriff Ben Thorn's version, however, was quite different. In a letter written in January, 1884, Thorn accuses Morse not only of attempting to grab all the public glory associated with capturing such a notorious outlaw, but also of looking for the entire $2000 reward. Thorn wrote:

Charles Boles — Black Bart
(Courtesy California State Library)

After talking five hours and a half with [Bart] of 'Moses and the children of Israel' you withdrew in an exhausted condition — Capt. Stone and myself being more familiar with the evidence in the case against B. B. than with the exploits of Moses, soon demonstrated to Black Bart that his case was hopeless and to us alone (you being out of the room entirely) he made his confession & proposal to "go after it."

Harry did you glean a particle of evidence from any source in the world that could have had any possible weight in inducing him to make the surrender?

The testimony of Martin, which Thacker and myself discovered and furnished, the testimony of Mrs. C[ampbell] and others at Angel's [Camp] which I procured on my visit there on the 5th, the handkerchief, which Mr. Case and others found behind the rocks near the scene of the robbery, the laundry mark which was traced out by an experienced laundryman of San Francisco, the attaching of the moneys found in his possession, by W.F. & C. which deprived him of means with which to employ counsel, are the chief causes of his relinquishing his ill gotten gains and occasioned the oft-quoted remark of "let us go after it —"

When you indulge in so much venomous satire regarding my participation in the capture of B. B. you should have remembered some of the wild improbable statements which you caused to be published at the time, and in which you figured as the hero and which threw a decided 'glamour' over the whole business of the capture which we allowed to pass unnoticed & without offering a reply.[49]

Though the *Examiner* obtained the letter, and portions were printed to embarass Morse, for some reason crucial passages controverting Morse's account of how he 'broke' Black Bart in the San Andreas jail cell did not see print. Apparently the *Examiner* was more interested in showing how Morse tried to cheat Thorn out of his reward share than in proving him a liar.

Relative to his confession and sentence, Bart said that no one was present when he acknowledged his crime except Sheriff Thorn and Captain Stone. Harry Morse had talked with him for nearly six hours, urging him to confess. Thorn told him that the chain of evidence was complete, that:

He could not beat the game... "Besides all he told me," Bart said, "I know he could easily obtain more evidence and I confessed. I was glad to do so, for I didn't want any more suspense. If I had made a fight, my sentence might have been twenty years and I would have come out of jail a broken-down old man. As it is, I will be less than 52 when I come out, and will have a chance to redeem myself."

Whatever happened during the grilling, Bart confessed to a lot during the moonlit 20-mile carriage ride from San Andreas to Funk Hill. "This was

Charles Boles — Black Bart
(The Pony Express)

where I committed my first robbery. I wonder if this will be my last," he remembered thinking, while waiting for Reason McConnell's stagecoach.

He had Morse's word he would only be tried for the latest holdup, but talked around the issue for a while, reminiscing about robberies committed before 1879. Richard Dillon, Hume's biographer, theorized that Bart had a faulty knowledge of the statute of limitations. Another reason could have been his desire to cooperate with Morse and Wells, Fargo; with his guilty plea and sentencing coming up within days, he helped them close the books on their backlog of unsolved cases.

Hume circulated a list of twenty-two robberies he believed Black Bart had committed. His revised 1888 list shows twenty-seven, plus the ill-fated twenty-eighth (Bart confessed to a twenty-ninth robbery in San Quentin).

Perhaps the compelling reason Bart pled guilty to the one robbery was his fear of the Postal Department. He had rifled the U.S. mail during every holdup; convicted of any other robbery, he might be prosecuted by the government.

Once started, Bart couldn't stop. He talked at length about his preparations for the holdup. He had gone to the Patterson Mine in Tuttletown and learned through casual conversation the date and time the amalgam would be shipped. He had walked the stage route from Tuttletown, looking for the most likely spot for the holdup. He had stayed one night at Reynolds Ferry, forgetting that travellers don't ask for room keys at country inns, unless they have something to hide. He'd found his perfect site, exactly where he'd robbed his first stage eight years earlier, and set up a 'sleeping camp,' as he called it, nearby. He brewed coffee during darkness, when a small campfire could be concealed, its smoke unseen.

He had timed the stage for several mornings. Once the territory had been scouted, he had moved his camp (the one the posse found) nearer the stage road.

Three days before the amalgam was to be shipped, he spotted another man stepping from the brush, with a kerchief covering his lower face. Perhaps the man was a competitor in the road agent business. Bart had two ideas, he joked. He would let the other highwayman rob the stage, then hold the man up himself. Or, if the pickings were slim, he could capture the man, turn him over to Wells, Fargo, and collect a reward. The lawmen did not share Bart's sense of humor. But the unknown man vanished, and Bart was left to rob the stage.

It was now about 6:45 in the morning. As Bart finished the conducted tour of his campsites, the Sonora to Milton stage plodded by, driven by Reason McConnell. One can only imagine the looks that passed between the two men, having met so recently under such different circumstances.

Asked about his poetry, Bart wouldn't comment on its quality, but proffered he enjoyed 'versifying.' He'd planned to leave a new poem at the Funk Hill robbery, and in his interview with the *Call*, Morse revealed that Bart recited part of it to him. Alas for history, no one was interested enough to write it down or ask for a copy.

Bart took particular pleasure in describing his relationship with the San Francisco Police Department. His normal dining place, the New York Bakery, was only two blocks from Central Station in City Hall, and was frequented by off-duty policemen. He named several, specifically Dave Scannell, "who had been a nice fellow." Once his coat had been stolen; when Detective Edward Byram recovered it for him, Bart tipped the officer for his help. He was startled when asked if he hadn't been afraid to take such chances, considering his activities: "Why, no, they didn't know who I was. I never associated with any but good people, and none of them ever dreamed what my business was!"

Then Bart led the lawmen to the butt of a hollow log under a buckeye bush, where lay, disguised by dirt and leaves, a bag with $4100 in gold amalgam, consigned to the Shelby Smelting & Lead Co. of Stockton; a package with $330.25 in coin; another with $60 in gold dust. After placing the recovered treasure safely in the wagon, Bart and the detectives drove to Copperopolis. The express shipment was taken to San Andreas and handed over to Wells, Fargo agent E. C. Roworth. Morse wired Wells, Fargo's Division Superintendent, Leonard F. Rowell (Hume had just arrived in Bakersfield):

> Black Bart throws up the sponge. Stone, Thorn and myself have received the stolen treasure. Inform Thacker.

Morse and Captain Stone returned to San Francisco, while Sheriff Thorn escorted Bart back to San Andreas.

Chapter 18
Calaveras County
Friday/Saturday, November 16-17, 1883
The Sentence

Bart spent the rest of what remained of that night, and the next, in cell No. 3 of San Andreas' brick jailhouse. On Friday morning he was taken before Judge P. H. Kean, where he waived bail and pleaded guilty to the November 3rd robbery. The following day in Judge C. V. Gottschalk's courtroom he waived the right to a jury trial, again entered a guilty plea, to the Funk Hill holdup — but intimated it was his first offense — and denied being Black Bart. The *Calaveras Weekly Citizen* commented that this speech "seemed to have no effect whatever upon the Judge, and was considered rather weak by the lookers-on;" but in fact the law honored the understanding which Harry Morse all but guaranteed Bart — a light sentence in return for the amalgam and the guilty plea. Charles E. Bolton (as he insisted his name was) was sentenced to six years in prison.

Looking through James Hume's published catalogue of crimes against Wells, Fargo the sentence seems about average — for a one-time offender who cooperated with the law. The Goodwin Act, renewed by the California Legislature in 1880, allowed months of credit deducted from a court sentence for good prison behavior. For a six-year sentence twenty-two months might be credited, leaving the prisoner an incarceration of four years, two months. The *Citizen* was probably correct that Bart "seemed rather pleased with the sentence."

He was transported back to the San Francisco City Prison to spend one night before going to San Quentin. On the first leg of the journey, from San Andreas to Milton, Sheriff Thorn allowed him to travel without handcuffs or chains.

According to Mrs. D. A. Ramsden of Ahwahnee,[50] his fellow passengers were a Chinese gentleman and a Miss Bunt, next to whom Bart sat:

> He was a model prisoner all during the trip to Milton and gave no trouble to Thorn, who placed no restrictions upon his movements, but allowed him to leave the stage at the different stage stations where they stopped to water the horses or change them for fresh ones… At one place he went into a store and bought a large bag of candy which he presented to Miss Bunt, which she, of course, accepted in the spirit in which it was given.

One wonders whether Mrs. Ramsden's maiden name was Bunt.

Bart and Thorn took the train to Stockton, then another to Oakland, arriving at the San Francisco ferry slip at 8 a.m. Then Thorn, accompanied by Morse and either Thacker or Stone, "took their friend to a fashionable restaurant and banqueted him for over two hours, regardless of the impatience of his waiting friends at the prison."[51] Then on to City Prison. As news of Black Bart's presence in the city spread, a crowd gathered and when the brigand passed through the throng "there could be heard exclamations of 'That's the man! Why, I've seen him a thousand times.'" Those with legitimate business, or who claimed it, or who looked presentable enough, were admitted to the prison booking area; the remainder of the swelling crowd milled about in the hall or outside.

The first to push her way to the front as 'Bolton's' name was registered, accompanied by an unidentified female friend, was his faithful landlady. The meeting was evidently unexpected by Bart, who exclaimed with surprise, "You here!"

"Weeping copiously, [Mrs. Henry] fell upon his neck and cried, "Oh, Mr. Bolton, I never would have believed it if you had not confessed to it."

One writer poignantly described the fifteen minute conversation:

Asking permission from prisonkeeper Sergeant Patrick McDonough to see him was a tall handsome lady clothed in a sealskin, her handkerchief to her eyes to stop the flow of tears. She was his landlady, who looked reproachfully at the worthy crowd, and conversed with her friend. They exchanged a few whispers together, saying the best of friends must part and so the stately landlady shed a few more tears, more heartily than the first, pressed a long lingering press upon her robber friend's hand, and left a dead and awful silence pervading the prison, only to be broken by the prisonkeeper's quick and skillful turn of the locks that in another moment separated her from Black Bart for six years.[52]

That is not exactly what happened, as Bart was placed in cell No. 1 of the row known as 'the hole in the wall,' and the door left open so visitors could enter at will. For two hours he received the press and public cordially, and "appeared pleased to think that he had become, as it were, the hero of the hour." He regaled the press with the story of the other potential holdup man, whom he felt he had frightened off.

The photographs taken a few days earlier in Stockton had become best-sellers, and not a few San Franciscans were surprised to see the image of a longtime acquaintance, now identified as the most famous of road agents. To their credit some old friends of Charles Bolton showed up to greet him. The gesture moved Bart; to one he said, "I cannot call you my friend now. After this I have no friends."

Asked why he hadn't forced the driver to break open the express box, he replied:

It would have taken him three weeks, and I was in a hurry just then. There was no time to waste. As it was, I was surprised that I got through so quickly. When I got through I was weak, so weak a child could have captured me, and after I got in the brush I could hardly walk. Still, I made these things [indicating his legs] go along very lively. If there had been anyone behind that gun who knew how to use it, I would be a dead man today. Indeed, I am sorry there was no Carver behind it.

He was referring to W. F. 'Doc' Carver, a famous sharp-shooter in Buffalo Bill's first Wild West Show, that had just opened in Omaha in May, 1883. Then Bart commented wistfully:

I only wish that one of the balls fired after me from the Copperopolis stage had been well directed. I laughed at them as they whistled by me then. No one knows how deeply I feel my disgrace. If the man with the gun had killed me I would have been buried there, and the world would never have known who I was. I had a presentiment that I was going to danger when I saw the stage coming down the hill, but once in the road with my gun at my shoulder my curiosity overcame me, and I felt bound to see what was in that box.[53]

A bystander blurted out, "Ain't you sorry for what you've done, Mr. Bart?"
Bart became moody:

I do not care for the years of imprisonment, nor shovelling sand or whatever I will do at San Quentin, but the shame of my old friends finding me out hurts me more than all. There isn't a man in this city can say he ever saw me do wrong or ever met me in questionable places. I never drink, smoke or chew; all my friends are gentlemen, and I never associated with other than gentlemen. To be sure, I can't claim to be perfect. They do say I will rob a stage occasionally. But no one can say that I ever raised my gun to do anyone harm. I merely carried a gun to intimidate the driver. As for using it — why, for all the gold that road ever carried I would not shoot a man. I could easily have killed that driver while he was popping at me. And it was a loud call — two bullets passing through my clothing.

Bart spoke well of his jailers, presumably with sincerity, and the now wry raconteur reserved special words for Sheriff Thorn:

I never before took to men whose company was forced on me, but Mr. Thorn, Mr. Stone and the gentlemen with them did everything in their power to make me comfortable. In fact, I grew so attached to them I could not stay away from them. When I went to San Andreas, I stopped at Mr. Thorn's hotel to be near him and because it is a temperance house; and I have never been in a better-kept hotel. When I went to bed at night I never took the trouble to bolt the doors. I knew they would attend to all that.

He continued to deny being Black Bart: "In every paper I pick up I see those big black headlines, Black Bart. Why, when I wake up in the morning I expect to see in big letters on the wall of my cell, Black Bart. I don't know but what they are here now," he queried, scrutinizing the autographs of 'Wheeling Red' and 'Texas Pete,' two predecessors in the cell. Obviously, if he ever acknowledged his road identity publicly (though he was beginning to have some fun tiptoeing around the subject: "They say I rob a stage occasionally"), Bart thought he could still be tried for some of the earlier holdups (the statute of limitations had run out on the robberies prior to October, 1880).

While talking to the scribbling press, Bart stopped in mid-sentence when San Francisco Police Detective Chris Cox appeared at the cell door: "There's a man I've seen a thousand times!" "You bet you have, old man," Cox responded as the two men shook hands. Then Bart laughed, reminding the abashed but goodnatured law officer of the many tables they had shared at the New York Bakery.

Finally, around 10 a.m., Thomas Ware, the unwitting agent of Bart's capture, arrived. The two men shook hands, "and held their hands locked for quite a long time," and Ware congratulated Bart on looking well. Suddenly the outlaw seemed to wilt. Tears filled his eyes, and he gasped out "By God, I can't choke this thing down." Sensing that the prisoner now wished privacy, the visitors withdrew.

For up to two hours the throng outside the jail had waited for a glimpse of the famous robber. When police conducted a swarthy man with a wild black beard in a deerskin coat to a waiting van, the crowd was satisfied they had seen Black Bart and rapidly dispersed. They had actually seen a ward of the court being escorted to the Home for the Care of Inebriates.

The Town Crier columnist for the weekly business and mining newspaper, *San Francisco Newsletter and California Advertiser*, added some levity to the day:

> The arrest of Black Bart, the hero of twenty-three stage-coach robberies, appears to develop the fact, that in the placid intervals during which he was not employed in the cheerful pastime of leveling double-barreled shot-guns at stage-drivers and corraling treasure-boxes, he lived in San Francisco and passed for a mining man. This apparently disarmed suspicion where naturally enough it ought to have excited it. However, all persons who call themselves mining men are not necessarily bad, yet the probability is that the next time one of Wells, Fargo's stages is robbed every one known to the police as a speculator in Arizona or Nevada mining securities will be summarily arrested. We cheerfully advise the next stage-robber who may succeed Black Bart and prefer to spend the intervals between his hauls in this burgh, to let it be understood quietly that he is either a retired pork-packer from Cincinnati, or agent for the Pacific coast for P. T. Barnum, traveling in search of Aztecs for the show.

Charles Boles — Black Bart
(Courtesy California State Library)

That night, while Bart lay in a San Francisco jail cell, Hume, Morse, Thorn and Thacker celebrated their success at Ned's, a fashionable San Francisco restaurant (expensive, too — the feast cost Wells, Fargo $18.75 — probably $200 in 1992 purchasing power). The following morning his last known photograph was taken, showing a more gaunt, considerably older-looking man than was seen only a week earlier. Then Sheriff Thorn escorted Bart to the Marin ferry, and to San Quentin.

J. B. HUME,
Special Officer.

OFFICE, ROOM 1, WELLS, FARGO & CO'S BUILDING,
Sansome and Halleck Streets.

RESIDENCE, 810 McAllister Street.

Wells, Fargo & Co's Express,

San Francisco, Nov. 26th, 1883

To Agents of Wells, Fargo & Co.

Since the conviction and incarceration of CHARLES E. BOLES, *alias* CHARLES E. BOLTON, *alias* "BLACK BART, the Po 8," for robbing WELLS, FARGO & CO'S EXPRESS, numerous inquiries have been received from Sheriffs and other officers, inquiring as to the identity of BOLTON *alias* "BLACK BART." This inquiry has doubtless been occasioned by the statement of the prisoner when pleading guilty before the Court, to a particular robbery—that it was his first offence, and that he was not "BLACK BART." All officers will readily understand the reason of such a statement, viz: To excite judicial clemency. The man CHAS. E. BOLES *alias* BOLTON (of whom we herewith append photograph and description) is " Black Bart, the Po 8."

DESCRIPTION.

Received November 21st, 1883.

Number of Commitment—11,046.

Education—Liberal.

Nativity—New York.

Crime—Robbery.

Term—Six years.

County from—Calaveras.

Age—50 years.

Occupation—*Mining.*

Height, 5 feet 8 inches, in stockings.

Complexion—Light.

Color of Eyes—Blue.

Color of Hair—Iron Gray.

Heavy Mustache—Nearly white.

Heavy Imperial—Nearly white.

Size of Foot—No. 6.

Weight—160 lbs.

Size of Hat—7¼.

Does not use Tobacco in any form.

Does not use Intoxicating Liquors.

Does not use Opium.

Respectfully

B. B.

A notice sent to Wells, Fargo agencies explaining the identity of Black Bart.
(Courtesy Wells Fargo Bank)

174

Chapter 19
San Francisco — *November-December, 1883*
Controversy

Six years in prison may have been a fair sentence for a one time road agent, but Black Bart (almost nobody doubted 'Bolton' was Black Bart, despite his denials) had robbed over twenty stagecoaches. Though he turned out to be a jolly man with winning ways, his sinister shadow, celebrated through the press and local legend, would soon become a Sunday supplement staple. The scourge of Wells, Fargo was finally behind bars, but his story furnished the San Francisco press with a controversial topic for years.

There was the subject of the reward. How much was to be collected for his apprehension? Who was to get it? A *Chronicle* reporter, multiplying the first $800 reward total (Wells, Fargo, $300; the State of California, $300; the United States Government, $200, for the pillaged mail sacks) by the holdups Bart was originally thought to have committed (23), came up with $18,400. This figure failed to take into account either the statute of limitations or Bart's single conviction.

For nabbing Bart on the streets of San Francisco and (at least according to his own account) breaking his will in the San Andreas jail, Harry Morse received $228.75, plus $99.50 in expenses (included was board at the Russ House in San Francisco) plus $20 he paid to the laundry bookkeeper. As company employees neither James Hume nor John Thacker could claim any reward, although the latter was paid $65 in unnamed expenses. Sheriff Thorn could and did, receiving the same sum as Morse, $228.75. Besides $105 paid to driver McConnell, hunter T. P. Martin was granted $20, while Captain Stone received $100 in expenses.

It has not been possible to determine just how Wells, Fargo arrived at the figure of $228.75 each for Morse and Thorn. A typed copy of Wells, Fargo's General Cash Books covering the period October, 1883 through February, 1884 lists these rewards specifically, along with the others. But $561.50 does not compute into any of the reward figures published. Wells, Fargo's policy was to offer as a reward one-fourth of the total of any monies recovered from a robbery. Morse (if he was not considered a quasi-Wells, Fargo employee) and Thorn should have been eligible for $540.97 apiece ($4327.77÷4=$1081.94÷2=$540.97). Deducting all the expenses, or parts of them, does not come up with either $228.75 or $561.50, no matter how the pie is sliced.[54]

175

Wells, Fargo & Co.'s General Cash Books listed the total expenses and losses in the Black Bart case as $4866.50, less bullion and treasure recovered, $4327.77, for a total loss of $538.73. Additional expenses were: $62.50 for the two photographers; $5 for R. F. Gallagher, shorthand reporter in the examination of C. E. Bolton; McDonald & Mead of Milton, $5 for horse and driver for Thacker in pursuit of the Sonora State robber; McDonald & Mead, $5 for horse and buckboard for Thacker; John H. Olbrick, $2 for repairs to iron stage safe; $9.50 United Carriage Company, J. B. Hume.[55]

Wells, Fargo could close its books on Bart with satisfaction. After paying out rewards and deducting all expenses, the company had incurred a net debit of only $653.23 to catch 'the gentleman bandit' and bring him to trial.

Another person was rewarded after Black Bart's capture. Donna McCreary, who provided the first accurate description of the outlaw five years earlier, was now twenty years old, the bride of a Mendocino County neighbor, George Vann. While Bart was in City Prison, by coincidence the new Mrs. Vann was in San Francisco, staying at the Hancock House. Hume sent an elegant silk dress and other gifts to her, courtesy of Wells, Fargo & Co. The cost of Mrs. Vann's dress is not listed as a reward figure in Wells, Fargo's General Cash Books. According to a newspaper report these gifts were sent by various Wells, Fargo officers.

~

As if $18,400 wasn't bad enough as a mistaken reward total, this sum passed into legend in countless newspaper and magazine articles as the aggregate amount Black Bart had stolen during the eight years he preyed on the express company. In fact, during his entire career the highwayman never even approached this figure. He might have topped it if his attack on the Oroville stage in 1882 hadn't been shortcircuited by George Hackett's quick trigger finger, as that haul would have been $18,000 (perhaps $23,000) and more. By far the most he ever got away with was $4700 from his last holdup, and he had to give $4100 of that back.

A completely accurate total of what Bart stole can never be established. Wells, Fargo agents were usually exact to the penny as to how much was in the express boxes, but often no figure was reported to the public. The government apparently never tabulated how much he took from registered letters. The road agent's total from robbing stagecoaches probably wasn't even $5,000 — a far cry from the individual $50,000 holdups of the 1850s and 60s. Considering his thirteen year career — eight years as a bandit and almost five years in prison — Charles Boles might have made more money if he had been a school teacher.

Hume knew what Bart had stolen from Wells, Fargo; if $5,000 is a fair estimate, the decision to bargain for the $4100 missing from the Funk Hill holdup seems logical. It represented about what Wells, Fargo had lost to Bart, money long since spent for meals at the New York Bakery, clothing befitting a mining executive, transportation to holdup sites. The money was gone, but the company could close its books on some earlier holdups (including a few unconnected to Bart before), and be rid of their most pesky gadfly — for at least four years, possibly forever, if his arrest and time in San Quentin impressed him enough.

There was also the fact that Bart, once he regained his usual control, was a charming, middle-aged gentleman. Banks have never been the world's most popular institutions. Even if he was not necessarily a Robin Hood, a courteous bandit who refused ladies' purses

The Wasp, San Franciso's literary magazine, put a romanticized Black Bart on its cover.

and gentleman travellers' wallets — who liberated money from a rich monolith — was something of a popular figure.

From its founding, Wells, Fargo & Company was more respected in California than most other financial organizations. Full value was given for the gold dust it bought; full restitution for valuables entrusted to its care; in general the company behaved as television commercials portray its early days. But Wells, Fargo was not immune to the criticism levied at the powerful by the public:

> In some quarters Wells Fargo express charges were regarded as exorbitant taxes exacted by a ruthless business monopoly... Consequently, the activities of highwaymen were tolerated by too many otherwise honest Mother Lode citizens. They saw these affairs simply as instances of one thief robbing another.[56]

The *Tuolumne Independent and Oakdale Wheat Grower* suggested "that by fair treatment, the company could gain sympathy of the people who live in the vicinity of the stage operations and make stage robbery a more dangerous pastime." When Hume asked a Milton resident what he'd do if he saw a stage being robbed, the man replied, "Why, I'd turn my back and walk away."[57]

Freight charges actually seem low, considering that the goods were fully insured, with instant reimbursement if lost. In 1875 the express charge to transport a bag of gold coins worth $300 from Sonora to San Francisco was $1.75; $100 worth of gold cost $1.00. Perhaps more subtle grievances existed against the express company.

So the prospect of Black Bart on trial might not have been pleasant for Hume or Morse (who could have changed their minds after seeing the robber's sorry showing in the San Andreas courtroom). The Wells, Fargo detectives offered what they thought was the best deal for all concerned, and they were probably right.

But the press didn't think so. William Randolph Hearst's *Examiner* charged Hume with a 'perversion of justice.' Joseph Henry Jackson suggests the *Examiner* was anxious to paint Hume in a bad light, not so much because a deal had been made with Bart in exchange for a lighter sentence (though that was the ostensible reason for the paper's 'high moral tone'), but because Hearst's reporters had not been let in on the case when Bart was arrested. The robber was booked into the San Francisco County Jail under a false name (besides the one he gave himself), then spirited out before dawn the next day to Calaveras County. Nary a Hearst newshound was in sight (or a reporter from anywhere else, for that matter, though both the *Chronicle* and the *Call* got information the night of the 13th that 'Mr. Fleming' was, in fact, Black Bart). Eventually, Hearst tired of badgering Hume and Morse, and the Black Bart case died down temporarily.

But Harry Morse and Ben Thorn had their own private war, and the *Examiner* got wind of it, probably thanks to a leak by Thorn himself. Even though Thorn's one surviving letter[58] quotes two Morse letters in full, the exact situation is still difficult to reconstruct.

In December, 1883 Wells, Fargo had approved the rewards of $228.75 each to Morse and Thorn, but these had not yet been paid, nor had the State of California rewards (the smaller rewards had been given out). On December 14th, 1883 Morse wrote to the Calaveras County Clerk asking whether Thorn would be claiming part of the State reward. To Thorn, who apparently felt Morse self-aggrandized events prior and subsequent to Black Bart's capture, it must have seemed that Morse was now trying to claim all the money as well as the entire credit; the sheriff fired back a missive calling Morse "mean, cowardly, [and] unmannerly." Morse repeated his request, this time directly to Thorn, demanding "upon what grounds you back your claim?"

Thorn's answer was that on the day he had delivered Black Bart to San Quentin the two lawmen had agreed to divide the Wells, Fargo reward; that Morse had renounced any claim to the State reward, saying if anyone deserved it, John Thacker did.

In a December 23rd letter Morse questioned whether Thorn deserved any part of the reward, citing the sheriff's mistaken circulation of the 'Italian's' description, alleging also that Thorn possessed the famous handkerchief for over a day before Thacker discovered the laundry mark (in fact, Morse revealed his own ignorance of the events in Calaveras County; the handkerchief was in agent Case's custody for most of that time, not Thorn's).

Thorn called Morse's latest dispatch "impudent, insolent, malicious and malignant...venomous *false in detail*." He provided his own chronicle of events, asking Morse at one point:

> What, pray, did *you* have to to do with the arrest more that to invite the man to walk down to Hume's office? Who took B. B. into custody and escorted him to the Station House? Who escorted him to San Andreas if not the man who arrested him, Captain Stone?

However, then Thorn himself fell into a bit of histrionic memory loss. Toward the end of his long letter (after agreeing Thacker certainly deserved part of the reward but concluding Morse did nothing except stand in front of the right laundry at the right time), Thorn claimed that he drove hunter T. P. Martin to Stockton "at my own expense," and returned Martin home "at my own expense." In fact, the sheriff received $273.90 from Calaveras County for expenses incurred with Black Bart: a mileage fee of $218.70 for his travels from November 3rd to 14th; carriage hire for both Martin and the midnight drive to Funk Hill; meals for the prisoner and guards at San Andreas Jail; even fifty cents repayment for paying a barber to shave Bart.

The *Chronicle* jested about the controversy:

> In the quarrel the truth seemed likely to leak out after all. Police Captain Stone, who had kept quiet, seemed to be the man entitled to the reward. It is not on record that Mr. Morse recovered from this literary walloping sufficiently to take his pen in hand to let Mr. Thorn know that he was alive, and hoped he was the same. Neither does it appear that anybody wanted to fight. Perhaps it was all Pickwickian.

On December 29th, 1883 the Controllers Department of the State of California sent a warrant for $300 to Harry Morse (stating as the kind of service the 'arrest & conviction of Black Barth'). Morse kept quiet about it, probably not wishing to fuel any more sparks, either with Sheriff Thorn or about himself.

Chapter 20
Marin County — *November, 1883-January, 1888*
Prison

On November 21, 1883 the doors of San Quentin closed on prisoner No. 11,046, Charles Bolton. But despite his use of an alias, his real identity soon became known to his wife, children, and relatives. The inscription in the Bible found at the Webb House became a lead for the *Call* and the paper telegraphed to Decatur, Illinois for information. From there Mary Boles was traced to Hannibal, via New Oregon. Or Mary might have learned about the story and contacted California authorities herself; a *Chronicle* article about Bart's capture was reprinted in the *St. Louis Globe-Democrat* on November 20, 1883. Boles himself told prison officials his birthplace was Jefferson County, New York. On December 20th he wrote to his younger brother Hiram:

> Yes its only <u>too true</u>. I am your brother lost & in disgrace—
> let this suffice for the present.
> Your once loved brother
>
> C. E. Boles

This must have been the lowest point of his life, worse even than the day and night his will was broken by the detectives. For whatever reason, he had decided to become a dead man to his loved ones, to pass through life in an assumed garb of success, close friend to no one, acquaintance to many, a failure in everything except holding up stagecoaches and receiving San Francisco's respect as a professional gentleman. Not only had he failed in that, but suddenly his failure was again known to his wife and family, his anonymity gone.

However, his mercurial temperament allowed him to recover from the depression and shame fairly quickly (though not permanently). On January 10, 1884, only three weeks after the forlorn note to his brother, he wrote to Reason McConnell:

> You will please pardon me for this long delay in acknowledging your 'kind compliments' so hastily sent me on the 3rd of November last, but rest fully assured, my dear sir, that you are remembered, and with nothing but the most friendly feelings as a man having done your whole duty to your employer, yourself, and the community at large. I have often admired your fine qualities as a driver, and only regret that I am unable to compliment you on your

marksmanship. I would like to hear from you, however, if consistent with your wishes, and, my dear sir, you have my best wishes for an unmolested, prosperous and happy drive through life.

Bart signed the letter "I am, dear sir, yours in haste," and added as a P.S. "But not quite in so much of a hurry as on a former occasion." There is no record that McConnell answered the letter, nor did Jimmy Rolleri, who according to family tradition received a similar one.

And after almost fifteen years of silence the husband and wife began to exchange letters again. They had a considerable correspondence, but only a few letters have survived. The great-grandaughter of Charles and Mary Boles related:

They destroyed most of his letters. Mother said she found her [Frances Lillian Boles Dillingham, the youngest daughter] crying one day when she was seventeen and she [Frances Lillian] told her about him [Black Bart]. We learned after we were grown. [Present-day descendants of other Bowles family members were also not told about Black Bart until they were teenagers].

The first letter, probably written in October, 1884 (the date is smudged), is missing a page:

My dear & loving family,
   I have received two letters, one from MaMa & one from Ida since I wrote last and the Photograph of My whole darling little family in one group. Great Heavens, only think, all on earth, yet dear to me, grouped together in this little circle, a union of tender loving hearts, to benefit & happiness of all. What a Magnificent picture & what a holy lesson it teaches. An example of affection love and constancy rarely equaled & never excelled & it is impossible with the language at my command to give you full credit for the heroic exertions put forth for the promotion of each other's happiness under the most discouraging circumstances & it is especially so with You My own loving Mary, for you had the care & responsibility of training & guiding our tender lives in the direction you desired them to be taken & of each other & for this I am so profoundly thankful that I can never find words to fully express My gratitude. My darlings when I got those Photos, I could do nothing but sit & look & gaze at them for hours. I would try to put them away & the first thing I would know I would be gazing into those dear eyes again that seemed as though they must speak and let me know how deeply I had wronged them. Although after careful search I could find nothing in their expressions except a look of "My dear Father I forgive you & love you as fondly & tenderly as when I was a prattling happy child basking in the sunlight of your affections over 17 years ago." This I read in each kind eye & treasure it up in the sunniest brightest & warmest niche in this poor unworthy heart, there to remain while I have a heart to beat & a brain to think. If you could know how much I have looked at those pictures & how I cherish the three little tots, last seen May 1st, 1867 & look first upon one &

then the other you may possibly imagine Something Near the train of thought they set in Motion ...

The second letter (slightly edited) was written on November 10th, 1884:

My dear Mary & loving family,

I wrote last night but failed to send it as useless & now feel in a different mood consequently I will try again & I will start by thanking you for all your loving letters & telling you of my getting a good loving letter today from our darling Baby [Frances Lillian] & I was very glad to hear of her good health & she sent me HGBs [Hiram Boles] letter to you also. I am as well as usual & had the pleasure of a good visit with the only real true friend I have on Earth outside of the limits of our dear little family circle. He seems as much interested in all of you as in Me & I believe more sometimes. I know you would like his frank open Manly countenance.

I have just come from Supper. Had Soup, vea [smudged], Milk, Bread, Butter, Roast Beef, Squash fried & boiled Potatoes, Pickles, Macaroni & a nice dish of bread Pudding to wind up on & this is our usual bill of fare & same thing Sundays. And when the gas [light] is turned on it almost makes me think of being in town at a regular Restaurant & do you not think I appreciate it to the fullest extent & perhaps you would be surprised to know that I wear the Same Clothes that you saw me in My Photo or nearly so. The same coat, vest, Hat, Shirts, Collars, Cuffs but Prison Pants, but they would never attract the least attention anywhere only where the people are accustomed to seeing them on Prisoners. So you see there is nothing to be desired considered as a Prisoner. Now do not make up Your Mind that this is the lot of all Prisoners. But they are all treated humanely. Yes My dear family I am wearing the very identical Laundry Mark on My Shirts Collars & Cuffs every day that led to My Capture & imprisonment & this is a facsimile of it (Fxo7). That simple little thing Changed me from a respectable honored Citizen, to a Notorious outlaw and villain in the twinkling of an eye in the estimation of the people.

But My dear family in reality I have not changed in the least. I did allow Myself to go along under the strongest protest of conscience & under the most extraordinary circumstances. But my principles & habits are the same as when I was your honored protector — never having done any Man a personal wrong or deprived him of a farthing [the smallest English coin] unlawfully.

My own dear family, I am very proud of you when I think of your heroic exertions in this cold world in support of each other & I love you more every letter I read from you for I discover new beauties of character & nobleness in every one of your affectionate letters to me. They are so transparent, I mean beautifully transparent because I can see so clearly & distinctly all the beautiful attributes necessary to constitute a loving noble kind & affectionate woman [his youngest daughter, Frances Lillian]. So mindful of the welfare of her dear MaMa & her sweet sister. So little self & such a great big warm heart for others. How I hope she may be fortunate in the Selection of a Companion for life & have the protection of a Man worthy of her affections. Eva & Ida don't be jealous.

This language would apply with equal force to either of you. I must close so goodnight. CEB

I have just looked at my watch & it is just 7 & I will write to Lillie tonight. CEB

In a later letter he writes to Frances Lillian, who has become a milliner:

I would like to be there now. I think you would soon have a Wig customer. You are dealing in wigs and frizzy mustaches & the like. You ought to be able to get up a pretty good <u>Dude</u> & <u>Dudine</u> by this time. I suppose you have some of that breed in H [Hannibal] as well as we have in S. Francisco, in fact what would a City be without them.

Granted these letters are from a body of missing correspondence, but they reflect the frustration one has with Charles Boles, both as man and legend. An interesting item, the identity of his visitor with the 'manly countenance,' is not explained; the rest — syrupy, poignant sentiments, even an attempt at humor — sound like excerpts from a cheap 19th century novel. Boles is not necessarily being insincere. Though he treated his wife and family shamefully, they seem to have forgiven him, providing almost the only moral support he had while in prison. He was a disgrace and a failure, yet they accepted him again. Sitting in his cell, he probably believed all he wrote — at that moment; the blame will begin when he is released and expected to live up to sentiments expressed in perhaps hundreds of letters sent to his wife and daughters during his years behind bars.

But other aspects of the letters reveal a less-than-candid portrait. Charles Boles was a thief. He stole money and destroyed property belonging to others. Even if he had a legitmate grudge against Wells, Fargo — of which we have no knowledge — his actions were still reprehensible. His motive was personal gain, not to right a real or imagined wrong. He did personal harm to people, depriving them of far more than farthings. His destruction of mail undoubtedly caused individuals worry, if not actual suffering. Even if his weapon was unloaded, people fear for their lives when a shotgun is pointed at them. He deserted his wife and children for twelve years without word or dollar, and as far as is known never sent them anything except letters again. He was not quite their 'honored protector.' Charles Boles may have been charming but noble he certainly was not. One listens in vain for remorse.

At one point his letter-writing got him in trouble with the warden, showing a rare flare of temper. As the scene can be reconstructed, Bart wrote a letter to Mary, asking about the family's financial condition. Mary revealed that she no longer owned the house in Hannibal (purchased with money from the New Oregon, Iowa property years earlier). Mary's sister-in-law (her brother's wife) took advantage of her innocence in financial matters and cheated her out of the property. Bart sent a blazing letter to the sister-in-law. In response, Henry Johnson (Mary's brother, who must have been a party to the manipulation), complained to Warden Shirley and Bart's jailer, Captain Aull, at San Quentin. Shirley reportedly called Bart on the carpet, telling the prisoner that abusive letters were not permitted in his penitentiary. Bart's response was that Shirley might censor whatever he wrote, but the warden could not prevent him from writing what he felt.

The affair ended, but it proved costly to Bart, following his release. Captain Aull, an ex-Wells, Fargo detective, confided the story to his good friend, James Hume — but it became garbled. In the retelling Bart had written an intentionally abusive letter to his brother-in-law, to break off further communication with his wife and family! This convinced Hume that Bart, despite his engaging personality, was rotten at heart, perfectly capable of committing the crimes attributed to him.

Other than writing syrupy letters, Bart's only other known activity in San Quentin was to make a bird cage and a folding ivory toothpick[59] for Detective John Thacker.

He made few friends in prison: the prison physician, Dr. Rich, the druggist, Mr. Fuller, and an unlikely type, fellow stage robber, Charles Thorne (alias Dorsey). Thorne murdered a man during a 1879 holdup and received a life sentence, instead of death, because one juror, like Thorne himself, had been a member of Quantrill's guerila band during the Civil War. According to Hume, Thorne was "the worst man of all the 1,200 in [San Quentin]." The killer escaped in 1887 but Hume recaptured him three years later in Chicago. Strange company for a bandit who never loaded his shotgun.

The newspapers reported he received few or no visitors; a *Chronicle* reporter wrote that as of July, 1887 he didn't have a single one. But other accounts say writers Joaquin Miller and Ambrose Bierce called on Bart. He distrusted newsmen, but may have excepted Bierce, who was a commentator on Hearst's *Examiner*, rather than a reporter. As for Miller, he lived a life as self-invented as 'Charles Bolton, mining executive,' but nobody put him in jail for it.

A passage in the letter to Mary states that Boles had at least one regular visitor. The unnamed knight of the 'manly countenance' may have been Dr. J. H. Hostettler, a surgeon who also enlisted in the 116th Infantry in Decatur, Illinois in 1862 and probably doctored Boles's injuries during the Civil War. Both men served a similar length of time and were mustered out on the same day. They must have known each other reasonably well, possibly even before the War, certainly during their years in the Army. Hostettler, who had moved to Napa, California, is the only person named by a San Francisco newspaper as being a close friend of 'Charles Bolton.'

Boles might have also received visits from a fellow Webb House resident, Samuel Owen, a naval architect who had spent several years in Russia modernizing the Tsar's fleet. Owen's youngest daughter, Nellie (Elizabeth Eleanor), who was six in 1882, described their move to California in a 1954 letter:

> When we first came to San Francisco we lived for a while at the old Webb House, a small family hotel on 2nd street near Market. The neighborhood at that time consisted of small businesses, among them a bakery, a drug store and a few small restaurants, etc. At the Webb House also lived a kindly, quiet gentleman, Mr. Bolton, who had a permanent room there but who was away at times on business connected with his mining interests in other parts of California.[60]

Nellie recalled how her father's friend, 'Mr. Bolton,' gave her a five dollar gold piece with which she started a savings account at Wells, Fargo. She related that her two older sisters, Clara and Alice, had come into the Webb House at the moment Boles was arrested; they were going up the stairs while he was coming down, accompanied by two detectives. "The girls spoke to him, but he looked straight ahead and didn't answer, which was very unusual." Nellie also claimed she had accompanied her father to visit Mr. Bolton in San Quentin, when the prisoner wrote a poem for her (see Appendix V for the poem).

Only three month's after he entered San Quentin, Bart became immortalized for the nation as a whole in the Beadle & Adams Dime Library publication of W. H. Manning's **The Gold Dragon; or, the California Bloodhound:** A Story of PO8, the Lone Highwayman. The book bore no relationship to real events. In the scene portrayed on the cover, the hooded road agent is interrupted by a villain named Surly Steve Storms while burying stolen treasure alongside a stream. Storms tries to steal the treasure and the two men fight. Meanwhile, Detective Ned Neverfail comes out of the stream, takes the treasure and later arrests Bart. Surly Steve drowns, Bart is convicted and Ned wins the girl. In time Black Bart's real story would take on the trappings of a dime novel.

BEADLE'S Dime New York Library

COPYRIGHTED IN 1894, BY BEADLE & ADAMS.

ENTERED AT THE POST OFFICE AT NEW YORK, N. Y., AT SECOND CLASS MAIL RATES.

Vol. XXII. Published Every Wednesday. *Beadle & Adams, Publishers,* 98 WILLIAM STREET, N. Y., February 27, 1894. Ten Cents a Copy. $5.00 a Year No. 27

THE GOLD-DRAGON; or, THE CALIFORNIA-BLOODHOUND

A STORY OF Po-8, THE LONE HIGHWAYMAN.

BY WILLIAM H. MANNING.

AS BLACK BART FORCED SURLY STEVE BACK, NEVERFAIL GRASPED THE PRECIOUS BOX, DREW IT TOWARD HIM CAUTIOUSLY, AND THEN MAN AND MONEY VANISHED IN THE WATER OF THE POOL.

(Courtesy California State Library)

186

Institution. CALIFORNIA STATE PRISON   Reg. No. *11046*
NAME   *C. E. BOLTON*   Color *White*
Alias   *"Black Bart"*   Received *11-21-1883*
County   *Calaveras*   Sentence *6 years*
Crime   *Robbery*   Disch. *1-21-1888*
Occupation   *Laborer*   Paroled
Previous Record   *No previous prison Record.*

Num. Order	MARKS, SCARS, AND MOLES
	Sm. mole L. Cheek Bone
	Scar rt. top forehead
	Scar in. left wrist
	Tat. Shield R. up Arm
	Gunshot wounds R. abdom
	Other Description: High cheek bones
	Heavy eye brows. Head: Large & Long
	Forearms heavy & tuft of hair on
	breast. Prom. Nose and Broad at Base

Chapter 21
San Francisco and Points Southeast
January 21-February 28, 1888
The Release

As often happens in northern California in January, heavy rain beat down on the day Black Bart, having served his term with credit for good behavior, was released from San Quentin. The *Examiner, Chronicle,* and *Call* all sent correspondents to interview him, but the *Call*'s story contains so many inconsistencies it is obviously fake; the reporter could not have interviewed Bart at the prison itself.

According to the *Examiner,* Bart "was very nervous that morning, as though he was trying not to feel too hopeful lest an unforseen thunderbolt strike him." At 8 a.m. Warden McComb (who had succeeded Shirley) called Bart into his office, congratulated him on his new freedom and expressed the hope that prison time had served as a warning, that henceforth Bart would lead an honest life. Bart wore the same dark suit he had been arrested in four years and two months earlier. His gold-headed cane, his silver watch and gold chain, gold collar and cuff buttons were returned, and he was given $5, the amount presented to all outgoing convicts.

Bart arrived at the Ferry Building in San Francisco at 9:30 and held an impromptu press conference. An *Examiner* reporter first asked him if his imprisonment had seemed long. "Not very long to look back on," he answered, "but it was an awful long time in passing." Avowing that prison had left him a changed man, he thanked the prison officials for their kindness and tried to clear up his domestic situation:

> Since my incarceration I have understood that a great many people were of the opinion that I had taken to the road because of domestic difficulties. Such, I assure you ... is not the case. I have for many years had a faithful wife, who has been true to me at all times and she still clings to me. [Is some irritation detected in the choice of 'clings'?] I have also three daughters, who have now grown to womanhood, who entertain the most tender feelings for me. They have been well brought up, and received all the benefits of a first-class education, and I look forward to a very happy reunion with my family (*Chronicle*, 12/22/88).

Then Bart returned to a familiar, self-serving theme, articulating the underlying reason why he continued to deny responsibility for any other holdups:

> It has also been said that during my criminal work I have been guilty of robbing people outside of the corporation of Wells, Fargo & Co. That I positively deny. I never at any time injured any person outside of the express people, and Wells, Fargo & Co. are the only persons living to whom I owe one-quarter of a dollar. I know that the mailbag which was on the stage that I stopped near San Andreas — and of course you are aware that is the only stage robbery with which I have been connected was cut open when found, but I tell you truthfully that I didn't cut it. I never intended to tamper with the mail or to injure private individuals in any respect. The mailbags which were rifled must have been cut open by the stagedriver or some of the numerous detectives who were hunting arduously for me.

Bart was still afraid Federal authorities would try him for the Funk Hill mail robbery. He needn't have been worried. The U. S. government never showed any will to put him on trial for his hefty haul of registered mail. In a later interview with the *Examiner* Hume confirmed the government's attitude:

When the [Wells, Fargo] express is robbed, the shippers are reimbursed as soon as the amount is known; but for the people who intrust their money to the United States mail, there is no redress. Their loss is irrevocable. The Government never repays them or makes the slightest effort to recover the money or discover the offender.

As Bart turned to go, one reporter asked if he intended to write more poetry. With a twinkle in his eye, the waggish tendency still there, Bart responded: "Didn't I tell you that I had abandoned crime of every kind?"

He planned to rest four or five days before beginning the trip east to visit his family — they could expect him at St. Louis by February 3rd.

Leaving the reporters he boarded a Haight Street trolley up Market Street and rented a room at the Nevada House, a small hotel at 132 Sixth Street run by Mrs. Emily Burling.

The next day inquiring minds noted in the agate type of the *Examiner's* personals column the following cryptic entry:

> Black Bart WILL HEAR SOMETHING to his advantage
> by sending his address to M. R. Box 29, this office.

The ad has never been explained. Could a theatrical manager have placed it? A relative or unknown lover? Perhaps publisher William Randolph Hearst, eager for an exclusive interview, at the very least wanted to stir up a bit of dust with the brief item's mysterious air, and placed the ad in his newspaper himself.

A week later *Examiner* columnist Ambrose Bierce celebrated Bart's literary decision, in one stanza of a 40-line poem:

> What's that? — you ne'er again will rob a stage?
> What! did you so ? Faith, I didn't know it.
> Was *that* what threw poor Themis in a rage?
> I thought you were convicted as a poet.

On January 31st, ten days after his release, Bart wrote the following letter to Mary Boles:[61]

> My dear loving Wife and Children: After waiting all these days hoping to be able to comply with your wishes and my own most ardent desires, I most sincerely regret that I MUST disappoint you. My dear it is UTTERLY impossible for me to come now. O my constant loving Mary and my darling children, I did hope and I had good reason for hoping to be able to come to you and end all this terrible terrible uncertainty, but it seems that it will end only with my life. Although I am "Free" and in Fair health, I am most miserable. My Dear family I wish you could give me up for ever & be happy, for I fear I shall be a burthen to you as I live no matter where I am. My loving family I would willingly sacrifice my life to enjoy your loving company for a single week as I once was. I fear you will blame me for not coming but Heaven knows it is an utter impossibility.

I love you but I fear you will not believe me & I know the world will scoff at the idea & I am not prepared to prove my assertions. I am too sensitive for this world & not fit to try the next.

I have not called on any of my old friends & have only met by chance those I have seen. They seemed delighted to meet me and have had many invitations to call on them but I feel as though it would not be right to handicap them with my company, "Notwithstanding their earnest requests." O My Dears, you cannot tell how I feel with the papers making all kinds of remarks about me & reported interviews that never took place it is simply astonishing what nonsense they will put into one's mouth, but the trouble is they will make him swallow it for it goes to the World & if he should pay any attention to it, to try to correct through the press, they would only double the dose.

All this you may have seen [—]'tis all bosh. But the fact of my not being able to come home is the greatest disappointment to me almost of my life. As you know I have tried to point out to you that it would be better for me to stay away and do all I could for you, and I really thought so, and I am afraid you may think I did and do not intend to come home at all. But if I thought I should never see you again, Miserable as I feel I know my miseries would be increased beyond endurance. Now my dear when I can come I cannot tell. But if I live you will surely see me before another Christmas Anyhow and if Possible sooner.

Oh my dear family how I would like to be able to come Now and it was the hopes of this that have kept me silent so long.

At just over a century's remove, this is likely the closest we will ever get to Charles Boles, who became Black Bart. Even so, its ambiguity allows several interpretations. Given the cruel abandonment of his family, after five years in the Montana mines, he had become dead to them. He returned to life, in what must have been a horrible shock, only because his well-worn Bible revealed his real name. His wife, who presumed him dead, discovered her husband was not only alive, but a famous criminal.

His emotion seemed genuine, though the cynical may find the letter an attempt to keep his wife at bay while he found means to disappear again from her 'clinging' arms. Joseph Henry Jackson believed Bart was essentially a weak man; if so, the letter was a vacillating ploy to cruelly postpone the inevitable disappointment Mary must suffer.

But it also shows Bart in a different light. He had been a failure in the Gold Rush, an unsuccessful farmer, a courageous soldier, but, if we can believe the letters sent to Mary from Montana, a fairly successful miner. When he vanished, there were rumors of gambling losses. The eight years in San Francisco as Charles Bolton were the only times of his life when the world saw him as important. He was, he said, a mining executive, a gentleman. No one believed otherwise. His arrest proved him a fraud, a liar, a common criminal. The fall from grace must have been excruciating, though Bart kept a stiff upper lip through the mercifully brief eight days between arrest and incarceration. In San Quentin, at least he didn't have to see his former friends.

In his next letter to Mary, Bart wrote:

I got a letter the other day from the manager of the Oakwood Theatre and Dietz Opera House, saying he had a chance to make some coin. He requested me to give him my address so he could see me and arrange [Was this connected to the *Examiner*, advertisement, mentioned earlier?]. He claims to have known me well in former years around the 'Stock Boards.' But I cannot, of course, lend myself to any dime museum racket. My stay in the city has been quiet, and if the papers would let up, I would not care so much, for I can't strike back very well. Now, my dear, I hope you will not think, or attribute my not coming home to any lack of desire on my part, or lack of affection for any of you, for I appreciate your wonderful constancy and affection above all things — it's all I have to console me in my lonely, lonely hours. All other relations are as 'ropes of sand.' Only think of a once loving sister, only a few miles away, and never bestowed a line, or likely a thought on her once loved brother simply because he was in trouble and in need of a sister's sympathy.

Well, my dear, these are all sad reflections and I must drop them. Direct as before to San Francisco, California. O, my dear how I do hope you may retain your health until I can come to you. I think this climate would suit you much better than Missouri. Now, my dear, take good care of yourself and don't worry about me for I shall do the best I can. But, oh, my dear, how I do regret not being able to come to you. My dear, the clouds look dark and gloomy and the real struggle of life is at hand and I must meet it and fight it out. It will not be long at the longest, but it promises to be a terrible struggle. Let come what will I must see my own loved Mary and our loving children once more if it is but for a day or an hour — only to see you face to face and imprint a kiss on each of your constant, faithful, loving lips and look into the depths of those tender, loving eyes and then see and read for myself written in tears of love and sympathy these words: 'My dear husband, my dear father, I forgive you.' When that time comes — then, and not until then, can I expect the first ray of sunlight to enter my poor bleeding, desolate heart. Now, my dear Mary and loving children, may God bless you. Good night.

Charles

Someone with a different personality might have profited by the notoriety. After all, Bart was not lying when he reiterated that he'd never harmed a soul. He was, on his release, a bankable item. But clearly the role of celebrity embarrassed him. And what would he receive if he went to Hannibal except headlines declaring the famous stage robber had come to Missouri to visit his family? The greatest emotion in this letter, though unwritten, is the wish to sink into the earth, to become invisible.

An ambiguous sentence has led writers to conclude that Bart had a sister living in the vicinity of San Francisco Bay. After praising Mary's 'constancy and affection,' Bart wrote, "All other relations are as 'ropes of sand.' Only think of a once-loving sister, only a few miles away ..." The intimation is surely there, but in the convoluted grammar of the nineteenth century the sister might have lived a few miles from Mary, in Missouri. Beyond this reference nothing is known of her (she would have been Maria Bowles Bradshaw), but obviously she didn't wish to tarnish her respectability by acknowledging that her brother was Black Bart.

(San Francisco Examiner)

The last letter Bart wrote to Mary, published apparently as she wished, begins in mid-sentence, minus the first page(s):[62]

of my lodgings here. That's all right. I have made no effort to avoid them [presumably detectives who were observing his movements] or any one else yet — but when I do Mr. Detective will find his hands full to keep track of me. Not that I care for anything only this contemptible annoyance by his constant presence, and I know too if they can they will put a job on me if I remain among them thinking that my having served a term it will be easy to fasten the second on me. But I don't propose to allow them to succeed in anything they can concert against Me.

Now my dear I hope you can see the necessity of the move I am about to make. My Dear you certainly can forego getting letters every week or two for awhile, and then my Dear as I said before I will come to you if I live.

My Dear I got the paper you sent me and thank you a thousand times for it, for I wish everybody knew all the circumstances under which our terrible trouble was brought about, and I thank you for your statement and feel grateful to the publishers for their kind words of encouragement and only wish the world at large could find it in their hearts to deal with me in the humane, sensible, and lenient manner the Editor of the [Hannibal] *Courier* has done. For such language appeals directly to all that is Manly and worth redeeming in the human Character, and I most heartily appreciate the kind and lenient sentiments therein expressed.

My loving Mary, if we had come in contact with nothing but such sentiments in the past years of my life it would have saved me from a life of Sorrow, Sadness, and Disgrace, and you from a life of unutterable Sorrow and Hardship, and our loving children from a life of Poverty, Humiliation, and Care. But the future must be attended to and let the past take care of the dead past. I will write Mr. Holcomb [?] a few lines although I have never received a word from him yet.

Eva [a daughter] I thank you for your very kind letter. Oh, how I wish I could shake this feeling off forever — it will follow me to my grave and if it ceases there I shall be in luck. Tell Oscar [Eva's husband] I thank him for his kind letter and would like to see him and hope to before many months.

My Dear Family I am completely Demoralized, and feel like getting entirely out of reach of everybody for a few months and see what effect that will have. Oh my dear Family how little you know of the terrible ordeal I have passed through, and how few of what the World calls good men are worth the Giant Powder it would take to blow them into eternity. Thousands that under your everyday life you would call good nice men are until the circumstances change to give them a chance to show their real character. I have reference now to those that have charge of our Public Institutions. For instance you might go about them as a visitor and meet men there that you would think the very essence of official purity. But go into the Hospital and there see what they are doing for those that need their care, and you will find 99, yes 99 in every hundred that would not turn his hand over to save a prisoner's life.

But why talk about that. I am disgusted with those things.

I must now close after telling you again not to worry about me, and all may come out better than I expect, at least I hope so. Now may Heaven bless you and all our loved ones. Good Night. Your unhappy, unworthy husband.

C.E. BOLES

Unfortunately, the complete files of the *Hannibal Courier* burned in the 1890s, so we can't know how the paper's editor dealt with Black Bart in a "humane, sensible, and lenient manner," or what was written about the circumstances that brought about "our terrible trouble."

We can also only guess at what set off the letter's querelous self-pitying tone. Bart obviously thought the authorities were out to get him again — but why? And who? It would have been prudent for Hume to carefully watch what Bart would do during his first weeks of freedom. Was the ex-convict so paranoid to blow this perfunctory, yet understandable surveillance out of proportion, or were less savory dealings in the air?

Whatever his reasons, early in February, a few days after writing the final two letters to his wife, Boles moved out of his boarding house.

He travelled south, down the San Joaquin Valley, to Modesto, Merced (on Feb. 22nd), and Madera. His prison release was publicized in California newspapers, the photographs taken in Stockton had been widely circulated for over four years, and he was recognized wherever he went. He finally registered as 'M. Moore' at the Palace Hotel in Visalia. Proprietor Daniel Canty recognized 'Mr. Moore' and notified Visalia's *Weekly Delta*, which published the following item in its March 1st issue:

PERSONAL
"Black Bart" has been in Visalia several days.

On February 24th Chris Evans and John Sontag held up a train at Pixley, near Visalia, and killed one person. Wells, Fargo agents swarmed to the area. Bart wouldn't have been suspected of the crime, but he might have been spooked by the lawmen's presence. Two days before the newspaper appeared, Boles checked out of the hotel, telling Canty to hold his valise until it was called for at a future date. Then he left Visalia — and was never seen nor heard from again.

Palace Hotel, Visalia

Chapter 22
California — *July-December, 1888*
The Last of Black Bart

The Visalia hotelkeeper notified James Hume about Bart and the luggage. Hume noted, probably with some annoyance, that Bart had dropped out of sight. The valise contained two pairs of cuffs (with Fxo7 laundry marks), two neckties, a pound of coffee, packages of crackers, cans of tongue and corned beef, pickles, sugar, and a jar of currant jelly.

On July 27th the stage from Bieber (in Modoc County) to Redding was robbed by a lone masked gunman. The express box yielded only $31.75, but estimates of the money contained in the rifled U. S. Mail sacks ranged from $300 to $400. In his San Francisco office James Hume became uneasy, but wasn't ready to claim that the scourge of Wells, Fargo was on the road again — although Bart had robbed that stage line twice. After all, once Bart's holdup methods had been publicized, he would have spawned numerous imitators.

Some other robberies in southern California near Santa Barbara and San Luis Obispo, where Bart had never worked, began to arouse the press; Hume was certain Bart wasn't responsible. But on November 8th, on the road from Downieville to Nevada City, near Nigger Tent,[63] a lone gunman relieved the stage of three mailbags and the express box. In the box was a gold bar weighing 127+77/100 ounces, valued at $2200, as well as $20 in gold dust.

Now Hume was worried. A trip to Downieville and conversations with the driver and passengers seemed to confirm that Bart was operating again. The agent had Bart's valise sent from Visalia. The contents pointed to an extended trip in the wilderness — and proved the man who disappeared from Visalia was Charles Boles — but offered no clues to solve the recent holdups.

Hume still wasn't certain, but on November 13th he asked the Southern Pacific Railroad to send the following notice to its conductors:

The within is an excellent photograph of C. E. Boles, alias C. E. Bolton, alias Black Bart the Po. 8, the notorious express and mail robber, and was taken November 20, 1883, at the time of his commitment to San Quentin, and would have been considered a perfect likeness of him at the time of his discharge, January 23, 1888.

Of course he may have changed his appearance by altering the cut of his beard and mustache or by dyeing it, as it is now naturally almost white.

You are requested to keep a lookout for him, and should you discover him on your train, note carefully where and when he took passage, and what his destination is as indicated by his pay or his ticket, and wire these particulars immediately to J. B. Hume, Special Officer, Wells, Fargo & Co., San Francisco, Cal. Notify the agent at the station where he leaves the train, of his name and character.

This is important and you are requested to give it your earnest attention. Do not excite suspicion nor give information to outside parties. Allow your brakeman and newsagent to familiarize themselves with the photo and description.[64]

The next day Hume issued a circular, detailing the July and November holdups:

WILL HE WOO HER AGAIN?

The Wasp expected Black Bart to rob stages again.

We have reason to believe that the robberies described above were committed by C. E. Boles, alias C. E. Bolton, *alias Black Bart, the Po8*. We have not sufficient evidence to warrant a conviction or arrest, but are desirous of locating this man. Make careful inquiries, get your local officers interested. *Do not arrest*, but wire any information obtained at once, to the undersigned.

He may, however, have been trying to lull the actual thief into a false sense of confidence. The robbery method was similar to Black Bart's, and if the fake Bart thought he had fooled Wells, Fargo, he might make further mistakes. Six days later the Eureka to Ukiah stage was stopped, with a loss to Wells, Fargo of $684.75, and an estimated $1000 from the mail.

The San Francisco newspapers, however, were quite certain the road agent was back at work again and the *Chronicle* trumpeted three-columns with "BOLD BLACK BART. The Poet Robber Again at Work. Three Stages Surrender to His Shotgun. Episodes in the Highwayman's Ante-Prison Life." The story ended by quoting part of another circular Wells, Fargo had sent to its agents (but was not specifically directed at Bart):

The State and Wells, Fargo & Co. have each a standing reward of $300 for the arrest and conviction of each offender. A reward of $550 will be paid for the recovery of the bar, or proportionately for any part thereof. The Government has a standing reward of $200 for each person convicted of robbing the United States mail.

If arrested, or if further information is wanted, address J. B. Hume, San Francisco.

Not to be out-gunned, the *Examiner* came back on November 29th with:

HUME IS SURE OF IT. THE DETECTIVE'S IDEAS OF BLACK BART'S RESIDENCE. A CUNNING BRIGAND — Though Detective Hume does not stickle at the use of forcible expletives in speaking of Black Bart, one may see that he had a good deal of admiration for that persevering and energetic brigand. He was asked yesterday by a reporter what led him to believe that Black Bart was the perpetrator of the recent robberies.

"Have they the earmarks of his other work?"

"I cannot tell you that, but I know that Black Bart is the man,' was the reply. The 'know' was emphasized."

"I suppose Black Bart has altered his appearance since he came out of the penitentary?"

"He probably has had his mustache shaved off and allowed a beard to grow over the rest of his face. I cannot say, though.

"He is an accomplished stage robber and pursued the business so long and successfully that we have no reason to believe that he would be willing to earn his living by actual honest work, and the recent numerous one-man stage robberies occurring in this State bear so many characteristics of the Po8's artistic handiwork, that we are fully convinced that he has resumed his former mining operations and is again prospecting for bullion in our treasure boxes.

"He is too subtle and keen to risk suspicion by selecting any small town as a place of residence, for the reason that his frequent absences would be noted and discussed and he would naturally desire to avoid particulars in regard to his trips, his mine, etc., and, as it is a well-known fact, this is much more difficult to accomplish in a small town than in a city where one scarcely knows the name of his next-door neighbor, much less his business, habits or pursuits. For these reasons we believe that he has selected some such city outside of the State of California (we know he is not in San Francisco) as Denver, Kansas City, Omaha, Salt Lake, Tucson or even Chicago or St. Louis, and without creating surprise or suspicion makes these periodical trips for the purpose of 'cleaning up' his mine and replenishing his exchequer and then returns to lead the same apparently innocent, blameless life which he pursued in San Francisco."

But as Hearst knew quite well, a newspaper mustn't leave its readers in the lurch. If Bart was out there robbing stages, and Wells, Fargo didn't know where he was, the *Examiner* would have to find him — or else fabricate a story! Which is what the newspaper did.

First it planted a short item in its Saturday, December 1st issue, attributing a sighting of Black Bart in Lake County to George Vann, Donna McCreary's husband. Vann 'told' an *Examiner* correspondent that on November 22nd:

> [He] was out on his range, looking after his stock, when his dogs bayed at something in the bushes, and when he went to see what it was, [he] found a man lying down, and asked him what he was doing. The stranger informed Vann that he had come down from a sheep ranch, and becoming tired, had lain down to rest. The next day Vann told someone that "the stranger looked like 'Black Bart,'" he having seen him at McCreary's several years ago, when the celebrated highwayman came through the mountains on about the same route.

Then, to boost circulation for its Sunday edition the next day, Hearst went full-bore with a five-column 'interview:'

> WHAT BART SAYS/The Ex-Highwayman's Story of His Life and Strange Exploits/ Hume is Contradicted/An 'Examiner' Man's Adventure With the Road-Agent Poet in the Mountains/Why Bart Took to the Road/How a Great Detective Made a Reputation/A Robber's Midnight Ride.

Whew!

The 'interview' itself (Appendix IV), while interesting as an example of Hearst's emerging newspaper style, adds little of a factual nature, but provides grounds to speculate about the enigmatic history of Black Bart. It contains outrageous events, like the hardy reporter being rescued from a raging river through Bart's superb horsemanship (there is no evidence the real Bart ever rode a horse, though as a farmer and miner he'd probably mounted a few in his time). It does relate some curiously accurate information, however. Mary Boles' inheritance from John Bowles is implied, information undocumented until the 1980s. But an *Examiner* reporter may have discovered these facts subsequent to Boles' imprisonment and not found them newsworthy, until the 'interview' was written.

One Hearst fiction from this 'interview' has become an apocryphal story in Bart lore: As a young miner Bart asked for a meal at a farmhouse. The farmer gave him a dish of table scraps intended for the farmer's dogs. When Bart set down the plate uneaten, the farmer taunted that he didn't believe in encouraging tramps, whereupon Bart exhorted: "This is the first time I ever asked anybody to give me anything, and it will be the last. Hereafter, when I want anything, I'll take it."

Perhaps the reason for the purported interview was Hearst's antipathy to Hume, which showed itself five years earlier when the *Examiner* criticized the handling of Bart's arrest and guilty plea. Hearst had castigated Hume for purportedly making a deal with Bart, to unofficially acknowledge other robberies he'd committed in return for a lenient prison sentence. The story wasn't far off the mark, but imputed less honorable motives to Hume than was the case.

Now the *Examiner* writer had Bart denying he'd made a deal. He'd confirmed one particular robbery for Hume, then said, "[A]s for the rest, you can scratch off whatever you like. I don't care what you do; if you want to clear up your books that is your business." Now Hume was a liar to his longtime employers; all those Black Bart crimes struck off the 'current' file were still unsolved.

Beyond that Hearst stuck another pin in Hume — the detectives had been kind to Bart because they figured they could make a handsome profit by publishing his memoirs. When Bart "scornfully rejected" the idea, they "were not so friendly."

The 'interview' continued, with Hume and his associates attempting to trick Bart into revealing where he'd hid jewelry from various robberies. They concocted a story that one diamond was a precious heirloom, when Bart knew the gem in question was being returned to a diamond merchant. "He wouldn't give it up, and he allowed the schemers to see his contempt for them."

If Hearst's objective was to get Hume irate enough to let loose new information about Black Bart, he was successful. The following day, under the headline "MR. HUME GETS ANGRY," the Wells, Fargo detective characterized the purported interview as:

a thorough falsehoood, made up of distorted and villainous lies, and the man who wrote it is a low, malignant, contemptible cur. That interview was the boldest of inventions, and was invented by a sneak too cowardly to sign his name in order to vilify me… In the first place, the writer of the article never saw Black Bart and the twaddle it contained was therefore manufactured out of whole cloth. Secondly, it was written solely to injure my reputation as a private citizen and as a detective.

But in his anger Hume finally confirmed the substance of his 'deal' with Bart in 1883:

After Black Bart's conviction I told him in the presence of Ben Thorn of Calaveras County, who is an honest man … and one other person [Harry Morse, whose friendship with Hume had become strained by 1888] that I had him on my books charged with twenty-one robberies [in fact, Hume's initial count was twenty-two]. I asked him to tell me which he had committed, in order that I might see if there were any other stage robbers to look after. "You don't intend to use them against me?" he asked. "No," I answered, "we are done with you." Then he confessed to the twenty-one robberies and seven more. Later, in San Quentin, he confessed to another one, making twenty-nine in all. I never said a word about his helping me out, for I needed no helping out.

Hume could define 'help out' any way he liked, but Bart had helped him out, and possibly Hume helped back. As to the diamond story, Hume corrected it. He tried to get Bart to admit that a diamond the bandit had presumably pawned or sold, and now belonging to a man in Oakland, was in fact stolen property, but Bart had refused to cooperate.

The detective was then asked, "What, in your opinion, could have inspired the writing of the article?"

"I do not know," replied Hume, "unless it was animosity toward a man who never injured the author. But it is a dime novel story which will delude no one. Why, Black Bart himself, as accomplished a scoundrel as he is, wouldn't have stooped to anything so low."

After pointing out numerous other errors Hume concluded his interview with the *Examiner* reporter:

> Before you go, I want to say again that the anonymous scoundrel who directed that attack against me is a vile miscreant, a cowardly contemptible cur. I say it again, and I live here at 1466 Eighth street, Oakland, and my office is room 28, over Wells, Fargo & Company's, and I'm always in.

After this salvo the reporter ended the story with a one word comment: "Wow!"

While Hume and Hearst fired broadsides back and forth, someone robbed another stage, this time in Sonoma County, seven miles north of Ingram (now Cazadero), the terminus of the North Pacific Coast Railroad. The coach from Mendocino City was relieved of $1100, plus registered mail, including a letter containing $300. The *Examiner* shrilled "BLACK BART AGAIN," though several aspects of the holdup argued against him. The stage was forced to stop, not by a masked bandit catching up the lead horse, but because a large log had been tugged across the road. When a deputy sheriff from Santa Rosa discovered the highwayman had stabled a horse near the holdup scene, and rode away from the robbery on horseback, Hume concluded the brigand wasn't Black Bart.

About the same time a Paso Robles weekly printed a poem found near the scene of a minor holdup, one not blamed on Bart. Hume examined the poem and pronounced it a fake, as the handwriting didn't match Bart's. This was only the first of many bogus Bart verses that appeared over the coming decades.

Hume told a *Chronicle* reporter that Bart had probably committed the first three robberies (in July near Redding, November 8th Ditch Hill, and November 20th Eureka-Ukiah); but had immediately left California, on November 23rd; this was the last holdup seriously attributed to Bart.

Then Hume seemed to change his mind, but that was a ploy. The agent turned his suspicion from Bart to J. A. Wright, alias John A. Garvin, who had committed five stage robberies in 1876 and 1877, been caught and convicted in 1877, served nine years of a fifteen-year sentence, and was released in October, 1886. Wright worked alone, like Bart, but used a horse — and held a grudge against Wells, Fargo, blaming the company for thwarting his frequent appeals for a pardon or commutation of his sentence. Further, his known movements tallied with the robberies.

To keep Wright off guard, Hume focused attention on Bart, but a friend inadvertently leaked the story. The *Chronicle* interviewed San Quentin Warden John McComb, who told the reporter that Hume had visited the prison to check on Wright's dental records, for positive identification of the highwayman.

This confused the public even more but without anything new the story began to grow old. Hume essentially killed it, telling an *Examiner* reporter that when Bart "was last seen, on April 6th [1888], he was leaving the state and bound for the [Far] East," though the detective never produced any evidence to verify the statement.

The *San Francisco Post*, apparently desperate for readership, tried raising a new issue (one that is still with us):

> Black Bart proves that his hand has not lost its cunning by a few years' confinement. What is the use of turning professional criminals loose when he is certain to return to the business at once? Better have the indeterminate sentence as soon as possible.

Hearst fired one last shot at the Wells, Fargo detective. On December 13, 1888 the *Examiner* made an unsubstantiated accusation — which has also passed into Bart lore, as fact — that following the Po8's release from prison Wells, Fargo began paying the highwayman a monthly stipend, to keep him from robbing them again. The figure of $400 per month has even been written, which would have been a large amount of money at the time.

It is wryly pleasant to think of Black Bart retiring on money from his long-time nemesis; of Wells, Fargo shelling out in a given year as much as Bart had taken from their express boxes in eight. But beyond Hearst's boundless imagination, sensationalism, and bad taste, there is little to the suggestion. If the story was valid, why would Hume have spent time and money warning Wells, Fargo agents and trying to locate the bandit?

A *Chronicle* reporter asked Hume if "Black Bart, after his release, was in the pay of your company?"

"The detective smiled in a sarcastic manner and replied: 'I am astonished at you asking such a question. If it were so don't you think he would have been only too glad to say in his letter to his wife that he was working instead of writing in such a despondent strain?'"

Joseph Henry Jackson scoffed at the idea:

It grew as such tales do; it took root and has become firmly fixed as part of the Black Bart legend. But it dies harder than any of the false statements that have been made about Bart. There is nothing people hate so much as having their fairy tales taken away from them.[65]

Wells Fargo Bank historian Robert Chandler made a succint statement on the subject:

Wells, Fargo's payoff of Black Bart is absurd. Black Bart was successful for so long because he was a loner and not known as a criminal. Once his cover was blown, he could only run — but not hide.[66]

~

On December 11th the *Chronicle* published:

A Model Husband. "Black Bart" Shown in a New Light. Protest Of His Wife: And now comes to the rescue of the robber's reputation as a husband no less a person than his wife, who, in words that carry with them in every line the evidence of being penned by a sincere, broken-hearted, but loving woman, pathetically begs the people of California, through the CHRONICLE, not to hastily pass judgment upon her erring husband, but to believe that whatever contempt he may have had for the law, he has a heart which still beats for the unhappy wife who has been mourning his absence all these years and wearing out her life in the hope deferred which maketh the heart sick."

The following letter from the wife of the noted Black Bart, received by the CHRONICLE yesterday, tells its own story:

HANNIBAL (Mo.) December 5, 1888

To the Editor of the Chronicle — Sir: I have just finished reading your long article of November 28th about C. E. Boles, and I drop my work to tell you that falsehood, base falsehood, runs all through it, from the time it pretends that he wrote an unkind word to any one of his family here. It is true that he did write once to my sister-in-law here in Hannibal, who had cheated me out of my home here, and I presume he did say some pretty sharp things to her, and she certainly deserved it, for bad as he had done he would scorn to stoop to the deed she has to account for. Now about my husband's rejecting the friendship of his family. Not for one moment has he ever done it, to our most certain knowledge. I will send you the first letter [these letters began on Page 189] written after he left San Quentin, and I ask and beg of you, in mercy to a helpless though innocent family, that you publish it just as you find it.

Every one of us here believe to-day that Hume & Co. are after an innocent man now, for he had told us over and over again that while God gave him breath he would never lift his hand to do a dishonorable act to disgrace us further; and we know he refused to write a history of his life while in San Quentin, which probably would have been a source of quite a good sum of money. In the end, simply as he said, because he had done enough to make us unhappy; and for the future, if left alone, he would do all in his power to aid us and not disgrace us further.

Now, Mr. Editor, will you please publish these letters as willingly as the other side seems to be published.

Remember, we do not say Mr. Boles is not having an alias who is doing the work, as he had succeeded only too well in doing in the past, knowing well that it will be laid to him, but we believe it, and we shall believe him innocent until it shall be fully proven that he is not.

Now, as to making bad friends, I know that his most valued friends in San Quentin were Dr. Fagle and the druggest Fuller, from the former of whom I have received the most kind letter, speaking very highly of my husband while under him.

In conclusion, I ask once more that you publish these letters, that were not written for other eyes than our own. In memory to a sad, heart broken family, and inclosed find stamps for two papers to my address and a stamp for the return of these letters which I send. By doing this you will surely be rewarded in some way, I presume, either here or hereafter. Respectfully, MRS. MARY E. BOLES 117 Market Street, Hannibal. Mo.

Please remember that not one word or sentiment has ever reached us contrary to the sentiments of these letters. M. E. B.

Mary also asked the *Chronicle* to publish a letter (which refers to Charles' discharge from prison) that had been sent to her from a former neighbor in New Oregon:

We are truly glad to believe that the burthen you have long borne is likely to be lifted (partially at least) from your weary shoulders. I infer from your letter that Charlie is with you or will be soon. We think you were right in still holding to the almost forlorn hope of being united again.

Knowing Mr. Boles (as I think I do), I feel confident that nothing but the direst circumstance could ever have led him so far astray, and believing now that his eyes have been opened by such a sad, sad experience, I hope and believe he will take his bearings anew on which his craft so nearly foundered. And let me say I pity the depravity that would lay a straw in his way either by word, deed or insinuation: but on the contrary, all lovers of humanity should stretch forth a friendly hand to help him on his feet again.

W. H. Powell, Cresco, Iowa

The *Hannibal Journal* had printed this article earlier, on November 13th:

Black Bart — A "Journal" Reporter's Visit to His Family — Facts showing that the Famous "Lone Stage Robber" May not Have Been as Black as he was Printed. Twenty Years Test of a True Woman's Love for her Husband. The Wife's Letters and the Little Bible Worth More than Gold or Silver.

Fearing that the publication of sundry items which have recently appeared in our exchanges in regard to 'Black Bart,' the alleged famous 'lone stage robber' of the Pacific coast, might unnecessarily wound the feelings of his innocent and estimable wife and children, we concluded to defer to the matter until the wife, at least, could be interviewed, and that duty was assigned to a JOURNAL reporter last night.

The wife's name, as many of our readers are aware, is Mrs. Mary E. Boles.

The reporter's object was of course to secure such information as might be obtainable in regard to the movements and history of the famous 'Black Bart' since his release from the SanQuinten (California) penitentiary last January.

Ascending the stairway of a neat frame tenement house at No. 117 Market street, the reporter knocked at the door of the only room in which a light was burnng, but the lady who came to the door said that Mrs. Boles lived just across the hall, but as the rooms were dark she supposed that the lady was not at home. The news man, however, ventured to knock at the across-the-hall door and his perseverance was rewarded by the appearance of the lady whom above all others he was just then most anxious to see.

"Pardon me," said Mrs. Boles, "I was sitting at the window thinking, and had really not noticed that it had grown so dark."

A lamp was speedily procured, however, and Mrs. B. informed of the object of the JOURNAL's call.

"Yes,' said she, "I knew, or almost know, what you wanted before you told me. I absolutely know nothing more about my husband's whereabouts than is known to the public generally. The last letter I received from him was dated Feb. 21, and in that he said that if his life was spared, he would be with us by Christmas at farthest, and when I opened the door in response to your knock, I would not have been greatly surprised to find him in the hall, and oh! how unspeakably happy I would have been to find him there."

You have heard, Mrs. Boles, said the reporter, that your husband is charged with having returned to his old business of stage robbing since his release from prison?

"Oh, yes sir, I have heard that, but I cannot, cannot believe that it is true. I believe, and his children believe that he is innocent. In the very last letter we received from him, he declared that he would never again be guilty of an act that would disgrace his wife and children, and I believe he has been true to that promise."

How do you account for his long silence?

"He knows the detectives are again on his track, and that whether innocent or guilty, no mercy would be shown him should he again fall into their hands. You can easily see then why he dare not write, as the letter no matter where mailed, would be almost certain to fall into their hands. I believe he is engaged in mining in some secluded spot in the mountains, though of course I do not know. He may be dead. God only knows."

Do you still hope for the promised Christmas from him?

"Oh, sir, I hardly know what to look for. If he is alive and not pursued by the detectives I believe he will come. I know that he still loves us. The evidence in my possession shows beyond all doubt that he is still as devoted to us, as he was when we last saw him twenty years ago. A gentleman wrote to me soon after he was captured that all my old letters and the little pocket bible I sent him when he was in the army were found on his person. And then, too, my husband wrote me about the same time that he still had the letters and the bible and all the gold in California would not buy them, though some of the letters were worn into shreds. Oh, sir, do you believe that he would have taken care of my letters if he had ceased to love me? No, no, that could not be. If you would read the letters he has written since his release, you could but see the spirit of devotion that pervades them all. Then, again, in all the accounts that appeared in the newspapers about his robberies it was never even hinted that there was a woman associated with him. To the contrary it has been repeatedly said that he was unlike other men of his class in that respect."

"And there is another peculiarity about his history. He has never been charged with robbing a stage passenger or an individual. I remember reading of one case where a frightened lady handed him her watch and purse, but he handed them back to her and told her not to be alarmed, and that she had nothing to fear at his hands. It has been said that his depredations and robbing were confined exclusively to the Wells, Fargo express company. I do not say this to excuse him, for God knows that he has enough to answer for. But, oh, sir, he has some noble traits of character, and if they would only let him alone, I know that he would henceforth lead an honorable life. Here is a letter from the physician of the prison in which he was confined three years, and you can see how highly he was esteemed even under the unfortunate circumstances then surrounding him."

"Once, since his release, he wrote to me that it would probably be better for him to go off somewhere and never come near us again, as our association with him might disgrace us all. I wrote to him in return that we loved him as dearly as ever, and were willing to follow him to the ends of the earth. In answering this letter, he said that he once more had something to live for, and God helping him, would henceforth live for his wife and children."

The reporter was also shown a number of letters written by the husband to the wife which abounded in tender, loving passages as well as expressions of hope that the long separated family might again be happily reunited.

Mrs. Boles has lived in this city twelve or thirteen years and bears an excellent reputation. She is thoroughly lady-like in her bearing and manners and impressed the JOURNAL's representative most favorably. The story of her life is indeed a remarkable one, forcibly illustrating the truth of the adage that "Truth is stranger than fiction."

She has three daughters, two of whom are married and are living happily with their husbands here. The third lives with her mother and is an estimable young lady.

Despite his unspeakable behavior by disappearing and letting her think him dead, Mary defends him — Charles kept her letters and the Bible she had given him during the Civil War. Rather than dwell on the terror he struck in scores of stage passengers and drivers, she reminds the reporter that her husband never took a single wallet or purse. Though he is gone again, for almost ten months without a single word, she still expects him in Hannibal for Christmas.

Mary had written that she and the children "would follow him to the ends of the earth." She was the model of the submissive, doggedly loyal nineteenth century wife. Perhaps, after all, this unquestioning loyalty and devotion was what Charles Boles feared most — an unrelenting love that drove him twice, the last time for good, beyond "the ends of the earth," into oblivion.

Chapter 23
1889 and Beyond

As his biographer, Richard Dillon, states, James Hume "could have retired, famous, after closing the books on Black Bart." But he continued to supervise and coordinate the men who tracked down the bandits who attacked Wells, Fargo. Although the highwayman's days were waning, there were more stage holdups than train robberies (although the latter got more publicity) during the decade following Bart's final disappearance. One case, however, tarnished the great detective's reputation. His employer ordered Hume to aid the brutal suppression of farmers and small businessmen in central California by the Southern Pacific Railroad monopoly, which 'owned' governors, senators, and law officers. When the 'SP War' ended — with 'the Octopus,' as novelist Frank Norris called Southern Pacific, unworthily triumphant — Hume returned to normal law enforcement.

By the late 90s he was all but retired. In 1903 the faithful John Thacker took over Hume's duties, though Hume retained his title as Chief Special Officer. On May 18, 1904 he died at his home on Wheeler Street in Berkeley, where he had moved after his marriage. Part of his obituary in the *Chronicle* read:

> James Bunyan Hume, chief of Wells Fargo & Company's detective force and one of the best and most favorably known figures in Pacific Coast criminal work, if not in the whole police world of the country, died yesterday afternoon after a lingering illness during which, although his body was enfeebled, his mind never lost its keenness until the very last hours.

And Bart?

As early as December 4, 1888 Carson City's *Nevada Tribune* would publish this 'localism:' "There is no longer any doubt as to the notorious Black Bart being in this part of the State, as he was recognized in Reno by several persons, especially railroad detectives."

During the next twenty years rumors would locate him many places, including Japan, Australia and China. He would be seen in Oklahoma Territory in 1889 during the great land rush, in Mexico City and New Orleans, as a peaceful farmer in Nevada Territory during the 1890s. In September, 1897 police in Olathe, Kansas, arrested one H. L. Gorton, alias James Croombs, alias James Gorton, for stealing $400 from a merchandise store. Ten years earlier the same man had been arrested in Olathe for a crime committed in California and returned there to serve his time. One can't even guess why Gorton claimed to be Black Bart, except for the notoriety. John Thacker took the train to Kansas to see the criminal and wrote a letter to Hume saying Gorton looked as much like the real Black Bart "as a bird's nest is like a mile post." Another part of that letter bears repeating:

John N. Thacker

> As for the original Black Bart, he is out of the country. He served his time and it became my duty to look after him for a few weeks after he got out of San Quentin Prison. He went to Utah and then up to Montana and then to Hailey, Idaho. I think he had some business to settle there. Anyhow, he was as straight as a string. Finally he made a bee-line for Vancouver, and boarded the steamer, *Empress of China*, for Japan. He is in that country now.

It would be interesting to know where Thacker got his facts. Had he traced Bart during the intervening eight years, or was he repeating rumors that began to spring up?

Bart was seen during the '98 Yukon gold rush and at a ranch near Sweetland, California in 1900. A sheriff in Cripple Creek, Colorado telegraphed Hume that Bart was in town; Hume telegraphed back that Bart was not wanted for anything in California.

Rose Schwoerer of Vallecitos, who once worked as a waitress in the dining room of the Mitchler Hotel in Murphys, told this story to researcher Owen Treleaven:

> The Chinaman cook left long before the stage got in at night... Sometimes it would get in around seven o'clock; sometimes not until nine or after. It all depended on what time the train got in to Angels with the mail. So I had to be on hand to feed anyone who came in on the stage and wanted supper. Of course, if it was very late I'd go upstairs to my room over the dining room and then, if someone came to eat, Frank Mitchler would pound on the ceiling of the dining room with a long stick and I'd come down and wait on the customers. Well, one evening a stranger came in on the stage about seven, or seven-thirty and wanted supper. We never served steaks or fry orders so late; just stew or cold meat or vegetables — whatever we had left over. So I took

this customer whatever we had. I didn't pay much attention to him at the time, but I remember he wasn't a very tall man and he had white hair; balding in front.

The next morning he left on the stage for Big Trees and after he had gone Frank came to me and asked if I knew who it was I had waited on last night. I said, no. 'That was Black Bart,' he said... It was either 1909 or 1910, I don't remember which.[67]

In 1933 a *Santa Rosa Press Democrat* writer invented this ridiculous ending for his article 'Black Bart's Entrance To San Quentin 50 Years Ago Recalls Colorful Career:'

> For many years until his death, 'Black Bart' was a familiar figure in San Francisco. He still wore his high silk 'topper' and carried a gold-headed cane, strutting about the city with all the dignity that his 5 feet 8 inches in height allowed. Many old residents of the bay region recall his daily visits to haunts of friends in the North Beach section of San Francisco where he loved to chat and relate his daring career.

~

Mary Boles died from heart disease on March 9, 1896. She was listed in ten editions of the Hannibal City Directory:

1875-76	Mrs. Mary E. Bowles-Dressmaker Market at Houston
1881-82	Mrs. M. E. Boles (Widow) Resides 201 S. Maple
1885-86	Mrs. M. E. Boles Resides at 1255 Lyon
1888	Mrs. Mary E. Boles Resides at 117 Market[68]
1892-93	Mrs. Mary E. Boles (Widow of Charles E) Resides 715 Center
1894-95	Mrs. Mary E. Boles (Widow of Charles E) Boards at 715 Center
1895-96	Mrs. Mary E. Boles Boards at 715 Center Street
1897-98	Mrs. Mary E. Boles (Widow of Charles E) Died March 9, 1896

First listing herself as 'Widow' in 1881-82, when she thought her husband was dead, Mary withdrew that designation in 1885-86 when she knew he was alive. Beginning in 1892-3, to the end of her life, she appears specifically as 'Widow of Charles E.' In 1888 Charles disappeared again, and certainly never returned to his wife and family. A notorious stranger in Hannibal could not have gone unnoticed or avoided law enforcement agencies and the press. Hannibal's police chief wrote a letter to Wells, Fargo in May, 1928, stating that after his release from prison Boles returned to his wife and children; then they left and were never heard from again; a portion of that letter is definitely false as Mary and daughter Eva remained in Hannibal for the rest of their lives.

So in 1892 (probably late 1891, when the directory would have been tabulated), did Mary know that her husband was, this time, definitely dead?

And if so, where did he die? If not in Hannibal, in Japan? Or Idaho? Or Oklahoma? Numerous writers on Black Bart refer to an unnamed New York newspaper that supposedly printed Charles E. Boles' obituary in 1917 — but extensive research has not discovered that obituary. Was his death in 1891 or 1917, or sometime in between? It seems that Charles Boles — Black Bart — hid his whereabouts from historians far longer than he was able to hide from his wife. One would like to think the woman who loved him to the end finally became the only person who knew the circumstances of his real passing — and kept that knowledge from the world and posterity forever.

~

Ida Boles was listed in the 1880 Missouri Federal Census as a family servant in the household of Jerome B. Clement. She married John Warren in Hannibal in 1885. Warren was listed in the 1892 Hannibal City Directory as a wood worker for the Hannibal & St. Joseph Railroad Shops. The couple moved to Salt Lake City about 1894 and John L. Warren was in the 1897 Salt Lake City Directory as a laborer for the Portland Cement Company. It is thought they had one child. Ida's brief obituary was published in the *Deseret News*:

> WARREN-In this city, May 7, 1899, of Consumption. Ida M. Warren, wife of John L. Warren; aged 43 years. The remains will be shipped to Hannibal, Mo., for burial ...

Eva Boles married Oscar James in Hannibal in 1881. Oscar, who owned a large rooming house at 715 Center Street (where Mary Boles lived from 1888 until her death in 1896), died in 1891. They had four children, two of whom died in infancy. Eva listed her occupation as stenographer in the 1890 Missouri Federal Census. A portion of her obituary in the *Hannibal Courier Post*, July 17, 1922 reads:

> For 32 years in the insurance business in Hannibal, for the past 6 years she was employed by Plowman and Greenville Real Estate Company as an accountant and insurance clerk. Prior to that she was with the Triple Alliance Insurance Company, a fraternal organization for seven years. She was a member and regular attendant at Fifth Street Baptist Church.

(Frances) Lillian Boles is listed in 1880 Missouri Federal Census as a millinery clerk residing in the household of Charles Wentworth. The 1888 Hannibal City Directory shows her as 'Miss Lillian Boles, a seamstress, lives at 117 Market St.' She married Vachel Dillingham on May 24, 1890 in Delphos, Kansas, where a daughter was born in 1893. In 1900 the family was in Deep Creek Township, Woods County, in Oklahoma Territory. Lillian died near Homestead, Oklahoma on December 22, 1929.

Mary Boles, Ida Warren and Eva James are buried in Mt. Olivet Cemetery in Hannibal. The plot was purchased by Oscar and Eva James in 1883.

Mt. Olivet Cemetery, Hannibal, Missouri *(Photograph by William S. Richmond)*

Between Mary and Ida is an empty gravesite. Who the grave was reserved for is not known.

~

So like all stories, this one seems to end in a graveyard, except that gnawing questions remain: why did Charles Boles become a stagecoach robber; when and where did he die? Not to have answered these riddles leaves an nagging void. Perhaps we might have nosed about in more dusty old newspapers — which would have enhanced local color, but not cracked the enigma of this unusual man. Unfortunately, the questions cannot be answered and probably never will be.

One story about why Charles turned to crime is that his Montana mine was adjacent to a mine owned by Wells, Fargo. Because of mining laws the seam of gold belonged to the mine higher up, so Boles lost his claim. Believing Wells, Fargo had stolen from him, he decided to respond in kind.

211

But Wells, Fargo never owned a mine in Montana, nor does a court case exist concerning the matter.

A Bowles family tradition is that Charles sent money or gold 'back East' to Mary that was never received — and Wells, Fargo wouldn't make good the loss. Of course, the express company gained its reputation and wealth precisely because every shipment was insured, instant payment guaranteed for all losses. A very slim possibility exists that the story could be true. After the transcontinental railroad was completed in 1869, Wells, Fargo sold most of its western stage lines, but kept the express business. In Montana the new stage company became Gilmer & Salisbury. Apparently the three-month transitional change of ownership was very difficult — stage violence and robberies increased, even Wells, Fargo employees were involved and arrested. Charles Boles was in Montana during that time. When he sent hard-earned money to his wife, did an unscrupulous agent omit writing down the information in a receipt book and fail to give Charles a receipt? Wells, Fargo would have refused his claim, so did he decide to rob their treasure boxes to get back his gold?

What happened isn't known and one can only speculate about his motives for robbing stages. Only the U. S. Post Office and Wells, Fargo shipped money. Was it simply (as Willie Sutton, the infamous robber quipped about banks) "Because that's where the money is?" A suggestion that Bart was antagonistic towards all financial institutions, having lost his money when the Bank of California failed in 1875, doesn't wash either, as his first robbery was a month before the bank closed its doors. Was it the plight of a younger son, who got lost on the road trying to equal the achievements of his older brothers? Not likely.

Looking at Charles Boles is like trying to focus dust-covered binoculars using only one eye — we can't get a fix on the man. But in a larger sense, why should we really care? After all, he was one of society's troublemakers, an 'outsider' who wouldn't play the game, got caught and paid the price. We care about this will-of-the-wisp wayfaring stranger, who robbed stages "with the regularity of the Pacific tides," because the intrigue has lasted more than a hundred years — and will continue. 'The Black Prince,' as the *San Francisco Call* named him, has achieved a peculiar immortality, and, barring the discovery of some Bart lore in an antique trunk or attic, a final assessment just cannot be made.

The *Stockton Independent* tried to pen one, just after Bart's release from San Quentin:

> He is one of the most amiable rogues that ever 'stood up' in a stage or rifled a treasure box. He is a man of refined tastes and quiet manners. Endowed with a fair education, he is possessed of much shrewdness, but his actions immediately after his capture showed a lamentable lack of 'sand' in one

accustomed to success in his peculiar line of business. A vein of sentimentalism ran through his character, which rendered him, in the eyes of a certain class, the most popular highwayman of modern times.

The oft-quoted Joseph Henry Jackson wouldn't stand for much of that:

It does seem, though, that Bolton was a curious type, if not altogether a problem for the psychologist... That 'Po-8' idea is in itself an oddity, though a man who wrote the kind of wretched doggerel that Bolton seemed to think was poetry — or po8try — would be quite the kind to think 'Po-8' a really cute bit of work. And, of course, there is the matter of his occasionally signing himself 'Carlos' instead of plain 'Charles' — again a sign of a man who felt the need of opportunities to seem bigger than he was, more dashing than he looked.[69]

Some critics have been quite harsh:

Black Bart hardly measured up to the super-criminal myth that had grown up around him. He was a rather stupid man who figured out an elementary scheme of robbing and followed it... He tried his simple routine, and got by with it... As long as the pattern went smoothly, he was invincible, but when the pattern went wrong, he was in trouble.[70]

But though he had great disdain for Bart, calling him mean and pusillanimous, James Hume gave him the best epitaph of all:

Black Bart is the most remarkable stage robber ever produced in America. Cunning, endurance and bravery are combined in the man.

～

For three winter days in 1880, at two different times, Charles Boles stayed at the Sperry and Perry Hotel in Murphys. On Tuesday, February 10th, he signed the register as Carlos E. Bolton and gave his residence as Silver Mountain. On Wednesday, February 11th, his signature reads C. E. Bolton, from Silver Mountain. For both nights he stayed in Room 17. A week later, on Thursday, February 19th, he registered as C. E. Bolton, of San Francisco. Bart robbed no stages during those weeks, so he was in Murphys for other reasons.

Owen Treleaven investigated the signatures in Murphys and believed an entirely different person had signed the hotel register. Treleaven found the following entry in the Great Register of Tuolumne County: 'Carlos Edson Bolton, age 33, County of nativity, Vermont, Occupation, machinist, residence, Sonora, certificate from Alpine County. Date of registration, Oct., 1, 1880.' However, even Treleaven couldn't come to a definite conclusion, for he said, "But I'm comforted by a vague sense of something still screwy in it all; who ever heard of a man from Vermont named Carlos? I'll probably be sniffing around old records searching for something on that for ages." An analysis and comparison of the hotel register signatures with other signatures and writings of Charles Boles is inconclusive.[71]

Silver Mountain, in Alpine County, is one of the most remote areas in the Sierras, close to where Bart told Hume and Morse his mine was located, not far from the California-Nevada border. The stage line passing through Murphys ended at Markleeville, a few miles north of Silver Mountain. It is speculation, but perhaps Bart did own a mine in the Sierras. On the day of Bart's arrest in 1883, the *Stockton Republican* reported "The detectives think he has some mountain resorts which they will endeavor to locate." Maybe he stopped over in Murphys between trips to his property at Silver Mountain. Perhaps winter snows prevented the stage from leaving on February 11th, forcing him to remain an additional night.

On February 28th, 1888 could he have hiked east from Visalia, then doubled back north to cover his trail? Did he rob one or two more stages to pay for his mining costs at Silver Mountain? Was he able to alter or disguise his appearance so he wouldn't be recognized in remote Markleeville? Did Charles Boles, still digging for treasure, hide out far up in the mountains, dying alone in a scene reminiscent of grand opera? In the interview printed in the *Hannibal Journal* Mary had said:

> I believe he is engaged in mining in some secluded spot in the mountains, though of course I do not know. He may be dead. God only knows.

Another Bowles family tradition is that because of the shame he brought upon them, Charles remained incognito for the rest of his life. And where else could he have quietly passed his days but in secluded Jefferson County, far from detectives and reporters, living shielded and unrecognized after the 20-year absence, tramping Chaplinesque through the tranquil countryside. He would have been safe there; he could have stayed in the old country hotel owned by a relative; other family members would have fed and protected him. And when he died they might have secretly buried him in an unmarked grave near his parents in the Plessis Cemetery.

The monument to Black Bart at Copperopolis.

COPY OF INFORMATION
IN THE SUPERIOR COURT OF THE COUNTY OF CALAVERAS
STATE OF CALIFORNIA
THE PEOPLE OF THE STATE OF CALIFORNIA
against
C.E. BOLTON
Information for robbery

C. E. Bolton is accused by the District Attorney for the County of Calaveras, State of California by this Information of the crime of robbery, committed as follows:

That said C. E. Bolton on or about the third (3) day of November, 1883, and prior to the filing of this Information at and in the said County of Calaveras and State of California in and upon one McConnell there being, did feloniously make an assault, and him the said McConnell by force and intimidation then and there put in bodily fear, and from the possession and against the will of him the said McConnell by force, violence, and intimidation one lot of gold amalgam, being 228 ozs. and of the value of $4,104.00 and several parcels of U. S. Gold Coin valued at $553.00 in the possession of him the said McConnell but the property of Wells Fargo and Company, a corporation, doing business in this State, did then and there feloniously seize, rob, steal, take and carry away, contrary to the form, force and effect of the Statute in such case made and provided, and against the peace and dignity of the People of the State aforesaid.

William T. Lewis
District Attorney of Calaveras County, California
Names of witnesses examined before filing the foregoing Information,
Ben K. Thorn
Filed the 17th day of November, 1883, R. M. Redmond, Clerk.

~

Testimony taken at preliminary Examination of C. E. Bolton
Before P. H. Kean, Justice of the Peace, San Andreas Township
Calaveras County, California
PEOPLE vs C. E. BOLTON

charged with the crime of Robbery - on 3rd day of Nov. 1883-

Warrant read to him. Waived counsel and plead [sic] guilty

B. K. Thorn sworn.

Q. What is your name and occupation?

A. Ben K. Thorn, Shff. Calaveras County; California

Q. Do you know anything of a stage robbery in this county this month?

A. I do, on the 3rd day of this month on the road from Reynolds Ferry to Copperopolis in Calaveras County, California, the stage was robbed at Funk Hill.

Q. State what you know about it.

A. On the 3rd inst. I received a telegram from Copperopolis that the stage had been robbed that morning on the down trip. I went there, arrived then on ground after dinner. We found some things close to the rock where the stage was robbed, consisting of one paper bag containing some crackers, another paper bag containing granulated sugar - on the outside Mrs. Crawford's trade mark of name, also the case of an opera glass - belt, also a quartz magnifying glass - a razor, also a handkerchief containing buck shot, also two flour sacks - one from Sperry's & Co., Stockton, another Sonora brand of flour. Apparently a person had been lying at the base of the rock. We tracked around all day - we came across a man named Martin who lived about 3/4 miles from scene of robbery. (I forgot to say we found 3 dirty linen cuffs.) Martin said he had met an elderly man with gray whiskers near his place in the woods and had a conversation with him. Asked the man where he was going, said he was going to Jackson - where he lived. Had been to Tuol. Co. Chinese and Jamestown to see a party on business. He then inquired of Martin the way to Jackson and wanted to know if it would be necessary to pass through Angels on his way home, said no.

Also the same man was seen by Mr. Sylvester. Martin said he would know him if he ever saw him again. I went to Angels to procure evidence to lead to the detection of the robber - found at Mrs. Crawfords at Angels that a man described by Martin was at her store on the 25th of Oct., purchased there $1.00 of Knic Knack Crackers and 10 or 15 cents sugar (granulated) which she put in a bag similar to the one found at the rock. Conversed with others who had seen the same man at Angels at that date and having obtained all the evidence I could at Angels I started for San Francisco. The handkerchief on one corner in small letters had the following character F. X. O. 7. in capitals. Went to office of Wells, Fargo & Co., Thacker gave J. B. Hume the handkerchief and Hume gave it to Morse and Morse found the laundry of <u>Ware</u> where the handkerchief had been washed and identified the mark on it - while they were talking the defendant came by - Ware said that the mark was the mark of C. E. Bolton. Morse and deft. went to Wells, Fargo & Co. office. I, in the meantime, came back for Martin for identification and left Morse in San Francisco. I asked Martin at Stockton if he saw any man in the depot that time resembling the man he saw in the woods previous to this stage robbery. Looked around among 100 people, more or less and pointed out the Deft. as the man - we brought the defendant to San Andreas - put him in jail and night before last took him out in the Jailor's room and Morse had a conversation with him trying to get a confession from him. After Morse quit I talked with defendant a short time and he finally said - we will start, I said whereabouts is the treasure. He said close by where the robbery was committed.

Went and got a team and carriage - Stone, Morse and I and the defendant started and went to the scene of the robbery, arrived there morning of the 15th inst. - all went to the place designated by the deft. where he had hid or buried the treasure, searched around a little time and defendant pointed out to us, a log - in which he said the treasure was. We found it in the log as he said - opened the sack containing the packages - we found one large sealed package said to contain $4,100.00, another sack said to contain $330.25, another said to contain $60.00. Went back to the carriage with it in a big sack and returned to San Andreas.

Q. Did you have any conversation on the way back?

A. Bolton confessed that he had committed the crime.

Q. Did you make him any promise of reward or make any threats to do him any harm - or did you offer any inducements of any kind to tell him or make his confession?

A. I told him the usual practice of the courts, but I offered no inducements to him.

Signed   B. K. Thorn

Subscribed and sworn to before me this 16th day of Nov. A.D. 1883.

P. H. Kean,
Justice of the Peace.
Endorsed: Filed Nov. 16th, 1883
P. H. Kean, Justice of the Peace.

~

COPY OF COURT MINUTES, SUPERIOR COURT
CALAVERAS COUNTY, CALIFORNIA

Saturday Nov. 17th, 1883

Court met, pursuant to notice. Present Hon. C. V. Gottschalk, Judge, W. T. Lewis, Esq. District Attorney, B. K. Thorn, Esq. Sheriff and R. M. Redmond, Clerk.

THE PEOPLE etc.   )
)
vs.   )   INFORMATION FOR ROBBERY
)
C. E. Bolton,   )

Now comes the People by their Attorney W. T. Lewis, Esq, and defendant without counsel, the District Attorney informs the Court that defendant desires to plead guilty, the court thereupon asks defendant if it is his true name, that by which he is informed against, he answers that it is his true name. The Clerk under instructions of the Court then proceeds to arraign defendant by reading to him the information, and presenting him with a copy thereof, and is asked if he desires to now plead to the information. Whereupon he duly enters his pleas of Guilty as charged in the information, and waiving time asked the Court to then and there

Judge C. V. Gottschalk *(Courtesy Calaveras County Historical Society)*

pronounce judgment against him, and no legal cause appearing to the Court why sentence should not be pronounced against defendant, thereupon the Court rendered its judgment.

THAT WHEREAS, the said C. E. Bolton had been duly convicted of Robbery by his own confession; IT IS THEREFORE ORDERED, ADJUDGED AND DECREED, that C. E. Bolton be punished by imprisonment in the State Prison of the State of California for the term of Six Years. The defendant was then remanded to the custody of this County to be by him delivered to the proper office of the State Prison.

Book B. Superior Court Minutes, Page 76

Appendix II
Speculative Stories

Almost every area of northern California has a Black Bart tale. Some, like the little cabin above Guerneville, where Bart supposedly stayed the night before his first Sonoma County robbery ("when the sheriff returned to town he gave a public reading of the poem and Bart was standing in the crowd") are hardly worth investigating (although we did). Other stories one wants to be true, even though the odds are against them. These were not placed in the narrative; readers can decide for themselves.

The reminiscences of 91-year-old Frank Reader were published by Bob Paine in his column, "Fool's Gold," in the *Nevada County Nugget* in 1961. Reader's father owned a sawmill in Nevada County. One day (Reader remembers it as when he was five or six years old, therefore 1875 or 76) a man calling himself 'Martin' came looking for work. He turned out to be a good worker, and Reader, Sr. provided him with a cabin on the property. At the time almost all millworkers, like cowboys and other hired hands, shared dormitory-like arrangement, the 'bunk house' of many a western tale. Martin's taste for privacy might have had to do with hiding the loot from his forays into stage robbery.

Young Reader remembered Martin had a deep, pleasant voice, was a good dresser and a skilled ventriloquist. He worked during the spring and fall milling seasons for about four years. He kept to himself, not going with the mill gang to a saloon at French Corral which they frequented on Saturday nights, nor ever joining them for dances in San Juan. Reader, Jr. recalled Martin read Shakespeare, and was always interested in seeing copies of O. P. Stidger's *San Juan Times*, especially those which chronicled stage holdups. Reader Sr. once mentioned to Martin that he was short of funds and had to go to San Juan; whereupon Martin loaned him $300 in ten and twenty dollar gold pieces. Even at Reader Jr.'s young age he found it odd that a millworker who made $2.00 a day had that kind of money.

Reader Jr. was not clear if Martin left the sawmill after four years, but following Black Bart's capture the Reader family got news of Martin from another former sawmill employee, Beard Wooster. Wooster worked as a bookkeeper at the Palace Hotel in San Francisco. Wooster went to the jail to see the famous bandit and discovered it was none other than his old friend, Martin. Frank Reader does not seem to have been a historian or a Black Bart fanatic, rather an old man recalling a significant event in his childhood. Black Bart's whereabouts are unknown between 1875 and 1878, and Reader's account squares with the robberies Bart committed during those years. The footpad could easily have kept to the sawmill schedule, though what he did with his winters and summers remains a mystery.

Bob Paine ends his Column with:

Back to Black Bart. Released from prison, for some time it was all quiet on the stage front. Then on Nov. 8, 1888, the stage from Downieville to Nevada City was stopped on Ditch Hill near Nigger Tent by one man and robbed of $2,200. Wells Fargo immediately investigated and they reported it had all the earmarks of BB.

Then not long after that Nigger Tent holdup, Hattie Reader, Frank's young sister, saw a man approach the front porch of the Reader home. Hattie was home alone. No one was in shouting distance. She opened the door. Color left her pink cheeks. She was almost paralysed with fear. There stood Black Bart. Quiet, polite and soft spoken as he had been as 'Mr. Martin,' her father's sawmill worker. Please could he visit the cabin where he had once stayed? Yes, said Hattie. To recover hidden gold, perhaps. Who will ever know? Then he appeared at Hattie's door again. He said thank you and slipped a polished silver dollar in her hand. He walked slowly away toward North San Juan. No one ever saw Black Bart again.

~

A lasting story comes from Oroville, in Butte County, that Black Bart stayed at the Commercial Hotel on the corner of Montgomery and Lincoln Streets, or the Union Hotel on Myers Street. Both hotels looked out on Miners Alley, a notorious street where lay Sam Mullen's Gem Saloon [Seybold's Tavern occupies the spot today], a meeting house for miners and mine employees. Bart gambled at the Gem, deliberately losing to lull his opponents, so they might tell him about rich shipments of gold dust, of money leaving or arriving by stage. It's an interesting enough idea, but if the ploy worked in Oroville, why didn't Bart ever gamble in this fashion elsewhere? But Oroville isn't far from Woodleaf, where his legendary sweetheart lived.

~

As a young man Elisha 'Lish' Shortridge homesteaded 440 acres in Pocket Canyon, west of Forestville on the Santa Rosa-Guerneville Road in Sonoma County. He made his living by hauling lumber, rails and split timber from the forest areas to Petaluma; then it was shipped on river boats to the Bay area. If far from home at night, Shortridge would camp with his wagon and horses. One night, after picking up a load of wooden rails for fencing, and picketing his animals, he stayed in an abandoned cabin near Stewart's Point, south of the Gualala River, in northwest Sonoma County (About five miles east of Plantation, not far from Stewart's Point, is an old cabin on State Park land known locally as Black Bart's cabin). He was preparing his evening meal over a campfire when a man carrying a shotgun

A painting of Black Bart by Donald Clever that formerly hung in the Palace Hotel in Ukiah.
(Santa Rosa Press Democrat)

in the crook of his arm came into the clearing near the cabin. Following the custom of the country, Lish invited the stranger to stay the night.

"Just two things about him struck me," Shortridge said. "His voice was rather peculiar — kind of sounded like he was talking into an empty barrel. He had eyes like a hawk's, steel-blue, that seemed to look clear through you. Good-natured as he was, you could see he wasn't a fellow you could fool with; so, when he didn't see fit to explain anything about himself, I didn't ask him any questions. I thought maybe he was looking the country over, sizing up land and timber."

The next morning Shortridge saw his guest's shotgun standing in the cabin's corner. Curious, he examined the gun and to his surprise found the barrels bright and clean, as if they'd never been fired. More than 50 years later, in 1931, Shortridge told a *Santa Rosa Press Democrat* reporter that he complimented the stranger on the gun's condition. The man smiled, replying "Yes, it always gets what I go after. I never waste ammunition. I save money in other ways, too. I don't drink or smoke."

Before departing the traveler thanked Shortridge for his hospitality and inquired how much he owed.

"Nothing," answered the homesteader. "The country isn't thickly settled, and there's only a few places for us to put up on the road, but all of us know we'll be treated neighborly. The fellow that gets a bunk and meal today may be the one that gives 'em to somebody else tomorrow."

As the man started down the road, he hesitated, then turned and asked Shortridge "Did you ever hear of Black Bart?"

"Hear of him!" responded the rancher. "You bet I've heard of him! He's one of the main things talked about around these parts nowadays."

"Well," said the stranger, "I'm Black Bart. I've just thought that if you knew who I am you might accept something for your kindness."

Shortridge thought the man joking, "Sure, now, you ain't Jesse James or Joaquin Murietta or some other tough *hombre* we all thought was planted safe under the dirt?"

But with the smile gone and his jaw set firm the mysterious visitor came up close and uttered, "I'm not making fun of you. I am Black Bart."

Beginning to believe his ears, Shortridge responded, "Well, pardner, it's a damn fine thing you waited until this morning to tell me. You let me get a good sleep last night, anyway."

The shotgun bearer laughed, "I've never yet harmed a single person, and I've never taken a cent from a passenger. But a lot of these big companies rob the public all the time, and there doesn't seem any way of stopping it. I'm just getting back the part that belongs to me — that's all. You'd feel easier if I told you some other things, but it would be too risky."

With these words the bandit left. 'Pioneer' (as he was also known) Shortridge maintained that he kept quiet about the encounter until Bart was finally captured three years later and his picture circulated.

"I never said anything to anybody about meeting up with Bart until now," Shortridge revealed. "He didn't warn me not to, but I figured it was just as well to keep my mouth closed. It wasn't my job to catch him — he hadn't harmed me or mine. Besides, I calculated keeping still was the safest policy."

Hearing that Bart always carried an unloaded shotgun, Shortridge remarked, "Queer that thought never occurred to me until after Black Bart had gone to San Quentin, but then it came to my mind like a flash. His gun was unloaded, nor did any of his pockets bulge out as they would have if he had carried shells. Then I got to thinking things over, and I remembered what he said when he was leaving — that I'd feel easier if he told me something else, but he couldn't take the chance. What he meant was that he never loaded his gun while robbing stages."

The interview was reprinted in the 1937 *History of Sonoma County*; unfortunately editor Ernest Finley was unclear about when the incident occurred. If Shortridge encountered Bart just before the 12th robbery in 1880, and if evidence could be found that Shortridge told the tale in 1883, the story might be authentic. It does seem odd that Bart would reveal his identity to someone who might (but didn't) give the outlaw's description to the law. But by then Bart knew James Hume had a good description of him anyway. Otherwise, the remembrance of the stranger's manner and words ring true.

If Bart decided to hide out after the arrest and release described on the 'H. Barton' poster in 1880 (see Page 100), the wilds of Sonoma County would have been a good place to go. Cynics, of course, may suggest it was just an old man's fantasy, trying to ally himself with immortality as his own life visibly waned, attaching himself, however feebly, to an undying legend.

~

This story, excerpted from *San Francisco Bookstores*, a chapter in Gertrude Atherton's *My San Francisco* — A Wayward Biography, was written about 1940:

> Today there are many bookstores in San Francisco ... but in the 1880's the only ones I can recall were Bancroft's, A. Roman's, Doxey's and the smaller but far more fascinating one of C. Beach in Montgomery Street in the heart of the shopping district. That shop was very distinctive with its sign portraying green waves breaking on a rocky shore and very attractive with its nice sympathetic young clerk, Alexander Robertson — to become in his own time the dean of all that were to come.

Alec's favorite customer was one Mr. Samson, a mild-mannered dark man with an excellent literary taste and fascinating personality. But that pleasant acquaintance was brief. One day Alec opened his newspaper and was astonished to see the face of his interesting though somewhat mysterious friend on the first page. He was still more astonished, not to say horrified, to read that Mr. Samson was the notorious highwayman, Black Bart, who had been captured at last.

San Quentin News, August 4, 1944 *(Courtesy Wells Fargo Bank)*

Appendix III
Spurious Stories

'The Last of the West' was written by Frank Asbill in the early 1940's while he was serving a murder sentence in San Quentin. The location described is north of Covelo in Mendocino County, where the Asbill family was quite famous. This excerpt, edited for readability, is actually a better story than many Black Bart inventions:

Pierce and Frank Asbill always had the 'hi' air' ye' neighbor, get down, grubs on tha'y table, thor's hay in tha'y barn,' any living man or woman, white or black, injun or chinaman, outlaw, preacher, sheriff, runegade or gambler was welcome for a day or a year, just as long as he wished to stay.

At the Summit Valley ranch the log house was a great double log building, being really two houses in one with a shed-like driveway between them, a sort of a Missouri home. In the dining room there was a long table of whip sawed fir planks, with red or white oil cloth to cover it, where 20 people could be seated, and as a rule there was always a second setting at that table. Two fir logs were split in the center with two legs at each end, which were used as seats along both sides of the table. The large cooking stove was in the same room, with always two or more Wylackie squaw cooks and they were cooks, don't forget that, and just as neat as any white woman one ever seen. The food was brought in on great white porcelain dishes, one of them at each end of the table and both brim full of the finest meat in the land, then another filled with the milk gravy that only the mountain women knew how to make, whether they be a white lady or a squaw.

Once along in the latter Seventies, one day a saddle horse preacher rode up to the barn, put his horse in and came to the house. Next the sheriff came, he did the same. Then a beef buyer came also. Just before the three came, another rather tall, good-looking man came along the rail fence, which ran west from the barn, and which was the fence to the field in the meadow. As he leisurely walked along the stock-travelled trail, he bent down, picked up a rock and threw it at some scampering ground squirrel or chipmunk, which was darting along the pine rails of the old rough fence.

He walked up to the house, stepped upon the porch with a bow and removed his hat. The squaw asked him in. He stepped into the large square log room, took a seat by the large fire place in the middle of the room, and said to the squaw, "Is Pierce Asbill home?" She said, "He go Covelo get shep'sher, he com pretty soon now, he go like hall he come back same way." The fellow said, "I shall await his coming."

Pierce came back to the house, was sitting talking to the tall stranger who was a dark-complected fellow, one of these fellows that when he walked he'd put you in mind of a panther; he had a sort of a spring to his 'gait.'

The long crooked cow horn was blown for dinner, everybody washed at the back of the house in a long trough where the water ran out of a wooden trough into the larger one. There was always a roller towel which they bought by the gross and the half toothless comb, in the switch of the cows tail it was stuck in, did not last the Wylackie Injuns long with that black wire'ry hair.

The preacher, sheriff and beef buyer all walked in through the back door and to the table. Pierce Asbill and the tall stranger, who'd already washed up, came in from the other part of the house and took their places at the long table. Pierce spoke to the others, 'hi' air 'ye jen'tel'men' as he seated. He did not introduce the man that came in with him, for it was not western etiquette, especially in that particular gathering of men of such entirely different walks of life; but for Pierce Asbill not to introduce two men when they met was not out of the ordinary; that went for Frank also.

The sheriff was at Pierce's left and the stranger at his right. While they ate the stranger asked the sheriff if they'd captured the stage robber yet. The sheriff said "No, but they'd have him soon."

All the men stayed the night and the stranger and the preacher slept in the same bed. Pierce always laughed about that, "By-gad, if'en that preacher would a woke up to the fact that he was a sleepen' with that Black Bart the bandit, he'd a done some tall prayin' I betch'a.

~

On September 26, 1909 the *San Francisco Chronicle* printed a full-page article in its Sunday supplement titled 'Tales of the Last Frontier — Black Bart — Early Border Experiences of a Noted Detective by Francis Reno, Copyright 1909 by A. G. Chapman, Copyright in Great Britain.' If the authorship is unclear, the subject matter certainly is not, as it is complete fiction. The story is much too long to reprint in full but portions and paraphrasing will give a flavor of the writing:

It was during a temporary sojourn in the capital city of Mexico that I made the acquaintance of Jim Clarkson, or, as he was better known to the inhabitants of both California and Arizona, 'Black Bart.' Under the latter name for a period extending over four years this man, the most devil-may-care rascal that ever sung out to a traveler to 'stand and deliver,' held up stage coaches, plundered passengers and relieved the guards of the bullion in their care, the products of the gold mines, and set at defiance all attempts on the part of the authorities to catch him. At the time I speak of, the country around where Black Bart played his audacious pranks was thinly settled, and his chances of escape from the possees that took the trail after him were, as a matter of course, much greater than they would be at the present day.

Nevertheless, his exploits were none the less extraordinary on that account. In vain did the express companies offer large rewards for the apprehension of this daring malefactor, who appeared to take a delight in bidding his enemies defiance. Detectives famed for their cunning and skill in running down dangerous criminals came from far and near to join in the chase; sheriffs and deputies known in the Western country as men of proved courage and dead sure shots followed close on the heels of the elusive outlaw; but always he managed to give his pursuers the slip.

A heavily redrawn photograph of Black Bart that often appears in books as 'authentic.'

According to Francis Reno (or Chapman), Bart originally had three associates but during a quarrel two gang members died and the third left the country. Alone, Bart then "established a genuine reign of terror, and the sight of that tall masked figure standing with leveled gun, a lonely, sinister figure on the dreary landscape, appeared to exercise a benumbing influence on the hearts of men whose courage had never been doubted."

The story centers around two incidents. The first (while Bart still led the gang) is a stage robbery between Angels Camp and Milton. The express box contains $90,000 in bullion from the Utica mine. Five passengers are riding inside the stage: two military men, called 'Colonel' and 'Major;' a mine owner known as 'Cactus Bill' Crosby; a New England surgeon; a 'keen-faced' Chicago businessman.

The stage stops at Sullivan's Relay Station, for a change of horses and a drink of whiskey at the bar. Seated in the rear of the bar, "in the dim light of the room, the figure of a woman clad in deep black and wearing a heavy veil drawn over her face. She sat in a dark corner and seemed to shrink from observation." The woman boards the stage, driver Slamons telling the Colonel, "'Widow of Thompson, she is, him that was killed down to the Blue Moon mine last month, but she don't savvy a word of English, bein' French.'"

The stage pulls out, the passengers try to communicate with the Widow Thompson, but receive no response. The men begin talking about what a bad place the area is for holdups and about how much money each has. They all carry various sums of money, from $500 to $4000, the latter sewn into the Colonel's clothing. Dusk turns to dark, the stage road "wound its way around the face of a high cliff: on one side towered a wall of rock sheer three hundred feet, on the other sunk an unsoundable chasm." At that point the stage is halted by the 'crack of a revolver.' A highwayman tells the driver to throw down the box, the passengers to get down.

The last to descend was the widow —
but a widow no longer, for out of the
coach there sprang an active young
fellow, smooth shaven, dark, of slender but sinewy build, dressed in the
convential garb of the Western rider,
and carrying in his hand a nickel-
plated six-shooter. And this was Mrs.
Thompson — who did not speak
English. The former Mrs. Thompson
proceeded to search the pockets of
the luckless travelers and relived them
of their valuables...

Reno dates this robbery as taking
place in 1886 — when Black Bart was
actually in San Quentin!

A sketch 'drawn either from an actual
photograph or made first hand,'
by H. O. Lawson in the 1900's.

Bart is eventually found out and
captured as a result of "a white cuff
bearing the initils 'J. C.'" and "the cuff turned out to be the property of one
James Clarkson, a member of the Stock Exchange in San Francisco." Bart
goes to San Quentin, but "through an arrangement with the express
company ... he was pardoned after serving a year of his sentence.
According to the terms of his release [in 1890] he was obliged to leave the
United States and reside across the [Mexican] border."

The second part of 'Tales of the Last Frontier — Black Bart' takes place
in Mexico and contains so many ethnic slurs that a reader might wonder
if patriotism wasn't the article's underlying purpose. Reno, the detective,
has business in Mexico (to enforce the Chinese Exclusion Act) and meets
Clarkson after a monte game in a gambling casino. Reno wins big, then is
attacked by 'greasers' after he leaves the casino. Clarkson rescues Reno,
with the following conversation taking place:

"I like your style, Reno, and though I am never liable to meet you again,
I hate to sail under false colors. You may as well know who I am. I told
you my name was Jim Clarkson, but I used to travel under another that was
pretty well known and talked about in the States a couple of years ago. Did
you ever by any chance hear of an outlaw called Black Bart?"

"Heard of Black Bart? I should say I had. For an instant I was unable to
reply and stood staring open-mouthed at my singular companion. He
laughed in a tone that had something of restrained bitterness in it."

"I see you have." he said. "It would be an odd thing if you hadn't, being
a Western man. Well, I'm Black Bart, that was; an exile now, who must
never claim the shelter of the good old Stars and Stripes again. I envy you,

man, going back into God's country, while I must drag out the rest of my existence down here."

Reno ends by saying, "Whatever Black Bart's sins against society may have been, I felt that I, at least, had no cause to speak disparagingly of him."

The *Chronicle* would continue 'Tales of the Last Frontier.' The following week's episode was 'The Wiles of Quong Wong.'

~

Perhaps another more astounding (and purportedly true) Black Bart story has been written, but we haven't read it. Harry L. Doney maintained that a notorious and wanted outlaw, Jack Elmore, and not Charles Boles, was really Black Bart. In a long, three-part series, titled 'True Story of Black Bart Told For First Time,' published in the *Woodland Democrat* in 1961, Doney spun out a yarn that would, as the paper's editor said, "do justice to the TV westerns." Doney's manuscript, apparently written before 1906, was discovered after his death in 1945.

Doney relates what a friend, Bob Beard, had told him. In 1870 Beard mined in Montana when Jack Almer and two other men had been caught robbing a miner's sluice box. Instead of stringing them up, the miners drove the robbers out of camp. In the late 1870s Beard was mining in Churntown in Shasta County, and recognized Almer, known there as Jack Elmore. Almer/Elmore didn't recognize Beard, who told himself, "What are you up to in this country? I will watch you, old boy, and find out." Black Bart committed his tenth robbery on Bass Hill in 1879, not far from Churntown. No one suspected that Jack Elmore could be the culprit; but the seed was already in Beard's mind and he began to watch Elmore closely. But neither he nor anyone else could catch Bart robbing a stage. Sometime in 1883 Beard, Doney and a friend, Alec McMillan, conspired to capture Black Bart for the mounting reward. Beard proclaims:

> Now, my plan is that I make a trip down into the Churntown district and find out if Jack Elmore is there. If not, I will come back here, and after a while, I will go down again, for if he follows up his old game, he ought to be due there before long. It is now quite a while since his last 'hold up,' and he stays around quite a while before he makes another haul. If he is in that country now, I will stay and watch him, as I believe I can tell by his actions when he is about ready to take in the stage; and I can then send you a message by an Indian. Then you and Alec come down at once, prepared for business. By that time, I will have planned out the whole thing, and we will capture him in the act or soon afterward, while he had the plunder on him, and may also get his accomplices.
>
> To this Alec and I agreed, and we furnished Bob money to defray his expenses. He was instructed to report as often as convenient. All this was kept strictly secret, not a word leaking out...
>
> Bob was gone about a week, when one day he and Alec McMillan came in, with disappointment written all over their faces. Bob's first words were: "It's

all off. Black Bart is done for." What he told me was that Jack Almer, alias Red Jack, and two others men known as the Tuttle brothers, had been killed by a sheriff's posse near Prescott, Arizona, and that they had died game and fought to the last.

I said to myself, "Bob, that ends the game. No need of going further. I told no one of my interest in Jack Almer, but let me tell you, no one will ever hear of Jack Elmore again, nor of Black Bart, either, as they are one and the same."

Doney's tale doesn't end here. He wrote to a sheriff in Arizona and to James Hume, but received no replies. Both Beard and McMillan wanted Doney to drop the matter, fearful that Elmore's confederates in the area might take revenge (for what isn't stated). In 1906 Doney met an Oregon man, Edward Hall, from Prescott, Arizona:

I asked him if he had ever heard of Jack Almer, a noted highwayman. "Why, yes," he replied, "I saw him killed with the two Tuttle boys."" This of course interested me at once, and I asked him to go before a notary and make a statement under oath, which he did, and I have the document in my possession at the present time.

Doney insisted that Hall gave him the following deposition:

I was freighting from Prescott to Signal, Arizona during about the year 1883, and that time I met and became slightly acquainted with a person who was know there as Jack Almer. On a certain evening during the said year 1883, I was drinking some and I had several drinks of beer with said Jack Almer. After we had several drinks together, I stepped back to the water closet, and while I was there Jack Almer came back also. He said to me while we were there: "Kid, you don't know me, do you?" I said that I did not. He then told me that he was Black Bart. I took my teams that evening and drove out of Prescott, six miles and camped, so as to get an early start the next morning. The next morning I was hitched up and on the road when Jack Almer and the two Tuttle brothers rode past me. I recognized Jack Almer and spoke to him. The three men had barely got past me when the officers came up and commenced firing upon the three men. They killed the two Tuttle brothers and fatally wounded Jack Almer. I saw Jack Almer on the morning of the shooting, both before the shooting and after he was wounded and was lying in the wagon, positively recognized him as the same person with whom I was drinking the evening before, and who told me that he was Black Bart.

Doney concludes his story:

I will state that a man was afterward arrested for stage robbery, and pleading guilty to one charge, was sentenced to six years in San Quentin. This man acknowledged that he was Black Bart, and had robbed the stages twenty-eight times.

Unless Doney invented the whole thing, he seemed unaware that his informants were conning him.

Appendix IV
The *San Francisco Examiner* 'Interview' with Black Bart

The 'interview' published on December 2, 1888 was but a prelude to what William Randolph Hearst would print during the golden times of 'yellow journalism.' Undoubtedly fake, and rife with errors, it is nonetheless a clever invention.

What Bart Says

The Ex-Highwayman's Story of His Life and Strange Exploits

Hume is contradicted

An "Examiner" Man's Adventure With the Road-Agent Poet in the Mountains.

WHY BART TOOK TO THE ROAD.

How a Great Detective Made a Reputation.

A ROBBER'S MIDNIGHT RIDE.

_____, November 30

To Managing Editor Examiner, San Francisco:
Have seen the man of whom I spoke. Am under absolute obligation to conceal whereabouts. Will send interview if you guarantee strict compliance with conditions. As wires may leak, will forward under cover to _____ by Wells-Fargo.

Martin

SAN FRANCISCO, November 30

TO ____ ____, ___: Guarantee given. Send story as soon as possible. Hire courier to catch train at _____ if necessary. Don't spare expense to save time.

W. R. Hearst

The above telegrams passed between the editor of the Examiner and a special correspondent at a point which, for reasons that will appear, cannot be named. The correspondent had declared his belief that by going to a certain place named he could get information about Black Bart, who, the detectives say, has been robbing Wells, Fargo & Co.'s stages with his customary diligence and skill in the northern part of the State. He was not at liberty to say upon what he founded that belief, and in response to the suggestion that he might find it somewhat embarrassing to interview a gentleman who carried a shotgun and would have particular objections to being found, he replied that he did not believe Bart had taken to the road again, and as he was not going in search of him in the role of a detective, he was ready to take all the chances.

The telegram at the head of the column was the next that was heard of the correspondent, and it indicates the result of his trip. Following is his detailed account of the affair:

IN SEARCH OF BLACK BART

The particulars of my journey to where I now am cannot be given because it would be impossible even to describe the route or the character of the roads without giving clews which I am bound to withhold. Therefore I am somewhat hampered in my work and obliged to omit certain facts which ought otherwise to be stated. By accident the whole affair assumed a personal phase, which seems to make it almost necessary to tell the story in the first person. However, you can change that if your editorial judgment so dictates.

[The above was a note to the editor, but is published because it serves to introduce the correspondent's account without betraying confidence, and also explains the abruptness of the beginning of the narrative.]

After leaving the railroad, on my journey for the EXAMINER in search of information concerning the man whom Wells, Fargo & Co.'s detectives accuse of having robbed the stages frequently of late, I went to a ranch about two miles from the station and bought a horse, saddle and bridle and pushed on toward _____'s mountain ranch, where I expected to get reliable directions or possibly meet the man himself. Having known Bolton when he was a mining man, I hoped to be able to recognize him unless he had made very radical changes in his appearance. It was at least twenty-five miles to the ranch, and night came on before I had made half the distance. To make things still more uncomfortable, it began to rain copiously, and of course I was drenched to the skin.

I might have stopped at a house near the creek about half way, but thought it best not to lose any time, and, besides, I would have to lie furiously to ward off the questions that certainly would be asked a man applying for lodging in that part of the country at that time of night. To avoid country curiosity and to lose no chance of finding what I was after, I urged the horse on through the rain and mud, and when I struck the steep mountain trails I found that my animal was no good. He was all knocked-up forward, wheezed like an exhaust-pipe and kept me in constant fear of being pitched over his worthless head and breaking my own valuable neck.

AN ADVENTURE IN THE MOUNTAINS

It was somewhere near 9 o'clock P. M. when I heard the sounds of a horse's hoofs on the road ahead of me, and as the sounds came no nearer it was clear that somebody was traveling the same road and in the same direction. A little urging hastened the pace of my horse, and going down a steep place toward a stream I made out the figures of a horse and rider about half way across the ford. I hailed the man, and when he answered the hail I told him that I didn't know the ford very well and wished he would hold on and pilot me across.

"All right," he replied, "the rain has swollen the stream some and you'll have to be careful. Got a good horse?"

"No, he isn't worth a cuss. All bunged up."

"Well, I'll wait for you, stranger, right here. Come in a little above that rock and point straight for me."

Following his directions I rode into the stream and the horse picked his way with some trembling among the loose, rolling stones on the bottom. The water was breast high in the middle, where the stranger was, and just as I ranged up alongside and noticed that he was watching me narrowly, my fool of a horse stumbled, twisted his foreleg between two stones and went down. I fell out of the saddle on the side next to the stranger, and reaching for something instinctively I caught his stirrup. My horse was down stream from his, and rolling over in the water, was swept down by the swift current and lost to sight in a moment.

The stranger's tall, strong horse stood braced against the current, and when the man stooped and grasped my coat-collar he spoke sharply to the animal and in

'The Lone Highwayman of Placer County.'
A drawing often reprinted with articles about Black Bart that had nothing to do with him.
(*National Police Gazette,* October 6, 1880)

another moment we were in shallow water. As the rain had drenched me already, the ducking made no perceptible addition to my discomfort, but I had lost a horse, saddle and bridle for the EXAMINER, and had a five-mile tramp ahead of me.

I began to thank the man for his help, but he interrupted me with: "Don't mention it. That's a bad place at night. You've lost your horse, and that's something of a loss at this time of night, even if he wasn't worth a cuss. But, then, you might have broken your neck if you'd kept him, so perhaps you've got something to be thankful for. Where are you going?"

"I'm trying to get to _____'s place."

"H'm! Know anybody up there?"

"Yes, I've been acquainted with _____ for some years. My name is _____ _____. I'm from San Francisco."

The man told me to get up behind him, as he was going to the ranch, and as he leaned over to give me a hand, I thought I recognized the contour of his face, but I said nothing. When I was seated, and we had got along a hundred yards, he said abruptly:

"Still in the newspaper business?"

I replied that I was, and after a pause he said:

"I don't want to be inquisitive, but what do you expect to find at _____'s ranch that will be interesting to newspaper readers?"

"You."

"Well, I'll be there pretty soon."

There was nothing more to be said, but a good deal to be thought, and so we rode along in silence through the rain until we arrived at the ranch. There was a light in the window, and when we rode up to the house the owner of the place came to the door to meet us. Naturally, he was surprised at seeing me, but did not appear in the least disturbed. I was careful not to make any break in the matter of names and did not attempt to explain anything until I heard him address my companion as "Mr. Watkins." (That was not the name, but it will do.) Then I told the adventure at the ford and said I had come up to see Mr. Watkins about a mining proposition.

After getting into dry clothes and outside of a delectable hot rum punch, we had supper, and then our host showed us our rooms and bade us good night. As "Mr. Watkins" went in at his door he nodded over his shoulder to indicate that he wanted me to follow, and a few minutes later I went into his room. There was a queer, dry smile on his face, but no trace of uneasiness, as he motioned me to sit down. He opened the conversation.

FACE TO FACE

"It is some years since we met," he said, "and I believe the last time I saw you we were in a courtroom. I think you were writing down something for a newspaper," and again he smiled.

"Yes," I replied, "that was some time ago, and we were not very well acquainted then. But to-night we have become somewhat acquainted, and I am placed under deep obligation to you, as without your help I might have gone down stream with the poor old plug."

"Oh, it was only a bit of luck that my stirrup was there for you to grab. The rest was nothing. But you said you came up to see me. What can I do for you?"

"Give me an interview for the EXAMINER."

He looked at me intently for a moment, seeming somewhat troubled, and then said: "That's a job I don't very well like. I'm not much of a talker for newspapers, and I don't see what I can tell you that will do anybody any good. To speak plainly, I don't think it exactly a square deal for the papers to keep hammering away at a man after everything is all over. Now, what in the world put into your head to come up here looking for me?"

For reply I handed him the San Francisco papers containing Detective Hume's statements about Black Bart and watched him while he read them. Sometimes he smiled, and more frequently he frowned, and when he finished he said: "A little truth and a pretty strong dose of lie. I can deny a lot of this stuff, if that is what you want, but what's the use? You don't want to print that Black Bart says he isn't robbing stages because everybody would say, 'Of course he'd deny it; he wouldn't be likely to tell a reporter that he had gone on the road again.' And, besides, how are you going to print anything without letting people know where I am? You can see that I wouldn't like that. Here's Hume swearing that Black Bart is at it again, offering rewards and threatening imprisonment for life."

"I can fix it so that nobody will know where you are, and you can rest assured that there will be no chance of a leak in the EXAMINER office."

"Perhaps, but you forget those very clever detectives. You don't know how smart those detectives are, and you never will know unless you ask them and give them a chance to tell you. No, I don't take kindly to the interview idea. Don't you think you had better drop it and go fishing or something?"

"No, I'm fishing for news, and a man can't go back and tell fairy tales about that kind of angling. He must show up his string and have the weight verified by the man with the blue pencil. I've got to have an interview in some shape or go out of the business."

"Mr. Watkins" mused a while, the expression on his face varying with the thoughts passing through his mind, and at last he said: "It's a long trip to make for nothing, and I don't know but what I'd like to have some matters set right. But I've never been interviewed, and don't like to break the record. Now I don't want you to say that Black Bart said this or that. Write it some other way. Say that an intimate friend of his, somebody who knows him better than Mr. Hume does, told you what I am going to tell you."

"Very well," I replied, "I will keep your record unbroken technically, and I won't give any clew to your whereabouts, but you must leave the rest to my discretion, tempered by the necessity of making a proper news showing for my journey."

"All right. I suppose I must not hamper you too much. Now, then, Black Bart's friend — you'd better take notes — his intimate friend, the only man to whom he ever talked much about his life, said: Detective Hume makes a great many mistakes in his pretended 'Life of Black Bart,' some through sheer ignorance and some evidently for motives not wholly creditable. He takes some pains to abuse C. E. Boles, calling him a pusillanimous wretch, and declaring that there is nothing honorable about him. Let Mr. Hume's opinion be what it may, the fact remains that

From an article about Black Bart in the Amsterdam, Holland newspaper, *De Telegraaf.*
(Courtesy Wells Fargo Bank)

Black Bart never gained a man's confidence to betray it, never swindled a person in trade, and never plundered working people by taking what they produced, sheltering himself behind laws made to legalize theft. He robbed Wells, Fargo & Co. without pretending that stage robbing was a perfectly legal and commendable occupation. He took the chances of being shot, and at least was frank in his method of obtaining other people's property. I haven't heard him find any fault because he was sent to prison, but I know that what he saw and learned in San Quentin did not fill him with any profound respect for the men who execute the laws or the system which breeds them. All the thieves in San Quentin are not wearing stripes. The biggest robbers are not on the road with shotguns, but they make every man who works stand and deliver."

WHY BART LEFT HIS FAMILY

"But never mind that. Hume says that Boles left his wife and children at a town in Illinois at the close of the war and went to Montana. He didn't. He joined his family in Iowa and tried farming there until he found that it meant only starvation, and then he went West. His wife was a smart, capable woman, who could earn a living by dressmaking. Boles had some education but he had not learned a trade, and his army life did not increase his earning power. The only thing he knew much about was mining, and it was agreed between him and his wife that he should go back to the mines and try to make a stake."

"When he had anything he sent money home. The last time he wrote home before disappearing he sent all the money he had, but it never got there, as he learned from a letter he received shortly afterward from his wife. Then he disappeared and he had reasons for his action. He knew that if he was supposed to be dead, his father, who had property, would look out for his family. Hume describes the family as being 'pinched by poverty and distressed beyond description.' That is not true. Mrs. Boles probably did not put by any money, but she lived comfortably and got along very well."

"When Bart's father died, he left quite a lot of money, and Bart's share went to his wife. It was not a big fortune, but it was enough to assure the family of good living. His wife's name had been Johnson, and she had a brother who also possessed some means. The brother proposed to Mrs. Boles that they should combine their capital, buy a place and live upon and work the farm together, and they did so. While Bart was in prison, Johnson swindled Mrs. Boles out of her property. She was away from the place on a visit, and when she returned she found that her brother had installed a woman in the house and was running things to suit himself. He had taken advantage of her confidence and her ignorance of legal matters to get her property into his own hands, and she found herself practically evicted from her home and robbed of her means."

"Now we come to Hume's statement that Bart wrote a villainous letter to his son-in-law on a flimsy pretext, with the object of putting an end to correspondence with his family. That is a lie. When Bart learned of his brother-in-law's action he wrote an indignant letter to him. The letter was brief, and in a few words demanded restitution of the property to Mrs. Boles. No doubt Johnson found it unpleasant reading. Johnson sent the letter back to Warden Shirley, accompanied by a letter from himself, in which he practically admitted what he had done. Johnson wound up with a whining complaint and wanted to know if convicts were allowed to send out abusive letters. Warden Shirley handed the whole correspondence to Bart, not as a rebuke, but for his information."

"But Captain Aull was practically running the prison, and Bart was soon summoned before him. Aull began by telling Bart that he would not be allowed to write any more such letters. Bart replied: 'You will not be called upon to pass out any letters for me, but you can't dictate to me what I shall write to anybody. I will write what I please. When my letters come to you for approval you can pass judgment upon them, but not otherwise. I believe you are not Warden of this prison.' Then Aull put on his official dignity, and said he would not be talked to in that way. 'You have sent for me,' replied Bart, 'and opened a conversation. If you don't want to be talked to in my way, you can close the interview by sending me away, but while I am here I will say just what I mean.' That ended the conversation, and Bart sent out any letters he wanted to without regard to Mr. Aull's notions of propriety. Hume evidently got his story about the 'villainous' letter from Aull."

"Now, I can tell you why Hume, Aull and the rest of that crowd are so bitter against Bart. When he first went to prison they were all very friendly. The detectives had been getting a great deal of cheap glory on his account, and he was useful to them.

THAT FAMOUS CONFESSION

"You have heard of Bart's confession, in which he owned up to innumerable stage robberies. Here is the truth about that: After he was convicted Hume had a private talk with him — that is, it was supposed to be private, but probably somebody was within hearing distance. Hume said: 'Now this thing is all over, Bart, and nothing that you say can make any difference to you, but you can help me out. I have on my books a long list of robberies that nobody has been arrested for. You can admit to me that you committed them, and I can cross them all off.'"

"Bart declined to do anything of the sort. He said he was not confessing anything. Hume pleaded with him, saying: 'What difference does it make to you? All I want is to clear up my books and square myself. If you will say that you did them I can make my record clear. Now here's one case; I know you did that.'"

"'Yes,' said Bart, 'I did that one, if that is any consolation to you; and as for the rest, you can scratch off whatever you like. I don't care what you do; if you want to clear up your books that is your business.' And that is the substance of the much talked about confession. Hume and the rest of the crowd were very friendly after that. They conceived the great idea of inducing Bart to write a book about himself, giving the history of his life and his exploits. They were to superintend the job, and, of course, they were to be cracked up as the greatest detectives that ever lived. They made the proposition to Bart, and he scornfully rejected it. Then they were not so friendly."

"The detectives and Captain Aull were very anxious to get hold of Bart's diamonds and jewelry, and tried all ways to get them. They came to him with a nice story about his biggest diamond. They said it was a family heirloom, that tender and romantic associations were connected with it, and that the lady to whom it belonged was very anxious to recover it. It was a pretty tale, but it was a lie. Bart happened to know that the diamond had been sent with a lot of others for selection, and was being returned to the diamond merchant when he confiscated it. He wouldn't give it up, and he allowed the schemers to see his contempt for them."

"These great detectives ought to have been satisfied with their rewards. The men really entitled to the money were McConnell, the Copperopolis stagedriver, the hunter who helped him, and Harry Morse. McConnell got $100 and the hunter got a beautiful gun, which afterwards burst in his hands. How the rest of the pot was divided, I don't know. It was just an accident that put the clew into the hands of Hume and his associates, and then they had to get Harry Morse to follow it up and catch Black Bart for them."

"Perhaps the queeresi fatality was connnected with the discovery of Bart's true name. When he first went on the road, he carefully examined all his books and papers and destroyed everything that could reveal his identity, because he did not want his family to know anything about him if he should be caught. When he came to the Bible, which his mother had given to him, he tore out the fly-leaf bearing her name and his, and was about to destroy it, when something impelled him to desist. He knew it was indiscreet, but he could not tear that fly-leaf up, and so he opened the Bible in the middle and put the sheet between the leaves. But for that, nobody ever would have known him as C. E. Boles, and his family would have been spared a great deal."

HIS FIRST ROBBERY

"Let me tell you how my friend Black Bart came to go upon the road. He was traveling about, looking for something to do, and had spent his last dime. Being hungry, he walked up to a ranch-house where people were eating dinner, determined for the first time in his life to ask hospitality of a stranger. He was not a lazy, dirty tramp, but a traveler out of money and hungry. The owner of the ranch met him at the door and Bart spoke to him, not humbly or beggingly, but man fashion. He said: 'I have walked some distance, and being quite hungry, I would like to have dinner with you. I have no money.' 'Wait here,' said the farmer, as he went inside. Bart took a chair on the porch and waited, and as he sat there two or three dogs came sniffing about him. In a moment the man returned with some scraps of food in a tin dish, and handed the dish to Bart. Bart quietly took the dish and placed it down in front of the dogs."

"'Isn't it good enough for you?' asked the farmer. 'No,' replied Bart, 'I do not think such hospitality good enough for anybody.' The farmer said rather surly that he didn't believe in encouraging tramps. Bart got up and said: 'This is the first time I ever asked anybody to give me anything, and it will be the last. Hereafter, when I want anything, I shall demand it and take it.'"

"He left the place, and further up the road found another ranch. Nobody was in the house, but through the window he saw food on the table. He went in, ate all he wanted, and left a note, saying that he had taken a dinner, and telling the owner to send his bill if he wanted pay for it, giving his proper address. Of course, he never heard any more of it, and that may be counted as Black Bart's first robbery. After that he demanded what he wanted on the road, and usually he got it. He found stage robbing no trick at all. Why, if he chose, he could go out with no other weapon than an old stick and hold up a stage. George Hackett did take a shot at him once on the Lakeport road, but it was accident that gave him the chance. There were three horses attached to the stage, and Bart stood in front of the leader. This horse was nervous, and jumped around a good deal. Bart took his eyes off the box for a moment and glanced at the horse and, as he did that, the messenger fired. One of the shots struck Bart on the head and knocked him down, partly stunned, but the messenger did not follow up his advantage, and Bart got away."

A MIDNIGHT RIDE AND AN ALIBI

"Here is one case, illustrating his method of working. Never mind where this occurred. Bart went to a country hotel, where the stages stopped at night, and some time before the stage was due he asked the landlord to show him his room. He told the landlord that he wanted to take the down stage in the morning, and wished to be called early. Then he undressed and got into bed, leaving the candle burning. Half an hour after the night stage had come and gone he rang for the porter and asked for some water. When the porter had brought the water and gone away Bart got up and dressed, cut an inch off the bottom of the candle to make it appear that it had been burned a long time, and slipped out of the house unobserved. He went down to the river, where he had seen some boats, and paddled across the stream to a field where some horses were staked out. He selected the best horse, made a nose-bridle of the riata, mounted him, swam the stream, and followed the stage."

"Knowing the roads and lanes thoroughly, and having a good horse, he got around and ahead of the stage and waited for it at a turn in the road. As the stage approached his horse began to whinny, but he patted the animal's neck and quieted him. The stage came up and was halted, and Bart got what he was after. The stage was driven on, and Bart remounted and rode back at full speed, taking sideroads and cutting across open country. He forded the stream again, staked out the horse where the grass was green and thick, paddled back in the boat, slipped into the house and went to bed. Early in the morning the landlord called him and woke him up."

"When the down stage came along it brought news of the robbery, and Bart joined in the discussion that ensued. Suppose even that one of his cuffs had been found on the road where the robbery occurred. He could have proved by the testimony of the hotel people that he was in bed half an hour after the stage left that night, and the landlord would have sworn that he waked him up in the morning. Mr. Hume may take this as a confession, if he can locate the affair, and perhaps scratch off another unfinished case from his record-book."

"Now, I think that is all I can tell you. Where Black Bart has been and what he has done since he left San Quentin is his own business, and you don't want to know anything about it. You can say, however, that he never promised Mr. Hume or anbody else to do or refrain from doing anything whatever. He didn't ask anybody's advice about where he should go; that isn't his way. He is under obligations to none of that crowd, and he cares very little for their abuse. Goodnight."

Appendix V
The Bogus Poems

Black Bart left only twelve genuine lines of his poetry. He certainly didn't compose a poem for each holdup, though he might have written one for what turned out to be his last robbery. Fake Bart poems began appearing in late 1888, usually in small-town newspapers, when he was rumored to have taken up the highwayman's profession again. Where possible, the newspaper of origin is credited.

> This is my way to get money and bread
> When I have a chance, why should I refuse it ?
> I'll not need either while I'm dead
> And I only rob those who are able to lose it.
> — *Placer Democrat*

> I rob the rich to feed the poor
> Which hardly is a sin:
> A widow ne'er knocked at my door
> But what I let her in.
> So blame me not for what I've done
> I don't deserve your curses
> And if for any cause I'm hung
> Let it be for my verses.
> — *San Francisco Chronicle* (May, 1934)

Bart supposedly wrote the next poem between robberies, while treking on the Stillwater Plains in Shasta County, after he visited Jack Reid's cabin. Reid was absent, but Bart entered the cabin and ate some food. In exchange for what he'd taken, the bandit cleaned the house and washed the dishes. When Reid returned he found the following poem in a washed cup:

> Goodbye Shasta County,
> I will bid you adieu.
> I may emigrate to Hell,
> but I'll never come back to you.
> — (Unidentified clipping)

This poem appears in alternative versions; the original is probably in the *Yreka Union*:

> Lo, here I've stood, while wind and rain
> Have set the trees a-sobbin'
> And risked my life for that damned stage*
> That wasn't worth the robbin'
> — *Yreka Union*

*Printed in the newspaper as "that ...... stage."

> Here I lay, while wind and rain
> Set the trees a-sobbing
> To risk my life for a damned old stage
> That isn't worth the robbing.
> — *San Francisco Examiner*

The final poem may be genuine. As stated earlier, when she was very young Nellie Owen accompanied her father to San Quentin to visit Boles, who wrote the poem for her. The beginning letters of each line, read down, spell her name. Although the original burned in a fire that destroyed the Owen house in Berkeley, Nellie had memorized the poem and recited it to family members in 1961.[73]

> Never, oh never shall I forget
> Engraved in my heart is your image, sweet pet
> Like the sunbeams and dewdrops pure sparkling and bright
> Like the bright stars of heaven shedding forth their soft light
> In memory's casket you never shall lie
> Ever, forever, dear Nellie, goodbye.
> — San Quentin, circa 1883-88

Appendix VI
Black Bart's Love Life

Despite rumors of a mistress, probably concocted by San Francisco reporters to spice up their stories of his capture and imprisonment (like the description of his landlady's jail visit), no evidence has been found that Black Bart sought female company, either genteel or of the demi-monde.

After Bart's capture this romantic story was published in the November 19, 1883 *Sacramento Record-Union*. It contains some concrete detail but is most likely completely fictitious:

THE PO-8 OF THE SIERRAS
Black Bart Finds His "Mollie Darling" in Sacramento

The far-famed and notorious individual, the terror of the Sierras, who has singlehanded robbed more stages than any man on the continent, and who is known far and wide as "Black Bart, the Po-8," came to Sacramento about the middle of last August. He immediately secured a room in a lodging-house near the Post office, on Fourth street, between J and K, and for the first time, as recorded in his long career, was 'captured,' and became a slave to the charms of a woman, the object of his heart's idol being the temporarily-engaged chambermaid of his lodging-house, a woman well known on the streets of this city.

The po-8 spent the greater part of his time in his room writing and whispering words of love and devotion into the ear of his "Mollie darling." Cruel fate in this, as in many other love affairs, had placed an obstacle in the way of the entire twenty-four hours being passed in love's embrace, as at night the lovely maid had to hie herself away to the abode of her other admirer, who roomed on L street just a stone's throw from Sixth, leaving the poor poetical genius to pass the long weary nights alone. Although he had shown twenty-three different stage drivers that he "had the nerve," he doubtless concluded it would be a "cold day" for him if he got into a row with an ice man, even though the latter was but an employee in the cooling business.

Thus the last weeks of August were whiled away, and two other women were taken into their circle. When old John Robinson's circus came to the city the bold robber took the two to the show. On another occasion he took his adored to a shoe store on J street, where he had her tiny feet fitted with the best the establishment afforded, urging her not to think of price at all but to please her taste.

About the first of September, urgent business called the knight of the shotgun away, but not until a fictitious name was improvised for his "pet," in order that he might telegraph her, announcing his return, without the ice man "catching on." In due time the dispatch came, and on the 6th of September the po-8 returned, registered at the International Hotel, and remained over the 7th. A reception was given the distinguished individual at his room in the evening by the three women referred to above. At a reasonable hour, two of the females withdrew after having given the po-8 and his 'Mollie darling' their blessing for the night. It seems that there must have been at least one "cold night" scored against the ice man.

Nothing was seen of the polite old gentleman until the 5th of November — ten days after his last stage robbery — when he called at the hotel and got an old hat and valise, which he had left in charge of the proprietor. On that day he went to the tailoring establishment of Thomas Bromley, on J street, and ordered a $45 suit of clothes. He was again lost sight of until the 10th, when he called at Bromley's, received and paid for the suit.

As the ice man has been transformed from a vendor of frozen liquid to a fireman on Front street, and had to work nights, and must necessarily sleep day times, of course he can't tell who entertained the po-8 of nights and fed him during the days between the 5th and 10th of the month.

As soon as the new clothes were obtained to replace those worn at the time of the commission of the robbery, the po-8 had the appearance of a dude and was daily to be seen around the domicile of "Mollie darling's" tall friend, one of the trio referred to, and there can be but one conclusion as to who furnished consolation and food during the five days of seclusion.

Whether or not the detectives followed up the case and searched Susan's and Mollie's rooms for stolen property the reporter has been unable to learn; but if such has been done nothing was likely found, secrecy implored and granted.

~

(Courtesy Rosemarie Mossinger)

Through the years hints of a mysterious woman in Black Bart's life appeared, but they were never substantiated. In the 1940s the lively but badly-written *Pony Express Journal* printed stories about Black Bart and Mary Vollmer, based on an old legend in Woodleaf (Woodville). Until recently this was little more than another Black Bart tale. Then in 1970 the Woodleaf Hotel was renovated and a small paper note found behind loose wallpaper in an upstairs room. The ornately engraved Victorian card had a simple written message:

> Charley,
> Drop one pearl in memory's casket, for your friend.
> Mary E. Hall,
> Woodville, May 24, 1883

Unfortunately, the card itself was destroyed about 1980 when the hotel's records were taken to the local dump, but not before a professional historian photographed it. So its message, seen and verified by an expert witness, *is* authentic, and the card *was* discovered in the old hotel — that much is true. Furthermore, Charles Bolton was known to have stayed there, attested to by the Falck family, who owned the hotel in the 1880s (a plaque designating the building as an historic monument states that President Grant, Lotta Crabtree and Black Bart slept there). But is the 'Charley' on the note Charles Boles? Who was 'the belle of Woodleaf?' Mary Hall or Mary

Vollmer? Or did another Mary write a note to a different Charley? We don't know — but the appearance of 'in memory's casket' in two poems (see the poem to Nellie Owen in Appendix V) — if no relationship exists — is almost beyond the range of probability (the phrase might have come from a then popular, now unknown 19th century poem).

If there is a connection, the seemingly ridiculous story alluded to in the *Pony Express Journal* — that after his release from prison Bart married the widow Mary Vollmer (thereby committing bigamy) in Harrisburg, Pennsylvania — cannot be summarily dismissed. The *Journal* offered no documentation, except the statement in several issues that she was still alive in 1940. A school teacher named Mary Vollmer was listed in the Harrisburg City Directories in the 1880s and 1890s. It is not known if she ever visited California, nor has evidence of a link with Charles Boles been discovered. She died January 23, 1940. Proof of a love affair between Charles Boles and Mary Vollmer might substantially alter certain conclusions made in this book.

It is also possible that the editor of the *Pony Express Journal* was misled by an article in the December 12, 1888 *San Francisco Chronicle*. This consists of reprints of Mary Boles and Charles Boles's letters and an interview with James Hume — but it suddenly, with some confusion, shifts to the stage robber, J. A. Wright (see Page 201). Wright held up a stage on the Sonora-Milton line and had a female relative in Sacramento, who told Hume that the outlaw had gone back to Pennsylvania after serving his prison sentence. Perhaps this information about Wright was mistakenly transferred to Charles Boles.

Appendix VII
Black Bart Today

"Time has not dimmed the special appeal of this colorful outlaw, and in fact has probably increased it. The stories of his exploits remain a colorful thread in the tapestry of California's history."[74] Or put another way, "So legends grow and develop and change, adding a bit here and dropping a little there until they become something entirely new."[75] The public's interest in this mild-mannered man, yet "a synonym for elusiveness and mystery," continues unabated; children daily request information about him from their teachers and librarians, the original impetus for this book.

There is one known contemporary (out-of-print) novel about Black Bart, *A House Behind the Mint* by Laurie Huffman (Doubleday & Company, 1969). The book reads well and sticks to the facts, given the license granted to writers of historical fiction. The author probably didn't go beyond Joseph Henry Jackson's *Bad Company*, but that would have been adquate.

(*New York Times, March, 1948*)

Black Bart, a feature-length Hollywood motion picture was made in 1948, with Dan Duryea as Charles Boles and Yvonne DeCarlo as Lola Montez. Two other cast members were Percy Kilbride and Chief Many Treaties. *The Hollywood Reporter*'s review said in part, "The pace is brisk, the story credible and the performance persuasive." Credible for them, perhaps, but any criticism of the movie's historical authenticity would be an understatement. Montez, a famous dancer and courtesan of the mid-

19th Century, left San Francisco in 1856 and died in New York in 1861. It seems rather unlikely she would have known Charles Boles.

A fanciful Black Bart appears in a scene in the 1982 movie *A Christmas Story.* Supposedly a silent film was also made about the outlaw, but it has not been traced.

A syndicated television series, hosted by Col. Tim McCoy, apparently had one episode about Black Bart (which aired on San Francisco's KGO-TV in 1956). The 'Jim Hardie' character played by Dale Robertson in the 1950s TV series *Wells, Fargo* is modeled, often innacurately, on James B. Hume.

The character of Black Bart has inspired numerous plays. Representative are *BLACK BART or THE LONE ROBBER OF CALAVERAS COUNTY* by Melcena Denny, performed by The Troupers of the Gold Coast, which had a long run at California's First Theatre in Monterey, California in 1947, and *CURSE YOU, BLACK BART,* A Western Melodrama in Five Acts, by Tom Maxwell, performed at the Marines Memorial Theater in San Francisco in 1971.

A song, 'The Ballad of Black Bart,' written by Josephine and Margherita Sanfilippo, was recorded by Rich Jaqua on a 45rpm record, once available from TPA (Tin Pan Alley) Records, Sarasota, Florida.

(Courtesy David & Suzanne Brown)

For a while in the 1960s the Last Hurrah Restaurant and Night Club in Portland, Oregon featured a Black Bart Sandwich: roast beef, turkey breast, tillamook cheese, cheddar cheese, mayonaise, lettuce, tomato, on a french roll, all for $2.85 (customers could order Buffalo Bill and Jim Bowie sandwiches if they preferred).

A limited edition ceramic decanter (straight bourbon whiskey-86 proof) was produced by the McCormick Distilling Company of Weston, Missouri in 1974, part of their series, 'The Gunfighters.' The representation is extremely good and the piece quite rare. The bottle states

BALLAD OF BLACK BART

Lyric by JOSEPHINE A. SANFILIPPO
Music by MARGHERITA SANFILIPPO

2. Black Bart, he used no bullets, A shotgun he carried for fun:
   "Will you please throw down your treasure box, sir?"—Pointing his empty *Shot-gun.*

3. Black Bart, he was a poet, And this earned him early fame.
   He left at ev'ry holdup verses signed with his name.

4. Black Bart, he went to prison, and six years in jail he spent,
   With plenty of time to think of his sins, Plenty of time to repent.

5. Black Bart at last was set free, Wells Fargo had no more to fear;
   And on their pension Black Bart lived happily many a year.

(Back to Chorus)

(Courtesy Wells Fargo Bank)

on one side: 'From authentic paintings in the Overland Hotel, Reno, Nevada.' The hotel wasn't built until 1909, so Black Bart didn't sleep there. It was decorated in a western theme and torn down about 1980.

Expectedly, numerous advertising agencies have exploited Black Bart: one was the Sonoma Coast development, Sea Ranch, in 1974; another was

Aetna Insurance, who printed an ad called "The Hazards of Banking: The Pillaging Poet." Both Honeynut Cheerios and Rayovac Batteries used Bart in televison commercials during the 1960's.

Wells Fargo Bank itself, playing on what seems like a grand historical joke (but it was one of a series of historical characters), made Black Bart available for its customers' checks during the 1970s.

As for the 'public' Black Bart, quite a bit exists around California. The most authentic display is in San Andreas, where the Calaveras County Historical Society has exhibits and a research center in the restored 1868 San Andreas Courthouse. The jail where Black Bart was housed, the courtroom where he was convicted and sentenced, are in that building.

In San Francisco free guided tours are conducted at the Wells, Fargo Museum. Displays of a Wells, Fargo stagecoach and some Black Bart memorabilia can be seen. Research into the extensive Wells, Fargo & Co. records is by appointment only (plus payment of a modest fee), but the library is a goldmine of California history and Americana. Wells Fargo Bank also has historical museums in Sacramento, Los Angeles and San Diego.

In Oroville the Butte County Pioneer Museum displays a Wells, Fargo box robbed by Black Bart (either Robbery No. 5 or No. 9).

In Quincy the Plumas County Museum displays a small unmarked treasure box with the left end bashed in. It was received and is displayed as a relic of a Black Bart robbery.

In Shasta a display in the 1855 Courthouse Building, now a history and art museum, includes a .36 Colt revolver supposedly used against Black Bart.

In Weaverville the Wells, Fargo iron strongbox that Black Bart attempted to rob on September 1, 1880 (Robbery No. 13) is in the J. J. Jackson Memorial Museum.

San Andreas hosts Black Bart Day, including a parade, usually held the first week in September. San Andreas also has a Black Bart Inn and Saloon.

In Murphys three Charles Boles' signatures can be seen in the Murphys Hotel. Also, the Black Bart Players perform in the Native Sons of the Golden West Hall every year in April and November.

In Willits the Black Bart Gang performs western gunfight enactments during Frontier Days each July.

Cloverdale hosts Black Bart Days in May.

Duncans Mills goes all out, with a display in the Depot Museum, a Black Bart Day, usually in October, and a Black Bart Doggerel Poetry Contest in the Black Bart Tavern.

A few miles away, just outside Cazadero, is the Black Bart Cafe.

A road named Black Bart Trail exists in Redwood Valley.

In Los Angeles the Gene Autry Western Heritage Museum displays a shotgun supposedly used by Black Bart (given first to the Pony Express Museum in Pasadena by a Wells, Fargo official).

Concord (where Boles supposedly taught) had a Black Bart Festival as late as 1956. The motel opposite the questionable rock at Ridgewood Summit between Willits and Ukiah had a Black Bart dining room. The Palace Hotel in Ukiah had a Black Bart Saloon. Grass Valley had a Black Bart Motel. The Black Bart Chromite Mine once existed in Lake County.

Finally, Knott's Berry Farm near Los Angeles has a stagecoach (originally on the La Porte-Marysville line) that Black Bart supposedly robbed of its Wells, Fargo treasure box. A plaque on the old Concord (apparently written during the 1950's, figuring his death date as 1917) conjures up this fanciful legend:

HIS GHOST RETURNS

It is reported that Black Bart has a curious and intense liking for this perticular coach and though he has been dead these 40 odd years, there are some who say that his spirit often returns here.

And on nights when there is no moon, he can be actually seen lounging quite comfortable in the interior of this coach, and on occasion he sometimes climbs up into the drivers seat and plies the whip to the horses so vehemently that the coach and all go clattering down the road at a tremendous speed as though a hundred thousand (100,000) highwaymen were going to kill him and steal all the gold he had so boldly taken during his adventurous lifetime.

~

Thus the failed farmer, failed miner, failed husband and father, and, at the end, failed stagecoach robber, has been placed beside 'The Headless Horseman' and 'Pecos Bill' in the pantheon of American mythology. One can only imagine how astounded and thrilled — certainly amused — Charles Boles would have been with all the hoopla.

TO THOSE WHO COME AFTER ME

I took my name from Caxton's tale,
It suited me just fine,
And launched a life of lucre-lifting,
And dabbled some in rhyme.

For Uncle Billy Sherman
Was a Banker tried and true,
And with his Georgia "customers,"
He taught me all I knew.

I'd tried my hand at digging gold;
That work was cold and wet.
Wells and Fargo's treasure box
Is a better mine, you bet!

Jamie Hume's a clever man —
At least he does think so.
But I thumb my nose at Wells Fargo
And with their gold I go.

I learned that day as bullets flew,
And brought forth ol' Sheriff Benny:
Never go back to the scene of a crime —
Not that I'd committed any.

Before there were car license plates,
I was "F[o]X O 7."
To San Quentin went my road —
Not my idea of heaven.

Never one to hold a grudge,
Gifts to my Friends I gave.
To Jamie Hume went marmalade,
His breakfast toast to pave.

Since that time I've travelled on,
No one knows my fate.
A horde comes on, seeking clues,
Those fools I love to bait.

Now better known than Wells Fargo,
I humbly leave this zinger:
To those who come after me,
I wag my middle finger!

> Black Bart
> the Reprob-8

— Robert J. Chandler —

Notes

1 'Stagecoach West'
2 H. H. Bancroft: *History of California*
3 Brigadier General James F. Rusling
4 'Driving A Horse Drawn Stage Today Is Almost A Lost Art'
5 Ninetta Eames: 'Staging in the Mendocino Redwoods'
6 Hank Johnston: *Yosemite's Yesterdays*
7 Augie Heeser: *The Mendocino Beacon*
8 Owen Treleaven: 'Old Men in the Sun'
9 Robert J. Chandler
10 Robert J. Chandler: 'Wells Fargo: We Never Forget!'
11 Some writers, misreading Bart's commitment papers to San Quentin, have him born in 'Calaveras County, New York.' There is no such county in that state.
12 Jefferson County's only other famous person seems to have been James B. Liddy, inventor of the bedspring. Liddy worked in a carriage shop in Watertown. Coiled springs, used in carriage seats to soften jolts from dirt roads, had never been used for beds. But Liddy "seems not to have been a financial wizard as he realized no financial gain from his invention. Being a simple country lad, he had no idea of the commercial value of his invention and did not attempt to obtain patent rights." Lennon, Jefferson County Historical Society Bulletin.
13 The earliest surviving Bowles family letter, written from Shelfanger on October 19, 1830 by Robert 'Bowels' to his brother John in America, exhibits this skill, as do later letters written by Charles' younger sister, Maria.
14 After his capture Boles told reporters he'd come to California on the *John L. Stephens*, but this ship wasn't commissioned until 1853.
15 Numerous researchers have been incorrect about this location. The worst have said the state of Oregon; 'better' writers Oregon City, Illinois. Investigations in Ogle County in Illinois (Oregon City is the county seat) reveal nothing of Charles or Mary Boles' presence.
16 The Warrensburg house was dismantled in 1979 after being measured for eventual reconstruction by the Macon County Museum, but little interest has been shown for a monument to its famous resident.
17 Brigadier General J. N. Reece: *Report, Adjutant General of the State of Illinois,* Volume VI
18 Patrick Mooney married the great-aunt of the principal Bowles family genealogist, George J. Nixon of Salt Lake City, whose research was used extensively in this book.
19 A number of books and articles refer to this as 'Calina City,' a misreading of script that has caused innumerable wasted hours of research.
20 John Bowles signed his 'X' on his Last Will and Testament (he apparently never learned how to read or write) just a month before he died. Perhaps he had been induced to do it, but no particular family pressure is evident. He left his property to his wife, but made specific bequests to the children of his two presumably deceased sons, James and Charles, through their mothers. On his wife's death the New York property was divided among his three daughters and his youngest son, Hiram, the only living son (that he knew of).
21 Unlike Charles Boles' brother, John Hume thrived in California, becoming a successful lawyer in Placerville and later a member of the State Assembly.
22 Hume & Thacker: Official Report, Wells Fargo & Co's Express
23 Ash Williamson, according to the *Point Arena News*; Jack Morrison, according to journals of turn-of-the-century stagecoach driver, Jotham. L. Sedgley. Courtesy Cloverdale Historical Society.
24 E. L. Bacon: 'In the Days of Black Bart.' Courtesy Wells Fargo Bank.
25 Alvin Harlow: *Old Waybills*
26 George Ward, in the 1960's.
27 Sydney and Salina McCreary also owned a house on Burris Lane in Potter Valley; some writers have incorrectly located the site of the ranch.
28 Emma Thornton: 'The Children of William and Mary Sullaway'

29 Clyde Brewster: 'Lewis L. Brewster'
30 The town, earlier called Little Lake, had become Willitsville, and six years later would incorporate as Willits.
31 Henry Mauldin: 'History of Lake County'
32 Wells, Fargo & Company Archives: 'Advices, Posters, Etc. Relating to Robberies, Etc., August 1, 1882 to February 3, 1885.' Courtesy Wells, Fargo Bank.
33 Ibid.
34 Wells, Fargo & Company Archives. Courtesy Wells Fargo Bank.
35 Wells Fargo & Company Archives: 'Advices, Posters, Etc. Relating to Robberies, Etc., August 1, 1882 to February 3, 1885.' Courtesy Wells Fargo Bank.
36 Treleaven: 'Old Men in the Sun'
37 Letter written by Ben K. Thorn to Harry Morse in 1884. In the Alice Phelan Sullivan Library and Archives, Society of California Pioneers. Used by permission.
38 Treleaven: 'Old Men in the Sun'
39 Letter written by Ben K. Thorn
40 Letter from John Thacker to Oren Langemate, March 13, 1884. Wells Fargo Archives. Courtesy Wells Fargo Bank.
41 Joseph Henry Jackson: *Bad Company*
42 Treleaven: 'Old Men in the Sun'
43 Courtesy Wells Fargo Bank.
44 Wells, Fargo & Co. General Cash Books, November, 1883. Courtesy Wells Fargo Bank.
45 Letter written by Ben K. Thorn.
46 Information from 1927 letter written by Luke Fay, in Wells, Fargo Archives Courtesy Wells Fargo Bank.
47 Apparently some of Bart's clothing was left in his room and later stolen by a sneak-thief named Martin Kampfer, who was convicted of petty larceny in January, 1884.
48 Information courtesy Bancroft Library and Wells Fargo Bank.
49 Letter written by Ben K. Thorn.
50 Treleaven: 'Old Men in the Sun'
51 *The National Police Gazette*, 12/15/83
52 Pete Fanning: *Great Crimes of the West*
53 *The National Police Gazette*
54 Wells Fargo & Co. General Cash Books. Courtesy Wells Fargo Bank.
55 Ibid.
56 George Hoeper: 'Stage Robbery, A Risky Profession'
57 Quotations in Dillon and Hoeper.
58 Letter written by Ben K. Thorn.
59 Told to Owen Trealeven by Mrs. John N. Thacker. Courtesy Wells Fargo Bank. The toothpick is in the Wells Fargo History Room.
60 Letter written by Owen T. Stebbins, of Kentfield, California to Wells, Fargo in 1975. Samuel Owen was Stebbins' great-grandfather, 'Nellie' his great aunt. Courtesy Wells Fargo Bank.
61 Originally printed in the *Hannibal Journal* and reprinted in the *San Francisco Chronicle*.
62 Ibid.
63 In 1849 a black man erected a tent as a station on the pack trail from Camptonville to Downieville, in present-day Sierra County.
64 Courtesy Wells Fargo Bank.
65 Joseph Henry Jackson: *Tintypes in Gold*
66 Robert Chandler, letter to author, 6/30/1992
67 Treleaven: 'Old Men in the Sun'
68 Where she was living at the time of the *Hannibal Journal* interview, on page xxx.
69 Joseph Henry Jackson: 'A Bookman's Notebook,' *San Francisco Chronicle*
70 Noel Loomis: *Wells Fargo*, An Illustrated History
71 Courtesy Wells Fargo Bank.
72 Stebbins letter to Wells Fargo Bank, 1975. Courtesy Wells Fargo Bank.
73 Millie Robbins: 'Millie's Column,' *San Francisco Chronicle*
74 Joseph Henry Jackson: 'A Bookman's Notebook,' *San Francisco Chronicle*
75 Bill Anderson: 'Black Bart,' Dogtown Territorial Quarterly

REWARD

$1,000

IN GOLD COIN

Will be paid by the Sonora Stagecoach Company

for the arrest and conviction of the

notorious STAGE ROBBER known as —

BLACK BART

This dastardly villain cunningly conceals himself in a long linen duster - - artfully using a flour sack with eyeholes, over his head. He carries a firearm and according to his unfortunate victims is a man of gentle birth with the manners of a perfect gentleman.

He fancies himself to be a poet, leaving scraps of doggerel in the empty express boxes he has just robbed, and signing himself - B.B., P.O.8 Each line of the poems is carefully disguised as if written by a different hand, as you can witness by this artistic *fac simile* printed here.

Any information leading to his apprehension will be rewarded. *Address:*

THOMAS CRANE *Superintendent*
SONORA STAGE COACH COMPANY, SAN FRANCISCO **SEPTEMBER 1877**

A *fake* Black Bart Poster distributed during the 1930s or 1940s.
(Courtesy William Brazil, Jr.)

Sources & Bibliography

During the last 40 years probably a month hasn't gone by without mention of Black Bart in a publication somewhere. Unfortunately, many articles contain egregious factual errors. This is sometimes excusable, particularly when information is difficult to obtain, and mistakes do, of course, occur. One assumes that "He was leading a double life when captured, working as a bank clerk in San Francisco between excursions into the country to rob stagecoaches," as written in a recent major northern California history (*Santa Rosa*, A Nineteenth Century Town), is an oversight.

Then some writing is so bad it is amusing, like *The Hearts of the West*, written by Thomas Murphy in 1928. In this totally outrageous rare book, Black Bart is called "a notorious and bloody road agent" and heads a five man gang. At the end, California Joe kills Bart in a saloon brawl, by shooting him in the stomach. Then the state of California gives California Joe a $10,000 reward!

But one is not amused when contemporary authors transfer pulp writers' inventions into supposed reference works, as happened in the massive, three volume *Encyclopedia of Frontier Biography*, published in 1988. The worst writers, of course, make statements like, "Duncan's Mills and Point Arena, in the heart of California's gold-mining camps," and "he was born in New York state before moving West with his parents. Some accounts list him as a farmer, then a medicine drummer" — as John Wukovits did in a 1991 article. Though not criminal, this is a terrible disservice to readers. Wukovits, knowing neither geography nor history, has rehashed other writers' errors and fabrications (and created new ones), twisting the truth for monetary gain.

Another writer, Carl Breihan, made a career out of Black Bart (three known magazine articles, plus a section in his own book about western outlaws). Unfortunately, his research skills do not match his output, as he consistently made factual errors, particularly spellings, and worse created events that never occurred. He alone suggests that Charles Boles used 'Boulton' as an alias, and invented ridiculous stories, such as a room Black Bart kept at the Commercial Hotel in Ukiah ("and when this building was torn down in the 1930's, a pencil drawing signed Black Bart on the back side was found therein."). A Commercial Hotel did not exist in Ukiah prior to 1890.

Sometimes the inventions are amusing:

> Shortly thereafter, [Robbery No. 8] Bart had a narrow escape with the law. Several deputies and the Sheriff of Mendocino County thought they had him surrounded in the mountains when they saw him dash into an abandoned

cabin. They surrounded the cabin and on signal they all rushed the cabin only to find that Bart was not there. They looked around behind them and found that the crafty old gentleman had climbed out the chimney and was getting away in the Sheriff's buggy, leaving them stranded! This, by the way, was the only time Bart was known to use any other means of escape than his own two good legs.[76]

But they are still falsehoods. So readers desiring more information about Black Bart should be cautious — much of what they read may be fiction, if not flagrant lies.

Newspapers

The primary sources used to research this book were California newspapers published between 1875 and 1888. Information was also obtained from papers of later dates plus some out-of-state newspapers.

Amador Sentinel
Ashland (Oregon) *Tidings*
The Butte (Montana) *Daily Miner*
Calaveras Chronicle
Cloverdale Reveille
Daily Alta California (San Francisco)
Decatur (Illinois) *Herald & Review*
Deseret News (Salt Lake City, Utah)
Downieville Mountain Messenger
Grass Valley Union
Hannibal (Missouri) *Courier*
Hannibal (Missouri) *Journal*
Hollywood Reporter
Jacksonville (Oregon)
  Democratic Times
Marysville Daily & Weekly Appeal
Mendocino Beacon
National Police Gazette (New York)
Nevada County Nugget
Nevada (Carson City) *Tribune*
New York Times
Petaluma Weekly Argus
Point Arena News
Redding Indepedent
Redding Torchlight
Russian River Flag

Sacramento Union
Sacramento Record-Union
Saint Louis (Missouri)
  Globe-Democrat
San Francisco Bulletin
San Francisco Call
San Francisco Chronicle
San Francisco Examiner
San Francisco Newsletter
  & California Advertiser
San Francisco Post
Santa Rosa Press Democrat
Shasta County Democrat
Sonoma Democrat (Santa Rosa)
Sonora Union Democrat
Stockton Daily Independent
Stockton Republican
Trinity Journal
Tuolumne County Independent
Ukiah City Press
Ukiah Republican Press
Weekly Butte Record (Chico)
Willits News
Woodland Democrat
Yreka Journal

Books & Guides

Three works should be read by anyone interested in California outlaws and lawmen: *Bad Company* by Joseph Henry Jackson, *Wells Fargo Detective* by Richard Dillon, and *Badge and Buckshot* by John Boessenecker. These books deserve praise, both for their historicity and entertaining writing styles. Although the work is concerned primarily with southern Oregon, anyone interested in staging should read *Knights of the Whip* by Gary & Gloria Meier.

Atherton, Gertrude: *My San Francisco* — A Wayward Biography
(The Bobbs-Merrill Company, Indianapolis, 1946)

Bancroft's Guide for Travelers By Railway, Stage, and Steam Navigation
in the Pacific States (A. L. Bancroft & Company, San Francisco, 1871, 1874)

Bancroft, Hubert H.: *History of California*, Vol. VII
(The History Company, San Francisco, 1890)

Banning, William and George Banning: *Six Horses*
(The Century Co., New York, 1930)

Beebe, Lucius and Charles Clegg: *U.S. West*, The Saga of Wells Fargo
(E.P. Dutton, New York, 1949)

Block, Eugene B.: *Great Stagecoach Robbers of the West*
(Doubleday & Company, New York, 1962)

Boessenecker, John: *Badge and Buckshot*, Lawlessness In
Old California (University of Oklahoma Press, Norman, 1987)

Boggs, Mae Helene Bacon: *My Playhouse was a Concord Coach*
(Howell-North Press, Oakland, 1941)

Breihan, Carl W., with Charles Rosamond: *The Bandit Belle and
other Tales* (Hangman Press/Superior Publishing Co., Seattle, 1970)

Buckbee, Edna Bryan: *Pioneer Days of Angels Camp*
(*Calaveras Californian*, Angels Camp, 1932)

Carranco, Lynwood and Estle Beard: *Genocide and Vendetta*
(University of Oklahoma Press, Norman, 1981)

[Cassiday, Sam.] *An Illustrated History of Sonoma County,
California* (Lewis Publishing Co., Chicago, 1889

Colby, W. H.: *A Century of Transportation in Shasta County 1820-1920*
(Association for Northern California Records & Research, Chico, 1982)

Dane, George Ezra: *Ghost Town* (Alfred A. Knopf, New York, 1941)

Davis, Jean, compiler: *Shallow Diggin's*
(Caxton Printers, Ltd., Caldwell, 1962)

Dillon, Richard: *Wells Fargo Detective*, The Biography
of James. B. Hume (Coward-McCann, Inc. New York, 1969)

Drago, Harry Sinclair: *Road Agents and Train Robbers*
(Dodd, Mead & Company, New York, 1973)

Duke, Captain Thomas S.: *Celebrated Criminal Cases of America*
(Barry Co., 1910)

Early California, Northern Edition (Western Guide Publishers, Corvallis, 1974)

Escola, Nannie and Julia Moungovan: *Mendocino County Vignettes*
(Mendocino County Historical Society, Fort Bragg, 1967)

Fanning, Pete: *Great Crimes of the West*, 1929

Finley, Ernest. ed.: *History of Sonoma County*
(Press Democrat Publishing Co., Santa Rosa, 1937)

Gudde, Erwin: *California Place Names*,
(University of California Press, Berkeley and Los Angeles, 1969)

Harlan, George H., and Clement Fisher, jr.: *Of Walking Beams
and Paddle Wheels* (Bay Books Limited, San Francisco, 1951)

Harlow, Alvin F.: *Old Waybills*, The Romance of the
Express Companies (D. Appleton and Company, New York, 1928)

Hart, James D.: *A Companion to California*
(Oxford University Press, New York, 1978)

Hoover, Mildred B., H. & E. Rensch: *Historic Spots in California*,
3rd Edition (Stanford University Press, Stanford, 1966)

Hume, Jas B., and Jno. N. Thacker: *Official Report, Wells Fargo &
Co's Express* (H.S. Crocker & Co. San Francisco, 1885)

Hungerford, Edward: **Wells Fargo**
(Random House, Inc., New York, 1949)

Jackson, Joseph Henry: *Anybody's Gold*
(D. Appleton-Century, New York, 1941)

Jackson, Joseph Henry: *Bad Company*
(Harcourt, Brace and Company, New York, 1949

Jackson, Joseph Henry: *Tintypes in Gold*, Four Studies in Robbery
(The Macmillan Co., New York, 1939)

Jackson, W. Turrentine: *Wells Fargo Stagecoaching in
Montana Territory* (Montana Historical Society Press, Helena, 1979)

Johnston, Hank: *Yosemite's Yesterdays*
(Flying Spur Press, Yosemite, 1987)

Kneiss, Gilbert H.: *Redwood Railways* (Howell-North, Berkeley, 1956)

Langley's *San Francisco City Guide*
(The Directory Publishing Co., San Francisco, 1883)

LeBaron, Gaye; Blackman, Mitchell, Hansen: *Santa Rosa*,
A Nineteenth Century Town (Historia, Ltd, Santa Rosa, 1985)

Lee, Hector: *Tales of California* (Published by author, Santa Rosa, 1974)

Loomis, Noel M.: *Wells Fargo*, An Illustrated History
(Bramhall House, New York, 1968)

McGie, Joseph: *History of Butte County*, Volume I
(Butte County Board of Education, Chico, 1956. Revised 1982)

Meir, Gary and Gloria Meier: *Knights of the Whip*
(Timeline Publishing, Bellvue, 1988)

Miller, Donald C., *Ghost Towns of California*
(Pruett Publishing Company, Boulder, 1978)
Moody, Ralph: *Stagecoach West*, 1967
Northern California Atlas & Gazetteer
(DeLorme Publishing Company, Freeport, 1986)
O'Brien, Robert: *California Called Them* (McGraw-Hill, New York, 1951)
Reece, Brigadier General J. N.: *Report of the Adjutant General*
of the State of Illinois, 1900 (Journal Company, Springfield, 1900)
Robertson, Dale: *Wells Fargo*, The Legend (Celestial Art, Millbrae, 1975)
Shearer, Frederick, ed.: *The Pacific Tourist, 1884* (Adam & Bishop,
New York, 1884 & Bounty Books/Crown Publishers, New York, 1970)
Stevenson, Robert Louis: *The Silverado Squatters*,
in **Works of Robert Louis Stevenson,** Vol. XVI
(Waverly Book Company, Limited, London, 1925)
Thrapp, Dan L.: *Encyclopedia of Frontier Biographies*
(Arthur H. Clark, Glendale, 1988)
Wells, Harry L.: *History of Nevada County, California*
(Thompson & West, Oakland, 1880)
Wells, Harry L.: *History of Siskiyou County, California*
(Stewart & Co., Oakland, 1881)
Wilson, Neill C.: *Treasure Express*, Epic Days of Wells Fargo
(The MacMillan Co., New York, 1936)
Winther, Oscar Osburn: *Express and Stagecoach Days*
in California (Stanford University Press, Palo Alto, 1936, 1938)
Winther, Oscar Osburn: *Via Western Express & Stagecoach*
(Stanford University Press, Palo Alto, 1945)
Wolfe, Muriel Sibell: *Montana Pay Dirt* (Sage, Denver, 1963)

Articles

Alexander, Dick: 'Black Bart, A legend that will not die'
(*San Francisco Examiner,* January 21, 1990)
Anderson, Bill: 'Black Bart' (Dogtown Territorial Quarterly, No. 2, Summer, 1990)
'Arrest Stage Robber,' Biography and list of robberies
(Pony Express, September, 1946; March, 1953)
Bacon, E. L.: 'In the Days of Black Bart'
(Wells Fargo Messenger, September, 1912)
Boessenecker, John: 'George Hackett: A Terror to Road Agents'
(Old West, Fall, 1987)
Breihan, Carl W.: 'Black Bart' (True Frontier Tales, 1973)
Breihan, Carl W.: 'The Skittish Highwayman' (The West , 1970)
Breihan, Carl W.: 'Black Bart's Shotgun' (Real West, 1973)
Brewster, Clyde and Velma: 'Lewis L. Brewster' (The Covered Wagon,
1977; Shasta Historical Society, Redding, California)

Brill, Dick: 'The Legend of Black Bart,'
(*San Francisco Progress*, Saturday, November 30, 1974)
Buckbee, Edna Bryan: 'Black Bart, A Solitary Highwayman'
(Touring Topics, 1937)
Chandler, Robert J.: 'Wells Fargo: We Never Forget' (Quarterly of the
National Association and Center for Outlaw and Lawman History,
Vol. 11, No. 3 & 4 (Winter & Spring, 1987)
Davis, Bob & Sandy Banks: 'He Was a Gentleman, Too'
(*San Francisco Chronicle*, October 30, 1983)
Disbrow, Lewis B.: 'Black Bart,' (Central Illinois Genealogical Quarterly,
Vol. 18, No. 2, 1982; Decatur Genealogical Society, Decatur, Ill., 1982)
'Driver of Stage Coaches Black Bart Robbed Dies'
(*San Francisco Chronicle*, 1938)
'Driving A Horse Drawn Stage Today Is Almost A Lost Art'
(Wagon Wheels, February, 1968)
Eames, Ninneta: 'Staging In The Mendocino Redwoods'
(The Overland Monthly, Vol. XX, Second Series, No. 116, August, 1892)
Editorial: 'Black Bart' (Santa Rosa Press Democrat, November 9, 1967)
Gosting, Kenneth: 'Sierra Town Tips a Hat to Black Bart'
(*San Francisco Chronicle*, September 12, 1988)
Graham, Lulu: 'Holdup Days in Siskiyou County,'
(Letter to Pony Express, September, 1946)
Gunderson, Marsha: 'Echoes of Calaveras, Legend of the PO8'
(*Calaveras Enterprise*, August 10, 1983)
Heeser, Augie: (*Mendocino Beacon*, July 11, 1958)
Hoeper, George: 'Stage Robbery, A Risky Profession' (Las Calaveras;
April, 1991; Calaveras County Historical Society, San Andreas, Ca.)
Hopkins, Ernest J.: 'The Romance of the Counties'
(*San Francisco Examiner*, June 30, 1921)
Jackson, Joseph Henry: 'A Bookman's Notebook'
(*San Francisco Chronicle*, August 20, 1937)
Kraft, Ken and Pat Kraft: 'The Case of the Plodding Highwayman
or The Po8 of Crime' (American Heritage, 1974)
LeBaron, Gaye: 'Insight' (*Santa Rosa Press Democrat*, January 29, 1978)
LeBaron, Gaye: 'Insight' (*Santa Rosa Press Democrat*, April 23, 1978)
Lennon, Howard A.: 'Black Bart, Highwayman' (Bulletin, Vol. 12, No. 1
January, 1971; Jefferson County Historical Society, Watertown, N.Y.)
Nixon, Stewart: 'Black Bart, the Tidy Highway Returns'
(*Ukiah Daily Journal*, August 23, 1962)
Pacini, Bob: 'Black Bart Had His Day and His Century'
(*San Francisco Sunday Examiner & Chronicle*, July 20, 1975)
Robbins, Millie: 'Millie's Column, The Telltale Handkerchief'
(*San Francisco Chronicle*, November 25, 1968)

Schubert, John: 'Black Bart Revisited' (*Russian River News*, June 11, 1970)

Schubert, John: 'Stand and Deliver' (Journal of the Sonoma County
    Historical Society, 1991, No. 2)

Silva, Lee: 'Black Bart, The Bloodless Bandit'
    (in *Guns of the Gunfighters*, New York, 1975)

'Stagecoach West' (Aramco World Magazine, October, 1961)

Stanchak, John: 'Charles 'Black Bart' Boles'
    (American History Illustrated, 17:47-9, June, 1982)

Thornton, Emma: In 'The Children of William and Mary Sullaway'
    by Donna Brooks, (Siskiyou Pioneer, 1981; Siskiyou County Historical
    Society, Yreka, Ca.)

Truman, Major Ben. C.: 'Nights of the Lash: Old Time Stage Drivers of the
West Coast,' (The Overland Monthly, XXXI, 218-26, 308-18, 1898)

Wagoner, Rosemary: 'The Wagoner Family, Pioneers of Shasta County'
    (The Covered Wagon, 1962; Shasta Historical Society, Redding)

Wells, Bob: 'Black Bart's Outlaw Days are Re-Told'
    (*Santa Rosa Press Democrat*, November 8 & 15, 1964)

Wukovits, John F.: 'Elegant, elusive Black Bart delighted in taunting his Wells
Fargo victims with biting verse' (Wild West, Vol. 3, No. 6, April, 1991)

Court Records

Calaveras County Court Minutes, 1883:   *Information for Robbery*
                                          — *People v. C. E. Bolton*

Unpublished Materials

Letter from Charles Boles to Hiram G. Boles, 1883
    (Owned by Earl Bowles, Redwood, New York)

Seven letters from Charles Boles to Mary Johnson Boles, 1869-1888
    (Owned by Dick Reames, Aledo, Texas)

Asbill, Frank, 'The Last of the West'
    (Manuscript copy in possession of the authors)

Mauldin, Henry, 'The History of Lake County'
    (Manuscript in files of The Lake County Museum, Lakeport)

Treleaven, Owen, 'Old Men in the Sun'
    (Manuscript in files of the Calaveras County Historical Society, San Andreas)

Acknowledgements

Many people, some unnamed, provided information, photographs and help with this book. We thank them all. Our apologies to anyone inadvertently left off this list.

C. A. 'Doc' Alders, Alders Buggy & Wagon Service, Farmington / Lee Apperson, Sisson Museum, Mt. Shasta / Elizabeth Bailey, State Historical Society of Missouri, Columbia, Missouri / Mary Bertram, Macon County Historical Society, Decatur, Illinois / John Boessenecker, San Francisco / David & Debbie Bowles, Laytonville / Earl Bowles, Redwood, New York / William Brazill, Fort Bragg / David & Suzanne Brown, Plantation / Linda Brown, Cloverdale Chamber of Commerce, Cloverdale / Stanleigh Bry, Alice Phelan Sullivan Library and Archives, Society of California Pioneers, San Francisco / Robert J. Chandler, History Department, Wells Fargo Bank, San Francisco / Mike Chegwyn, Napa / Megan Coddington, Bill Wagner, Mendocino Historical Research, Mendocino / Kenneth Collins, Redding / Betty Davis, Butte County Pioneer Museum, Oroville / Carlo DeFerrari, Tuolumne County Museum, Sonora / Joe Doctor, Tulare County Historical Society, Exeter / Jess Doud, Napa County Historical Society, Napa / Linda Eade, National Park Service Library, Yosemite National Park / Liselotte Erlanger, Mendocino / Bill Fuller, San Andreas / David Haberstich, National Museum of American History, Washington, D. C. / Ginger Hadley, Guerneville Regional Library, Guerneville / Roberta Hagood, Hannibal, Missouri / Jean Hanson, Monte Rio Area Historical Society, Monte Rio / Kathryn Harris, Illinois State Historical Library, Springfield, Illinois / Suzanne Hartman, Fort Bragg / Brian Hembley, Dunsmuir Museum, Dunsmuir / Bill Horst, Visalia / Iola Huntingdon, Mt. Shasta / Donna Howard, Marion Taylor, Sandi Davis, Lake County Museum, Lakeport / Brian Kenny, Illinois Historical Survey, University of Illinois, Urbana, Illinois / Sylvia Kozak-Budd, Mendocino County Library, Fort Bragg / Jim Lague, Yuba Feather Historical Museum, Forbestown / Harry Lapham, John Schubert, Sonoma County Historical Society, Santa Rosa / Gail Lauinger, Mendocino / Lila & Bob Lee, Held-Poage Research Center, Mendocino County Historical Society, Ukiah / Robert Leu, San Mateo / Tracey Livingston, Ridgewood Ranch / John Lofgren, Eric Nelson, Sonoma County Museum, Santa Rosa / Alexander Lucas, Newberry Library, Chicago, Illinois / Anne McFarland, Cleveland Heights, Ohio / Hazel McMane, Alexandria Bay, New York / Eric Moody, Nevada Historical Society, Reno, Nevada / Carol Moore, J. J. Jackson Memorial Museum, Trinity County Historical Society, Weaverville / Daryl Morrison, Holt-Atherton Center for Western Studies, University of the Pacific, Stockton / Mark Morton, Mendocino Grammar School, Mendocino / Rosemarie

Mossinger, Challenge / Daniel Murley, Fort Ross Historic Park, Fort Ross / George Nixon, Salt Lake City, Utah / Richard Perry, California State Library, Sacramento / Helen & Don Perkins, Howard County Historical Society, Cresco, Iowa / Binah Polay, Mendocino Area Parks Association, Mendocino / Michael Potts, Caspar / Diane Powers, The New York Public Library, New York / California Quint, Sandi Cockerham, Shasta Historical Society, Redding / Marc Reed, Milwaukee, Wisconsin / Dick Reames, Aledo, Texas / Nellie Richard, Cresco, Iowa / William Richmond, Hannibal, Missouri / Louise Roberg, Cresco, Iowa / Douglas Roycroft, Fiddlers Green Books, Fort Bragg / Margaret Sanborn, Marin County / Robert Schneider, Cazadero / Richard Schwartz, Macon County Historical Society, Hannibal, Missouri / Oliver Seeler, Albion / Kathy Sisco, Modoc County Historical Society, Alturas / Julie Stark, Sutter County Museum, Yuba City / Mr. & Mrs. Charles Stone, Copperopolis / Mary Anne Terstegge, Tulare County Free Library, Visalia / Dee Tipton, Calaveras County Historical Society, San Andreas / Edwin Tyson, Searls Historical Library, Nevada County Historical Society, Nevada City / Dave Walter, Montana Historical Society Library, Helena, Montana / Fred Welcome, Shasta Historic Park, Shasta / Warren Wirebach, Historical Society of Dauphin County, Harrisburg, Pennsylvania / Alice Wittig, Mendocino Unified School District Librarian, Mendocino / Vada Wood, Ogle County Historical Society, Oregon, Illinois / Mickie Zekley, Mendocino

Facilities at:
Alice Phelan Sullivan Library and Archives, Society of California Pioneers, San Francisco / Bancroft Library, University of California, Berkeley / California State Library, Sacramento / California Room, Marin County Library, San Raphael / California Room, Sonoma County Library, Santa Rosa / Cloverdale Historical Society, Cloverdale / Cloverdale Regional Library, Cloverdale/ Duncan Mills Depot Museum, Duncans Mills / Family History Center, Church of the Latter Day Saints, Sacramento / Healdsburg Museum, Healdsburg / Held-Poage Research Center, Ukiah / Lake County Library, Lakeport / Lake County Museum, Lakeport / Library, California State University, Sacramento / Library, California State University, Sonoma / Mendocino County Library, Ukiah / Petaluma Regional Library, Petaluma / San Francisco Room, San Francisco Public Library, San Francisco / Peter J. Shields Library, University of California, Davis / Sutro Library, San Francisco / Wells Fargo Bank, San Francisco

Index